MW00714370

Dr. Macintosh's
Guide to the On-Line Universe

Dr. Macintosh's Guide to the On-Line Universe

Bob LeVitus
with Andy Ihnatko

Addison-Wesley Publishing Company

Reading, Massachusetts • Menlo Park, California • New York
Don Mills, Ontario • Wokingham, England • Amsterdam • Bonn
Sydney • Singapore • Tokyo • Madrid • San Juan
Paris • Seoul • Milan • Mexico City • Taipei

Many of the designations used by manufacturers and sellers to distinguish their products are claimed as trademarks. Where those designations appear in this book and Addison-Wesley was aware of a trademark claim, the designations have been printed in initial capital letters (for example, Macintosh).

The authors and publisher have taken care in preparation of this book, but make no expressed or implied warranty of any kind and assume no responsibility for errors or omissions. No liability is assumed for incidental or consequential damages in connection with or arising out of the use of the information contained herein.

Library of Congress Cataloging-in-Publication Data

LeVitus, Bob
      Dr. Macintosh's guide to the on-line universe / Bob LeVitus with Andy Ihnatko
         p.   cm.
      Includes index.
      ISBN 0–201–58125–6
      1. On-line data processing. 2. Computer networks. 3. Macintosh
(Computer) I. Ihnatko, Andy. II Title.
QA76.55.L48 1992
004.6' 165 — dc20   92–24401
                                                    CIP

Copyright © 1992 by Bob LeVitus

All rights reserved. No part of this publication may be reproduced, stored in a retrieval system, or transmitted, in any form or by any means, electronic, mechanical, photocopying, recording, or otherwise, without the prior written consent of the publisher. Printed in the United States of America. Published simultaneously in Canada.

Sponsoring Editor: David Rogelberg
Project Editor: Joanne Clapp Fullagar
Technical Reviewers: Leonard Rosenthol and David Alverson
Cover design by Jean Seal
Set in 11 point Palatino by Bob LeVitus himself

ISBN 0–201–58125–6

1 2 3 4 5 6 7 8 9 -MU- 9695949392
First printing, September 1992

For Lisa , Allison, and Jacob

Acknowledgments

First and foremost, thanks to my collaborator, Andy Ihnatko, who did all of the hard stuff, almost all of the research, much of the writing, and probably a lot more sweating than he ever expected.

Superduper thanks to our whizbang technical editors, Leonard Rosenthol and David Alverson. Nobody knows more about Macintosh telecom than Leonard and David. Leonard, in addition to inventing the telephone, the modem, Twinkies, Jolt cola, and much more, wrote much of my favorite commercial telecom program, MicroPhone II. David Alverson is the author of the phenomenal shareware telecom program ZTerm, and he is also a technical editor par excellence. These guys did an awesome job reviewing this book for technical accuracy; nonetheless, any errors you find are mine and mine alone (except the ones that are Andy's and Andy's alone <g>).

Thanks also to everyone at all the hardware and software companies mentioned in this book, too numerous to mention (you know who you are). Thanks for providing software and hardware, but most of all, thanks for all the good advice and answers.

Special thanks to my agents Bill Gladstone and Carole McClendon, and everyone at Waterside Productions, for being the greatest deal makers in the universe.

I'm running out of ways to say thank you, but I wouldn't want to forget the gang at Addison-Wesley—David Rogelberg, Joanne Clapp Fullagar, Amy Cheng, Abby Cooper, Steve Stansel, and everyone else. A good publisher is hard to find; I'm glad to have found you.

Last but not least, massive thanks to the wonderful folks at Apple Computer—John Cook and the public relations gang, Keri Walker and Doedy Hunter in product loans, and our evangelist, Martha Steffen. All I can say is thank you, thank you, thank you.

B.L.
Fall, 1992

Contents

Chapter 7

Chapter 8

Chapter 9

Chapter 10

Preface

You're standing in the bookstore holding this epic tome in your hand and wondering if it's worth buying. The answer is yes. If you want to learn to telecommunicate on the Mac, there's no better way than to buy a copy of this book and read it from cover to cover.

Andy and I love to telecommunicate and it shows; before we're finished, you'll love it too! Where other telecommunications books are somewhat technical and oftentimes confusing, we've done our best to make this a kinder, gentler telecom book—one that will spare you technical details you'll never need. Instead, our chatty, informal descriptions tell you what you need to know. In fact, our chatty, informal style should give you a pretty good idea of the way people write on line.

Why I Love My Modem

I love my modem—it's the one device I can't live without. Go ahead, take away my big monitor, my scanner, or even my 535Mb hard disk. But take away my modem and I'll surely cry. Take away my modem and you've cut me off from the world.

I telecommunicate about a dozen times a day. As a contributing editor for *MacUser*, I need timely feedback on Macintosh hardware and software from people who actually use it. My modem makes it possible for me to collect that feedback without leaving my desk. *MacUser's* "Help Folder" column is a collaboration between Andy and me. Modems make it possible for us to work together effortlessly, even though we're physically thousands of miles apart.

But a modem is more than a way to get Mac-related information. It is like a magic carpet—it can take you anywhere and teach you anything. Not only can you communicate with hundreds of thousands of computer users, but with a modem you can learn just about anything about just about anything.

Here's a list of a few of the things you can do once you attach a modem to your Mac:

- Transfer text or files between Macintoshes (and even those *other* computers) in different locations

- Send messages asking for help with your hardware or software and get answers quickly

- Read messages about hardware or software that interests you

- Send electronic mail faster and cheaper than by Federal Express

- Chat with real people in real time

- Download thousands of public domain and shareware programs, DAs, and fonts

- Order merchandise, including books, software, televisions, and hard disks

- Buy stocks and securities, or check their prices

- Search for magazine articles on specific topics

- Reserve airline tickets

A modem opens up the world to you and your computer. This book will help you select hardware and software for connecting your Mac to the world and show you hundreds of fun and informative things you can do once you're hooked up.

How I Learned What I Know

I live and breathe Macintosh—the Mac is a way of life for me. In the early days, I served as editor-in-chief of *MACazine*, one of the first, and always the most outspoken, of the Macintosh publications. Since that time, I have written several books: the first and second editions of *Dr. Macintosh*, *Stupid Mac Tricks*, and *Son of Stupid Mac Tricks*. I'm currently a contributing editor for *MacUser*; I write the "Help Folder" question-and-answer column (with Andy Ihnatko) and the "Beating the System" column about System software.

So you could say that my job for the past seven years has been to find information that helps people get more from their Macs.

Needless to say, I've spent a good part of that time on line, hunched in front of one of my Macs, using my modem to gather information, exchange files with other writers and editors, and keep in touch with friends and business acquaintances.

I'm a compulsive modem rat; for me, it's almost an addiction. If I don't prowl CompuServe, AppleLink, and America Online every single day, I become extremely cross, break into a cold sweat, and suffer withdrawal symptoms.

This book contains the best of what I've picked up over the years through my experiences as a modem rat, Macintosh lover, beta tester, editor, writer, advice counselor, consultant, author, and general all-around Macaholic.

How to Use This Book

The best way to use this book is to read it from cover to cover. If you are already using a Mac and modem, you may want to skim over the things you already know, but I recommend you read every chapter. A lot of good hints and tips are scattered throughout, not to mention good jokes and humorous parables. If you read only bits and pieces, you run the risk of missing one of the good parts.

The correct placement of much of the material was the subject of lengthy Bob/Andy debates. Does it make any sense to write "Make sure your modem supports the Trafalgar protocol" when you won't know what the Trafalgar protocol is until the next chapter? We ultimately decided, for example, to talk about what software to buy *before* we talked about how to use it. Should you become confused, feel free to skip ahead to pertinent chapters or glossary entries. But trust us—things will be made perfectly clear if you just hang in there.

If you come across a term you don't understand, check Appendix A, the Glossary, which appears near the end of the book. If you're looking for information about a specific topic, try either the Glossary or the Index. I've tried to make both as comprehensive as possible.

I'd appreciate your comments. If you don't have a modem yet, we can be reached in care of our publisher, Addison-Wesley Publishing Company, 1 Jacob Way, Reading, MA 01867. For the rest of you, my electronic addresses are:

- CompuServe: 76004,2076

- America Online, MCI, and AppleLink: LEVITUS

- GEnie: R.LEVITUS

Andy can be reached on CompuServe at 2511,204.

We're particularly interested in suggestions for how we can make the next edition of this book more helpful to you.

This book has been a pleasure to write. I hope you enjoy it, learn from it, and come to love telecommunicating as much as Andy and I do.

Bob LeVitus
Summer 1992

Postscript by Andy

Fortunately, this section is in the preface, indisputably the lowest-rent section of any book. Here I can safely tell you that I never learned anything of any real value in books.

Actually, I like to think this book has a lot of value, but this should just be a start. If you want the real straight dope, start asking questions. Ask everyone on local BBSs what *they* think about a certain modem or software package. Ask manufacturers. Go to meetings of your local user group. And foremost, *mess around*. Try things just for the thrill of it. Do things wrong *on purpose* just to find out what happens. In short, take nothing for granted and don't be afraid of the occasional spectacular failure. If you get your knowledge exclusively from books, you'll learn only what everyone else knows. Start experimenting, though, and you'll be introduced to new and exciting frontiers.

Andy Ihnatko
Summer 1992

1
Overview: What It's All About

What telecom is all about, what you're going to get out of it, and why you're going to love it.

Chapter 1 of this book, like *any* technical book, sells you on the basic subject and tells you what the book covers. A handful of pages of light reading, and you're on to Chapter 2. If you're in a hurry, or easily distracted, try reading only the next section, "Party Dogma," to get you enthused about life on line, and the section after that, which summarizes what's in the book. (Think of this section as the ultra-abridged Cliff Notes version.) The remainder of the chapter lets you peek over Andy's shoulder as he logs onto a bulletin board and does his thing.

Party Dogma

The world is a small place, and Andy and I have seen most of it. When the Berlin Wall came down, we were there. When earthquakes rocked San Francisco, we were there, too. How did we know the former Soviet Union was going to *become* the former Soviet Union? Folks in their military told us so.

Shortly after almost every major movie is released, we know all about how the film was made, what ridiculous demands were made by which ridiculous stars, what scenes were cut and why.

We know which laser disks fared badly in their transfer from film, and which have superior surround sound, usually within a day of their release.

Andy loves to tell the story of how he bought his stereo after the guy who designed the nation's top-selling receiver told him that his company's gear wasn't worth the money and recommended other, finer, products.

We once heard a rumor that one of our favorite writers was working on a new book he had stated publicly he'd never write; Andy talked to him personally to confirm it.

I realize this is getting long-winded, so I'll cut it off here. The point I'm trying to make is that all of the above was possible because we have modems hooked up to our Macintoshes.

You can define telecommunications any way you want, define all the protocols, hardware, and so forth, but it all boils down to this: *A modem hooks you up to the world and everyone in it.*

Just think of it. Every month Andy (in Boston, Massachusetts) and I (in Austin, Texas) write a column for *MacUser* (in Foster City, California). I write my bits here and modem them over to Andy there; conversely, he writes his bits there and modems them to me here. We log onto big services such as CompuServe (in Columbus, Ohio) and America Online (in Vienna, Virginia) to research the questions, searching every magazine ever electronically indexed (in dozens of countries) with just a few keystrokes. We often find exactly the piece of software (written by authors all over the world) we need for a particular solution on line.

We ask the top people in the business for information and they give it to us, saving us from an infinite series of secretaries, bureaucracies, or even worse, phone mail. And after all this, we send the completed manuscript to an editor cross-country via electronic mail. Without telecommunications, we'd be lucky to crank out one column a year.

The point is, a modem is a relatively cheap item that provides a solution to many, many problems. Try these on for size:

- **Get support from software and hardware companies**
  You'll be surprised at how many companies—Microsoft, Symantec, CE Software, and hundreds of others—provide some way (either directly or through a commercial on-line service) for The Rest of Us to contact them via modem. Rather than navigating through a confusing and user-hostile phone mail system to *try* to get the info you want, you can send an electronic message today that results in a long, detailed solution straight from the horse's mouth tomorrow. Or even later today.

- **Get loads of free and almost free software** Many program-mers write great, commercial-quality programs, then simply make them available to anyone and everyone without charge (freeware). Others allow users to make as many copies as they want, and to pay only a modest registration fee if they like the program (shareware). Utilities, games, spreadsheet templates, sample documents, and even com-plete, commercial-quality applications are available on line.

- **Access commercial databases** Anyone who's ever written a term paper knows that getting the facts requires work. Sometimes the best you can hope for is a list of books and magazine articles that have the info you want, but aren't available in a local library. Commercial on-line databases, however, can search most major magazines and newspapers published in the past twenty years for articles containing any keyword or phrase you specify. A solid week shuttling between libraries can be reduced to a couple of hours on your modem. Though some of these on-line databases cost an arm and a leg, the results are often phenomenal.

But these are all excuses to justify the expense. The real power of the modem is, again, the way it hooks people together. It's the ultimate party line, and possibly the last hope for the lost art of good conversation. That, my friends, is why Andy and I are so crazy about telecommunications.

Dr. Macintosh's Guide to the On-line Universe (Extremely Abridged Version)

This is the section where most of the book is summarized, so when you read about it in greater detail later on, your head will spin at a much lazier rate.

Chapter 2: The Hardware End

First, you have to buy a modem. This can set you back anywhere from about a hundred bucks to ten times that. The cheaper modems are basic, no-frills deals. More money buys greater speed (transmitting text and files four times faster than the entry-level model), better construction (less likely to melt when left on for twelve hours at a stretch), data compression (squashing down the data as it's being sent, making more effective use of whatever speed your modem's capable of), and error checking (able to recover from transmission problems with style and grace). How much money should you spend? Depends on what you want to do and how far you intend to go. And how rich you are.

Chapter 3: The Software End

The next thing you need is some software. You can find dozens of commercial, shareware, and freeware communications programs to suit every need. These range from simple, bare-bones programs like ZTerm, which claim to be simple, straightforward, and reliable communications programs, to MicroPhone II, which is powerful enough to be used to write your *own* custom telecommunication programs. In between are specialty programs that do one thing amazingly well, like VersaTerm, which is unsurpassed at bamboozling big mainframe computers into thinking that your humble Macintosh is really an expensive graphics terminal.

The software has a bunch of key components: file-transfer protocols, which allow your Mac to exchange files safely and reliably with whatever computer it's hooked up; terminal emulation, which is important for connecting to minis and mainframes; and user scripting, which at its most basic allows the program to type certain information into a BBS automatically and at its most complex can allow you to do away with all conventions of the original program and produce something totally customized.

Chapter 4: Your First Time

Once you've bought everything you need, it's time to install software and configure your modem for your first time on line. The less you spend on your hardware, the simpler this process is. In most cases, all you have to do is plug the modem into an electrical outlet, plug the phone cord into the modem, and turn it on. To get advanced features (such as compression and error checking) to work properly, you probably have to send some commands to your modem to ensure they'll work.

Chapter 5: Reading and Sending Messages

At last! You can connect to a BBS and start having fun. Your telecom program dials the phone and a BBS (bulletin board service) answers the phone, verifies that it's ok for you to use the system, and logs you in. You can read the public messages other folks have left, reply to messages that interest you, or even leave new messages of your own.

If the BBS allows more than one person to use it simultaneously, you can join an electronic conference—an open-mike situation where everyone types all at once, adding their own thoughts and comments to a live conversation.

Chapter 6: Downloading Files

While you're logged onto that BBS, you'll probably want to download some great new software. You'll find out everything you need to know to use your modem as a means of increasing the size of your software collection.

Chapter 7: All About On-Line Services

And you'll certainly acquire a wanderlust of sorts. In addition to BBSs, commercial on-line services, for a monthly or hourly fee, give you a larger range of services and a humongously greater user base. This category includes services such as CompuServe, America Online, GEnie, public access UNIX systems, BIX, Prodigy, and so on. Their biggest advantage is usually their greater size; they tend to be international in scope, without the regional quality of a local BBS. A Massachusetts BBS attracts folks from one area of Massachusetts; CompuServe and commercial services like it attract the world.

Chapter 8: The Strange and Peculiar Customs of the Natives

A word of warning: With exposure to a magnitude more users, you can offend a magnitude more fellow human beings. It helps to know the peculiar customs of the telecom enthusiast. It helps to know that telling someone to RTFM, PITA! is not usually regarded as cool behavior. ;-) (If that makes no sense to you, feel free to skip ahead to Chapter 8.)

Chapter 9: Advanced Telecommunications

Now that you're getting the hang of it, you can try setting up telecom sessions directly; you want to exchange a file personally with a friend across the country? You can fairly easily set up your Mac as a simple host system, which your pal can call up and interact with, just like a full-scale BBS. And why stop there? Try writing some telecom scripts or even your own full-scale telecom program!

   Or you can log onto the office mainframe, check your electronic mail, and/or send a message to a colleague. Or log onto one of the giant on-line databases like Dialog, where you can look up just about anything ever written for a price.

Chapter 10: It's Nothing to Worry About, Really

The last thing to consider, and it indeed should be the *last* thing on your mind as you start cultivating an interest in telecom, are the safety issues involved. It's *possible* that the software you download from a BBS or on-line service will contain a virus that can wreak havoc on your data. It should comfort you to know that most BBSs and all of the major on-line services take extraordinary precautions to reduce (I hesitate to say *eliminate*, though that's their goal) the likelihood of your catching a virus from one of *their* files.

Really, there's not much to worry about—the biggest dangers are in believing poorly researched articles, appearing in the noncomputer media, that try to convince you that danger lurks behind every corner. Read about it, but don't worry about it *too* much.

Anything you learn after that is just gravy. Don't forget to look at the Glossary and other appendices; you never know where you'll find some useful tidbit.

Over Andy's Shoulder: A Typical BBS Session

My biggest problem, as I set out on my first online session many years ago, was that I had no idea what to expect on line. I'd heard of messaging, and exchanging files, but I had no idea what I'd see and do on line. So you won't have to go through those same contortions, my cohort Andy has consented to allow you to peek over his shoulder as he does what he does when he logs onto his local user group BBS. A running commentary helps you follow along at home. So sit back and get comfortable because we're about to go (drum roll, please) on line with Andy.

On Line with Andy

I launch my communications program (ZTerm, in this case) and choose BCS•Mac from the list of BBSs I've taught ZTerm to dial (Figure 1–1). BCS•Mac is the Macintosh division of the Boston Computer Society; the BCS•Mac 9600 menu selection dials the BCS•Mac bulletin board and logs on at 9600 baud.

Dial
Directory... ⌘D
Save Setup
Dial Marked
Hang Up ⌘H
Athena
BCS•Mac 9600
BCS•Mac BBS
BCS•Mac v.32
Binex I

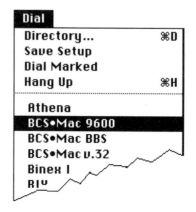

Figure 1–1: Preparing to dial the BBS

ZTerm dials the phone, redialing if the line is busy until a connection is established (Figure 1–2).

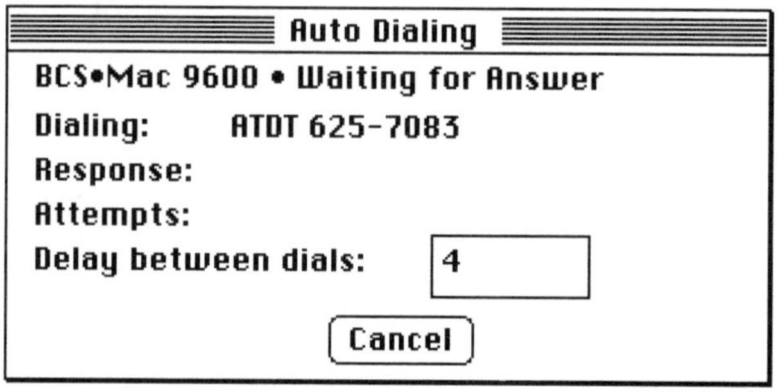

Auto Dialing
BCS•Mac 9600 • Waiting for Answer
Dialing: ATDT 625-7083
Response:
Attempts:
Delay between dials: 4
Cancel

Figure 1–2: Dialing and/or redialing

> Tip: The text that would appear in your terminal window—what Andy types and what the BBS types back—is set in 8-point Courier type.
>
> `Like this`

I hear a shriek from the modem, a beep from my Macintosh, and I'm connected! The first thing I see in my terminal window is

```
CONNECT 9600/ARQ/LAPM/V42BIS BCS•Mac BBS
```

The *CONNECT 9600/ARQ/LAPM/V42BIS* part comes from the modem and tells me how fast I'm going to be communicating, whether error correction and data compression are going to be used, and the like. The *BCS•Mac BBS* part comes from ZTerm and tells me what I'm connected to.

The BCS•Mac BBS then shows me its welcome screen (Figure 1–3).

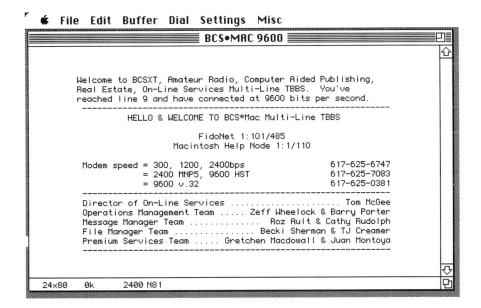

Figure 1–3: Welcome screen for the BCS•Mac bulletin board

The welcome screen varies from BBS to BBS; usually it tells a little about the BBS itself, who runs it, and so forth. The first thing the BBS wants to know is exactly who I am:

```
First Name? Andy
Last Name? Ihnatko
Searching User File ...
Calling From WESTWOOD, MA
```

The BCS•Mac BBS knows me well. Now it wants to know if I am who I say I am. I type in the secret password that only the real Andy Ihnatko would know, and the following text appears:

```
Enter Your Password: ********
TBBS Welcomes ANDY IHNATKO
Calling From WESTWOOD, MA
Your last time on was 3/16/92 14:31
You have read through message 3653
Current last message is 6744
You have called this system 967 times before
You are caller number 432932

* * Warning, system shutting down for maintenance in 157 minutes * *
You are authorized 157 mins this call
```

The BBS is satisfied that I'm the real Andy Ihnatko and lets me in. Of course, you're not given carte blanche on a BBS; usually it imposes a time limit (usually an hour or two per day per user).

Next comes a little business. Because the BCS•Mac BBS is a non-profit educational entity, it relies heavily on donated hardware. So it gives credit right at the top:

```
Type P to Pause, S to Stop listing
─────────────────────────────────────

Please support the companies that support BCS*Mac through donation of
products and technical support:
    eSoft, Inc. ............Producers of The Bread Board System (TBBS)
    GCC Technologies, Inc. ............................. Hard drives
    US Robotics, Inc. ..................................... Modems
    APS .................................. Hard drives & DAT software
    Hayes Microcomputer Products, Inc. ....................... Modems
    Prometheus Products, Inc. ............................... Modems
    Shiva Corporation ............... Net modems and Net serial modems
─────────────────────────────────────
```

Did someone send me a message since the last time I logged in? Just to make sure I don't miss any mail, the BBS automatically calls my attention to any new mail and gives me the opportunity to read it before I proceed:

```
Searching Message Base ...
Msg # From            To            Subject          Board Name
─  ────────   ─────────   ───────            ──────────

1037  ABNER LITTLE   ANDY IHNATKO     WHAT'S YOUR SIGN?   BEGINNERS
These 1 message(s) are marked for retrieval
```

I've got a message waiting for me, so I'll read it now:

```
Read Now(Y/N)? Y
Pause after each msg(Y/N)? Y
Msg#: 1037 BEGINNERS
3/17/92  07:44:08
From: ABNER LITTLE
  To: ANDY IHNATKO
Subj: WHAT'S YOUR SIGN?

Hey, Andy, what's your sign?  You sound like a Pisces...

   - Abner
<C>ubby, <F>wd, <D>el, <R>eply, <A>gain, <N>ext, or <S>top? R
```

Abner's a clever guy, isn't he? At the bottom of the message are all the things I can do to the message. I type **R** for Reply, and I see the following:

```
Change the Subject(Y/N)? N
```

The subject of the message (*Subj:* here) is a short phrase that lets casual browsers know what the message is about; this way, people scanning through piles of messages can look for interesting subjects without having to read entire messages that don't interest them. My reply is on the same subject so I'll type **N** to leave it alone. I see this text:

```
From: ANDY IHNATKO
Subj: WHAT'S YOUR SIGN?
Enter text of message.
<CR> by itself ends input.
```

Now I enter the message. Unfortunately, BBS systems generally don't give you a full-featured word processor for entering messages, so you have to enter them one line at a time:

```
01: My sign is "DO NOT BACK UP...SERIOUS TIRE DAMAGE WILL OCCUR".  This of
02: course under the Carolingian calendar.
03:
04:   - Andy
```

That's it. To send my reply, I type **S** to save the message, choosing from the following list:

```
<L>ist, <V>iew, <A>gain, <E>dit, <R>cpt, <F>ile, <Q>uit, <S>ave, or <H>elp? S
Saving message to disk...
<C>ubby, <F>wd, <D>el, <R>eply, <A>gain, <N>ext, or <S>top? N
```

No more new mail to read, so I can proceed to my next task! Like many BBS systems, the BCS•Mac BBS gives you the latest news about the user group and the BBS:

```
Searching  BCS  Membership  database.....
BCS MACINTOSH Multiline BBS — Newswire                    Updated 3/17/92
  ────────────────────────────────────────────────

   * TBBS 2.2 is here! Full-screen message editing, ZMODEM file transfers,
     and international netmail access are just a few of its new features.
     Many menus have changed; you may need to adjust macros.
   * (P)revious and (T)op may not work on some menus. We are working on a fix.
     (U)tilities will usually get you out.
   * No BCS*Mac Main Meeting this month because of the San Francisco Expo.
     Watch for the February Main Meeting with Apple's QuickTime development
team.
     * Design Group meeting Thursday Jan. 9 Read Msg #516 in <I>nfo <M>eetings.
     * SPECIAL OFFER - Be one of the next 100 new subscribers to Premium
       Services and get a free CompuServe trial membership. From the Main Menu
       choose (S)Premium Services, then (A)bout the Premium, then (4)CompuServe
       Special Offer.

  ──────────────────────────────────────────────────────────────────────

-Press Any Key-

BCS MACINTOSH Multiline BBS —   MAIN MENU
  ────────────────────────────

(I)nformation  ........  BBS help; BCS meetings and general info
(P)ublic-Files  .......  All callers can download these essentials

(M)essages  ..........  BCS Macintosh message bases
(F)iles  ..............  BCS Macintosh file libraries
(S)Premium Services  ..  Extended subscription features

(A)ctivists  .........  BCS volunteer work area
(W)riters  ...........  Submit an article to The Active Window
(J)umpToGroups  .......  Jump to BCS Main Menu (Access other groups)

(G)oodbye     (=)Utilities     (?)Help

Command: M
```

I think I'll read some public messages. I type **M** to get to the Message Base area of the board:

```
BCS MACINTOSH Multiline BBS — MESSAGE BASE Menu
─────────────────────────
Roz Ault and Cathy Rudolph, Managing Sysops

(R)umor Manager ....... Read/send general Macintosh messages
(C)ombined ........... Select message areas for combined reading

(B)BS Help Desk ....... Questions about how to use the BBS answered here!
(E)cho Manager ....... National & international message base

(M)ailbox ............ Private messages

(P)revious   (T)op-Menu   (G)oodbye   (Z)ap-Logoff   (=)Utilities   (?)Help

Command: r
```

To get to the public messages, I type **R** because BCS•Mac calls its public message area the Rumor Manager:

```
BCS MACINTOSH Multiline BBS — RUMOR MANAGER Menu
─────────────────────────
Roz Ault and Cathy Rudolph, Managing Sysops

(1)Beginners Come First !   ... Moderated by Andy Ihnatko
(2)Hardware Messages        ... Moderated by David Walsh
(3)Software Messages        ... Moderated by Glenn Parker
(4)Modem Madness Messages   ... Moderated by Roy Eassa
(5)Buy/Sell & Swap          ... Moderated by Craig O'Donnell
(6)Jobs/Help Wanted         ... Moderated by Steve Semple
(7)Rumors/News Messages     ... Moderated by Ilene Hoffman & Cathy Rudolph
(8)After School             ... Moderated by Jeff Carson
(9)Health'n Fitness         ... Moderated by Gretchen MacDowall & Rodney Smith
(0)Legal User Subgroup      ... Moderated by Harley Hiestand
(A)HyperCard Subgroup       ... Moderated by Bob Soron
(B)MacTech Subgroup         ... Moderated by Glenn Rosen
(C)Music Subgroup           ... Moderated by Rodney Smith
(E)BMUG<->BCS (MACQA)       ... A transcontinental message echo
(F)System 7                 ... National Apple System 7 discussion

(P)revious   (T)op-Menu   (G)oodbye   (Z)ap-Logoff   (=)Utilities   (?)Help

Command: 1
```

The message base is broken up into sections. The Beginners section looks interesting and professionally moderated, so I type **1**.

```
BCS MACINTOSH Multiline BBS — BEGINNERS Message Menu
─────────────────────────────
Moderated by Andy Ihnatko

(R)ead  ............. Read  messages
(S)can  ............. Scan  messages
(L)eave a Message .. Add comments and ask questions
(K)ill a Message ... Delete a message FROM/TO you

(P)revious    (T)op-Menu    (G)oodbye    (Z)ap-Logoff    (=)Utilities    (?)Help

Command:  r
```

You can read messages in any order you want, but right now I want to read the new messages that have been posted here since the last time I logged on:

```
Type P to pause, S to stop, N to skip to next msg
<F>orward or <R>everse Multiple
<N>ew Messages
<M>arked Messages
<S>elective Retrieval
<I>ndividual Message(s)
<A>bort Retrieve

Which One? N

Msg#: 6737  *BEGINNER*
3/16/92  00:14:51
From: MAX VIZSLA
  To: JOSEPH BLOE
Subj: REPLY TO MSG# 6713 (BOOT UP PREFERENCES)
You know, the lyrics to "Amazing Grace" fit the theme song from "Gilligan's
Island" perfectly.  That's something someone told me last week.

<->, <$>, <C>ubby, <F>wd, <D>el, <R>eply, <A>gain, <N>ext, or <S>top? S
```

This message is typical of the kind of the info you can get on line. Notice that the content of this message has nothing to do with the subject (which identifies it as a reply to an earlier message about BOOT UP PREFERENCES); well, that happens occasionally.

That's enough of that, so I type **S** to stop reading messages. The BBS zaps me back to the Beginners Message menu:

```
BCS MACINTOSH Multiline BBS — BEGINNERS Message Menu
─────────────────────────

Moderated by Andy Ihnatko

(R)ead ............ Read messages
(S)can ............ Scan messages
(L)eave a Message .. Add comments and ask questions
(K)ill a Message ... Delete a message FROM/TO you

(P)revious  (T)op-Menu  (G)oodbye  (Z)ap-Logoff  (=)Utilities  (?)Help

Command: T
```

About now I've got a hankering to download a file or two, so I type
T to get to the topmost menu and visit the file area:

```
BCS MACINTOSH Multiline BBS —  MAIN MENU
─────────────────────────


(I)nformation ........ BBS help; BCS meetings and general info
(P)ublic-Files ....... All callers can download these essentials

(M)essages .......... BCS Macintosh message bases
(F)iles ............. BCS Macintosh file libraries
(S)Premium Services .. Extended subscription features

(A)ctivists ......... BCS volunteer work area
(W)riters ........... Submit an article to The Active Window
(J)umpToGroups ....... Jump to BCS Main Menu (Access other groups)


(G)oodbye   (=)Utilities   (?)Help

Command: f

BCS MACINTOSH Multiline BBS — FILES MENU
─────────────────────────

Becki Sherman & TJ Creamer, Managing Sysops

(B)est of the Board ....... Files that every Mac User should have!

(F)iles Area  ............ BCS Macintosh Files Download Areas
(U)ploads/New Files ....... Upload/Download new files (untested area)

(A)pple Releases ......... Apple Computer,Inc., Macintosh System Software
(M)DN Files .............. Macintosh Distribution Network Files

(D)atabase of Files ... Search catalog of files available

(P)revious  (T)op-Menu  (G)oodbye  (Z)ap-Logoff  (=)Utilities  (?)Help

Command: u
```

All the newest files are located in a special Untested/New Files section. They're segregated because they're so new, no one has had a chance to examine them. They might be junk files with no data in them; they can even have a virus. Though it's unlikely that there will be any problems with anything you find in Untested/New Files, most BBSs give you a prudent warning:

```
BCS MACINTOSH Multiline BBS — NEW FILE UPLOADS
─────────────────────────────────────

Moderated by Becki Sherman

NOTICE : Files uploaded within the past 7 days may NOT have been checked
yet by our sysops for suitability of use or for lack of viruses.

(D)ownload/List .... View List of Files & Select for Download
(U)pload .......... Upload a File
(C)ut/Kill ........ Kill a File
(M)ove ............ Move a File to This Area
(V)iew directory ... Examine TBBS file (includes who uploaded each)
(!)Download ....... Download from Unprotected Directory
(*)Upload ......... Upload to Unprotected Directory


(P)revious   (T)op-Menu   (G)oodbye   (Z)ap-Logoff   (=)Utilities   (?)Help

Command: d

Type P to Pause, S to Stop listing

                     *** Newly Uploaded Files! ***
                      USE AT YOUR OWN RISK!

     *****************************************************************
     * Most of the files on this board are Stuffed (.sit) or Compacted *
     * (.cpt). You will need the applications UNSTUFFIT (for .sit) and  *
     * EXTRACTOR (for .cpt and many .sit files). Download them from the *
     * Public Files Area, accessible from the Top Menu.                *
     *                                                                 *
     *    You can stop this list at any time by pressing the 'S' key.  *
     *                                                                 *
     * Hint:  You can save time typing by using COPY and PASTE to enter *
     *           the name(s) of the file(s) you want to download.      *
     *****************************************************************


     CD_AUD_APP     16768   doubleclick audio cd tracks in cd rom drive  (3/13/92)
     RAGE.SEA      129408   Shoot holes in your screen  (3/14/92)
     PROGMKEY1.42    2048   Turns pwr key on kybd to progrmrs switch  (3/15/92)
     TIDBITS106     36123   Mac news for 3/15/92 Word 5 info text form  (3/16/92)
     MEMINIT.SIT    26240   &7 v2.0.2 Quietly shows foreground mem usage  (3/15/92)
     EFFN203.TXT    30000   ElecFrntFndn newsletter 1/7/92 #2.03 text    (3/16/92)
     CACHE040       43136   Turns on/off Cache for 68040 machines  (3/16/92)
     PEEK-A-BOO    198016   A Hypercard game that teaches mousing skills  (3/16/92)

     <D>ownload, <P>rotocol, <E>xamine, <N>ew, <L>ist, or <H>elp
     Selection or <CR> to exit: p
```

That Rage program looks interesting … I think I'll download it. First I tell the BBS how I want it sent by specifying a file-transfer protocol:

```
Select from the following transfer protocols:

T - TYPE file to your screen
C - ASCII with DC2/DC4 Capture
A - ASCII only, no Control Codes
X - XMODEM
O - XMODEM-1k
Y - YMODEM (Batch)
G - YMODEM-g (Batch)
S - SEAlink
K - KERMIT
W - SuperKERMIT (Sliding Windows)
Z - ZMODEM-90(Tm)

Choose one (Q to Quit): Z
```

I select ZMODEM because in most cases it's the most efficient of all protocols. Now I tell the BBS I want to download something—just a matter of specifying the filename:

```
<D>ownload, <P>rotocol, <E>xamine, <N>ew, <L>ist, or <H>elp
Selection or <CR> to exit: d

File Name? RAGE.SEA

File Name: RAGE.SEA
File Size: 129408 Bytes
  Protocol: ZMODEM-90(Tm)
Est. Time: 1 mins, 50 secs at 9600 bps

Awaiting Start Signal
(Ctrl-X to abort)
```

Once I give the command to the BBS, the BBS stands by until my telecom program is ready to receive the file. One of the features of the ZMODEM protocol (built into most telecommunications programs) is that it can automatically sense when a file is being sent and download the file without any intervention on your part. With protocols like XMODEM and YMODEM, you have to tell your communications program when to start receiving.

A dialog box appears on my Mac's screen (Figure 1–4), telling me that ZTerm is receiving a file and how the file transfer is going.

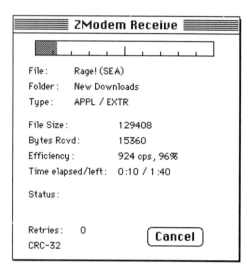

Figure 1–4: ZTerm's Receive progress indicator

After about two minutes, the file transfer is completed. Rage! is now a file on my hard drive, just as though I had copied it there from a floppy.

The BBS puts up its menu once again:

```
BCS MACINTOSH Multiline BBS — NEW FILE UPLOADS
──────────────────────────────────

Moderated by Becki Sherman

NOTICE : Files uploaded within the past 7 days may NOT have been checked
yet by our sysops for suitability of use or for lack of viruses.

(D)ownload/List .... View List of Files & Select for Download
(U)pload .......... Upload a File
(C)ut/Kill ........ Kill a File
(M)ove ............ Move a File to This Area
(V)iew directory ... Examine TBBS file (includes who uploaded each)
(!)Download ....... Download from Unprotected Directory
(*)Upload ......... Upload to Unprotected Directory

(P)revious   (T)op-Menu   (G)oodbye   (Z)ap-Logoff   (=)Utilities   (?)Help

Command: G
```

I've done all I want to do, so I log off by typing **G** for goodbye, and I see this menu:

```
BCS MACINTOSH Multiline BBS — LOG OFF MENU
_____


(Y)es . . . . . . . . . Log off now!
(N)o  . . . . . . . . . Don't log off now!
(M)sg to Sysop . . Leave a question for the System Operators

Command: y
```

The BBS wants to make sure I didn't accidentally hit the wrong key. I type **Y** to log off. Before I depart, the BBS has a final gift for me, a list of other local BBSs I may want to call:

```
Type P to Pause, S to Stop listing

Andy, if you liked this BBS try calling these other fine systems...

BCS Info Center          (617) 621-0882  |  4th Dimension          (617) 494-0565
BCS Telecommunications         786-9788  |  PhotoTalk                     472-8612
BCS IBM UG                     332-5584  |  The Graphics Factory          849-0347
BCS Comm/Amiga/HypMedia        729-7340  |  MacEast                       868-79

NO CARRIER
```

Finally, the BBS hangs up the phone. My modem sends the message *NO CARRIER* to my terminal window to let me know that the phone line is now clear.

Now I can play with the file I just downloaded, Rage!

Parting Shots

By now you should have an idea of what telecommunications is. We hope you're itching to get started. Although Andy's demonstration touches on some of the nifty things you can do with your modem, and hints at how easy it is to read and write messages and download files, his bout with a local BBS barely scratches the surface. It just keeps getting better.

2

The Hardware End

What you need to know to buy the modem best suited to your needs.

Hardware. It allows your computer to telecommunicate. It lets your computer talk to the hardware that telecommunicates. It solves the various problems that arise when the latter and the former aren't on friendly terms. In a nutshell, this chapter is about spending money.

We begin this odyssey at the baseboards of your home, condominium, apartment, or recreational vehicle, by looking at your phone jacks and phone lines. From there, we examine the modems themselves, and the array of features they can include—physical features, speed, compression, and error checking. Finally, we discuss how to select and shop for a modem that's right for you. Last but not least, you'll be provided with ample ammunition for dealing with dishonest marketing weasels.

Figure 2–1 demonstrates a basic Macintosh and modem setup. Simple, eh? Even the most advanced setup isn't much more complicated.

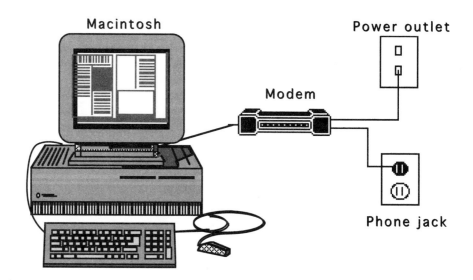

Figure 2–1: A typical Mac and modem setup

By the way, if you encounter a term you don't understand, you can consult the Glossary in Appendix A.

Phone Lines

One of the biggest myths of telecommunications is that you'll need to have a special computer-dedicated phone line installed. In fact, any working line will do just fine, whether it leads directly to your house or onto your desk through a huge office-wide telephone system. As long as there's a dial tone, your modem will be happy as a clam.

You can have a couple of special, optional phone lines installed, but for most of us they're a waste of money. The first is called a leased line, which is a phone line that connects you to a single, specific party directly, without requiring you to dial phones and work through telephone exchanges. Usually, you'd only make these arrangements if you wanted to link a company mainframe computer in Boston to another one in Chicago.

Remember the old "Batman" TV series? Commissioner Gordon's hot line to Batman (those red flashing phones they kept under cake covers) used a leased line. You wondered why Bruce Wayne answered before Gordon dialed a single digit? Now you know. You also now know why Gordon could never call Batgirl. Had he used a regular phone line, he might have figured out that Batgirl was actually his daughter. Such is life.

Some regional phone companies also offer, for a lot more money, a data-grade line. The definition of this varies from company to company. Sometimes you're buying a phone line that's been specially routed to run over fiber-optic lines exclusively (resulting in far less static); other times you're just buying a regular phone line and a promise that if your modem proves to work unreliably on it, the phone company will fix the line for free. Generally, data-grade or computer-grade lines aren't worth the additional expense.

Your Mac can talk to other computers with *radio waves* rather than phone lines. With packet radio, computers can broadcast text the same way ham radios broadcast sound. You need special equipment and an FCC license to get involved in packet radio, though.

If you want more information, seek out local radio enthusiasts or look in your Yellow Pages under "Packet Radio." If that's not successful, in Chapter 5 you'll learn how to post a public message on a BBS or an on-line service like CompuServe. Try leaving a message asking for information on packet radio and computers on your favorite BBS or in an appropriate CompuServe forum. (I'd start with the Ham Radio forum [go hamnet] or Consumer Electronics forum [go ceforum].)

Another alternative is cellular modems, now used in a few European countries. By the time you read this, they may be available in the U.S. as well. Check with your computer/modem dealer.

Protecting Your Connection

Modems don't *require* a special phone line, but if you share your phone line with family members, roommates, fax, or answering machines, a second line can save you a lot of grief.

Picture this scenario: You've been downloading a huge file from a commercial on-line service where you pay by the hour. As the last 1 percent of the file is coming through, someone in your household picks up the phone to make a call. Your modem immediately hangs up. Since the file wasn't transmitted in its entirety, you've spent $12.50 for 700K of worthless data (unless you used the ZMODEM protocol; see Chapter 5).

Or, if you have call waiting, as the last 1 percent of the file is coming through, another call beeps in. (Note: You can avoid the call waiting conundrum, as described in Chapter 4.)

Obviously, you avoid all these problems when you have a separate phone line installed exclusively for your modem. This will set you back about a hundred bucks for the installation and then twenty bucks a month for usage, so let's look at cheaper alternatives.

For most of you, a lost connection due to roommate interference is the most troublesome situation you may encounter. The cheapest solution is to preamble your modem sessions with a quick jog through the house, putting "Please don't pick up this phone!" sticky yellow notes on every handset. If you have more than two or three phones in your home, the second-cheapest solution is a lot less trouble: privacy boxes. These were originally designed to prevent people from snooping on your phone conversation by listening in on an extension. You plug one of these boxes into every phone jack on that line, and whenever any one phone goes off the hook, the rest of the phone jacks in the house magically go dead, neatly removing the possibility that you'll be disconnected by the actions of a roommate or spousal unit looking to have a pizza delivered. Privacy switches are sold by several different companies; one of them is Radio Shack's Teleprotector, for about eight bucks a box.

Another scenario: If you have multiple phone devices—a telephone, fax machine, and modem—connected to a single phone line, you may be tempted by the heavily advertised fax/voice/data switches that purport to automatically sense what sort of phone call is coming in and direct the call to the appropriate device. In many cases, you'll be spending a hundred bucks for a nearly useless box.

These devices work wonders with fax machines, due to the nature of the sound made by an incoming fax, but tend not to work with modems as transparently as they claim. In the majority of these boxes, modem calls are detected and switched only if the caller dials a special extra digit or two after the connection is first made. If you're considering one of these boxes, you should verify that the box can properly handle incoming modem calls without any involvement on the part of the caller, and verify that you can return the box and get a refund for any reason! (Actually, that's a good idea for any hardware or software purchase—always make sure you can get a refund if you're not satisfied.)

In summary, if this is your first modem, you don't need to invest in special phone lines and gizmos. If your enthusiasm for telecom blossoms (and it will) and you find yourself spending two to four hours a day (or, more likely, night) on line with your modem, you will inevitably have a second (or third, or fourth) phone line installed. Convenience increases by a factor of ten with a dedicated line—but hey, no need to rush things.

Phone Jacks

Modems use modular phone jacks—that place where you stick the phone wire in. That's not a problem for most of you. If you have a phone jack that looks like Figure 2–2, you're in good shape, and you can safely proceed to the next section.

Figure 2–2: A modular phone jack

If you're still reading this, you probably have old, Paleolithic-era phone jacks. Don't fret. Phone jacks are easily updated. If you have a four-pronged jack like the one in Figure 2–3, all you need is a simple four-prong to modular adapter, found in almost any store that sells phones. The better option is to remove that wall outlet and replace it with a modular unit. This involves removing the old jack with a screwdriver, unscrewing the four wires inside, screwing those wires into a new modular jack, and then sticking the new jack in the original hole.

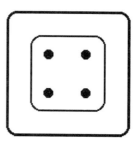

Figure 2–3: Old four-prong outlet

If you don't have anything remotely like the jacks described previously, you have a set that's been wired directly into the wall, without any easily removed plug at all. You folks have to replace that connector in a procedure similar to that of updating a four-prong plug to a modern connector. It's a safe, trivial procedure—so simple that complete installation instructions fit on the back of the card the jack ships on.

Whatever your problem, your solution definitely awaits you at your local Radio Shack or electronics store, and it shouldn't set you back more than five or ten bucks.

The Wire That Runs from the Wall Jack to Your Modem

Phone cords are phone cords. Buy it wherever you want. I get mine at Radio Shack where they have a wide selection of lengths and colors. Your modem may even include one. Frankly, I only put in this section so I could say I'd detailed the complete path from the phone company to your Mac, in order.

All about Modems!

An internationally recognized reference book explains modems this way: "Acronym for MOdulator-DEModulator." Enough said.

Just kidding. We can do better than that. A modem is a device that performs a simple task: It takes the numbers your Mac sends to it (numbers that represent characters, a program, parts of a graphic image, and so on) and turns them into a noise that sounds like static, then it pumps that noise through the phone lines.

Computers talk to each other on the phone the same way humans do: by making semiintelligible noises that each other can understand. The modem receiving this data takes that static, turns it back into those numbers that all computers recognize, and sends those numbers to the computer connected to it.

Two questions come to mind. First, if you have a Macintosh, don't you need a special Macintosh modem? Answer: no. Any computer with a serial port can use any modem. You can disconnect a modem from your Macintosh and use it with an IBM PC, or an Apple IIGS, or even a Commodore PET (built in 1976). Some companies sell a special Macintosh modem package, which includes a modem, a Macintosh modem cable, and some (usually hideous) free software to use with the modem, but that's just a marketing ploy. It may be convenient to buy everything in one package, but hardly necessary.

Second question: If you're using a Macintosh, does that mean you can talk only to other Macs? Answer: no. Early shakers and movers of the computer industry got together to set international standards for computer representation of text, ASCII (American Standard Code for Information Interchange). Therefore, every computer that sees the number 65 in ASCII mode automatically puts a letter A on the screen.

Let's pause here for an historical flashback sequence.

A Brief History of Modem Hardware

You old-timers can remember the days you could speak of the phone company in the singular. When Ma Bell tightly controlled all the phones, forcing folks to rent equipment exclusively from it, you could get an absurd modem called the DataPhone. This modem was about the size of a standard hard-shell suitcase, could transmit data only a little bit faster than you could type it, and cost *thousands* of dollars! And good luck getting the thing to work properly.

I mention this only because most folks have never heard of the DataPhone. If you saw one, you might start laughing. No, when most people think of a modem, they picture the kinds available in the seventies. These were more compact (shoebox-size), and they were great props in movies. To use them, you had to dial the phone, listen for the faraway computer to answer, and then slam the telephone handset into the modem's spiffy space-age acoustic coupler. Rent the movie *War Games* for a look at the quintessential late-seventies telecom setup.

The next technological breakthrough was the elimination of the acoustic coupler. Direct-connect modems could be plugged in between the wall jack and your phone, so establishing a connection after dialing from the phone involved simply pushing a button on the modem and hanging up the phone.

Notice a recurrent theme here: The human beings dial the phone, check to see if another modem answers the phone, and then finally switch the modem on line. Fortunately, the early eighties ushered in a wonderful new kind of modem: the smart modem, which is what we use today. Actually, *Smartmodem* is a registered trademark of Hayes Microcomputer Products, but it's come to mean any modem that can act on its own.

Modern Modems

Modern modems are now complete computers in themselves, with capabilities that far exceed those of any personal computer available in the seventies. Just as you give commands to your computer (Launch HyperCard, Print this document, and so on), through your computer, you give commands to your modem. Command the modem to dial the phone, and automatically it "picks up" the handset (metaphorically speaking), dials the number, and waits for an answer. If another modem answers, it connects to it automatically. If it can't connect for whatever reason, your modem hangs up the phone. Some modems can even tell you what happened.

If you want to be impressed by the sophistication of a modern modem or scared silly that it's an incredibly complex instrument, reflect upon the fact that the manual that came with your Mac is roughly half an inch thick. The manual that comes with a modem is usually one half to three quarters of an inch thick. This little box the size of a paperback book knows about thirty commands!

Why put so much power into a simple peripheral? Because a modem is often used in conjunction with a dumb terminal, which may look like a computer but is just a screen and a keyboard. When all you're doing is connecting to a mainframe and sending commands to the programs running on that big system, why invest in a whole computer system when a dumb terminal can do the same job for $150?

To get a modem working, all you need to know is where to plug it in. A modem is a sophisticated computer, but it's being controlled by an even more sophisticated computer, your Mac, which can shield you from all direct contact with your modem if you so desire.

Just as you don't need to know what /*Times-Roman findfont 24 scalefont* means to print a document on a LaserWriter, you don't need to know any of your modem's commands to use it effectively. (/*Times-Roman findfont 24 scalefont* is the PostScript instruction sent by your Mac to your printer, to tell it to use the 24-point Times Roman font.)

Modem Features

One of the reasons why telecommunications has become so popular is that a modem exists to fit every need and every level of interest. You can buy a perfectly adequate 2400 baud modem for well under a hundred dollars if you're just getting started, while other people giddily blow a thousand dollars on the latest, fastest, and most feature-laden modem.

(I know. I haven't told you what a "baud" is yet. Hang in there. We'll get to it in a second. If you can't stand the suspense, leaf forward to the section on speed or check the glossary.)

So many features are available, though, that it's easy to become overwhelmed. What follows is a field guide of sorts, a compilation of features—desirable, undesirable, and otherwise.

Physical Features

Most modems look like a paperback book, laid flat; originally, the idea was that you'd stack your phone on top of the modem. Now that we're in the design-conscious nineties, you'll see modems of every shape and size, leading to my first rule of thumb: Never buy a modem that you can't immediately identify as a modem. Many times modems with impressive angles and European styling cost more than plainer units with identical features, and you may find that more effort was spent on physical design than electronic design. On the other hand, I've heard people say nice things about the reasonably priced, European-style Logicode Quicktel Xeba modems (see Figure 2–4), though I haven't

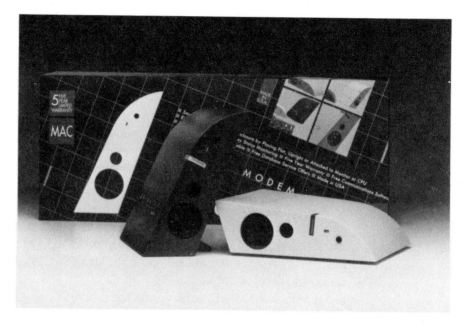

Figure 2–4: Logicode Quicktel Xeba Eurostyle modem

had the opportunity to put one through its paces myself. So take this "impressive angles and European styling advice" with however many grains of salt you wish.

Above all, avoid modems that plug directly into a wall outlet, rather than through a power cord. Both Apple and Hayes have come out with modems of this sort, and they're not as convenient as the sort that sits on your desk. It's important to have the unit close at hand, so you won't be crawling among the dust bunnies and Twinkie crumbs every time you want to make adjustments or check or change cable connections.

Prejudices aside, here are nice things to look for when you heft a modem in your hand at the computer store.

Switched Phone Jacks   In addition to the connector for plugging the modem into your phone line, there should be a second jack for plugging in a phone. This saves you the trouble of plugging a two-way adapter into your wall outlet. Furthermore, because the second jack is supposed to go dead when the modem is in use, when you or your loved one accidentally pick up the phone that's connected to the modem, it won't disconnect an important (and possibly expensive) on-line session.

Built-in Speaker with a Conveniently Mounted Volume Control   Imagine leaving the handset on the table and dialing a phone number. If the call didn't go through, you'd have no idea what happened. Was there a dial tone? Was the line busy? Did someone answer, then hang up? Similarly, a speaker in the modem allows you to listen in as the hardware dials and attempts to make a connection. Although the hardware can do its best to tell you when the line was busy or there was no dial tone, when you can hear the call's progress through the speaker, you're never in doubt as to why things went awry. A volume control knob mounted in front allows you to crank the volume down when conducting telecom sessions at 3 A.M. It's a simple feature, but it can save marriages. Although very few modems have it, it's worth looking for.

Indicator Lights   Why don't *all* modems have a bank of at least eight LEDs reporting at a single glance the operational status of the modem? One look at a modem with a full complement of lights can instantly tell you that the modem is off-hook it's currently connected to another computer, it's exchanging data at the highest speed possible, and data is moving both into and out of your computer. When you look up from your newspaper and see that all the lights have winked off, you know things have gone awry. This feature is so important that many modems for which LEDs are impractical (those installed *inside* your computer, for instance) come with software that displays a bank of simulated lights in the menu bar.

Resistance to Heat   If you intend to use your modem infrequently, heat resistance isn't that important, but if you're running your own BBS or intend to telecommunicate regularly, you want a modem that won't overheat. Look for a modem with either a metal housing (which dissipates heat handily) or a plastic housing studded with ventilation slots. Good ventilation generally isn't found on the cheapest modems, but the extra thirty bucks or so easily pays for itself if it prevents the unit from melting after being left on all night.

Other Goodies Not all modems are made alike; witness the modems made by USRobotics. Silk-screened on the bottom of the unit is a detailed reference sheet, listing all the modem's commands and operational modes. This feature has saved both of us more than once, as both of us schlep our modems from hotel to hotel sans manual! (As of last week, I have graduated to a wonderful PowerBook, which has an internal modem; more about it later in the chapter.)

Many modems also include a multifunctional switch up front, which you can set up to do many nifty things, such as immediately hang up the modem, switch the modem from data mode to voice mode (handy when you misdial and find that you've accidentally called an actual human being at 3 A.M.).

Speed

As nice and as useful as the aforementioned features are, the single most important feature of a modem is speed. Speed is really the feature that separates an $89 modem from an $899 modem.

Modems come in only one speed: not nearly fast enough. You buy a modem, see it in operation, and say "Wow! That's fast!" but two months later you'll want a faster modem. And as soon as you buy that one, you'll want an even faster one.

But that's not what you want to hear. Modem speed is measured in bits per second (bps), sometimes referred to as *baud* (*bits aud*ible). The higher this number, the faster the modem.

You want to know how to get a telecom enthusiast flustered and red? Proudly mention your 2400-*baud* modem. More often than not, you'll find bps and baud used interchangeably (even in modem ads), but *baud* isn't the proper term to use when talking about modem speed.

The simplified explanation is this: *bps* refers literally to how much physical data is being pumped through the phone line. *Baud* refers to how often the wave representing the transmitted data changes state.

In a nutshell, the two terms are used for two different aspects of data transmission. They are not synonymous.

The first popular consumer modems operated at 300 bps. As popularity grew and costs shrank, 1200 bps modems began to appear. Then 2400 bps modems were considered an extreme luxury, but soon prices fell to the point where it's the most popular speed these days, and no one makes modems slower than that.

Here we hit the wall. Engineers proclaimed that with the low quality of the phone lines in general use these days, 9600 bps transmission was a pipe dream at best; several produced detailed studies proving categorically that data transmission at rates faster than 9600 bps was physically impossible. But that barrier was soon breached, as were barriers above it.

Right now, only two modem speeds are commonly available: 2400 and 9600 bps. Any modem slower than 2400 bps will not sell, and 9600 is the fastest speed *everyone can agree upon*. That's an important phrase. What good is a 9600 bps modem that can only talk to other 9600 bps modems made by the same manufacturer? Central to the power of modems is the fact that every time a new speed or feature surfaces, the industry gets together and sets an international standard for data transmission at that speed.

> The organization that oversees modem-related standards is the CCITT, the International Consultative Committee for Telephony and Telegraphy, a branch of the United Nations. (The initials don't match because that's an English translation of a French name.)

Standards are important. For a while, the demand for 9600 bps modems and the lack of a CCITT standard for data transmission of that speed resulted in many modem makers coming up with their own standards. Hayes came out with a Ping-Pong protocol, USRobotics had HST, Microcom simply had its Microcom standard. They all worked at 9600 bps, but a HST modem worked at 9600 bps only with another HST, Microcoms worked at high speed only with Microcoms, and so on. This is no longer a problem, now that there is a CCITT standard for 9600 bps communications.

Before we list the standards, some soothing words: All modems are part of one big, happy family. You don't necessarily need a fast, expensive modem to make a connection to a 9600 bps modem. Almost all modems are downwardly compatible with modems of slower speed; when a 9600 bps modem answers a phone call from a 2400 bps unit, it slows itself down to 2400 bps.

Here are the standards:

- **Bell 103 (also known as V.21)**   300 bps communications. Just for backward compatibility.

- **Bell 212A (also known as V.22)**   1200 bps standard. Somewhat antique, but a few 1200 bps bulletin boards still exist.

- **V.22bis**   2400 bps. The most prevalent speed at this writing.

- **V.32**   9600 and 4800 bps. When folks talk of a high-speed modem, generally they mean V.32. The common speed is 9600; if 4800 bps is used at all, it's used as a fallback speed, when conditions are so noisy that the two modems can't swing 9600 bps.

- **V.32bis**   Includes V.32, plus speeds of 14,400, 12,000, and 7200 bps. This is as fast as you're going to get at this writing.

> Whenever you see V. in front of a number, it's a CCITT standard. The *bis* is a French word that means, in this usage, "modified" or "extended."

On the horizon is a new standard, called (for now) *V.fast*, which promises real speeds of 19,200 bps or greater.

In general, all modems maintain backward compatibility. Thus, a V.32 (9600 bps) modem also has V.22bis, V.22, and V.21 compatibility. The state-of-the-art modem you buy today will almost certainly be compatible with other, older modems.

Command Set

What commands does the modem accept? How do you tell the modem to dial a number? Answer the phone? Clearly, if a given telecom program is going to work with a broad range of modems, you need a standard set of modem commands. This is what you have in the Hayes Command Set.

Sometimes it's called the AT command set, because all commands begin with AT (when the modem sees ATH, for instance, it knows it's time to hang up the phone). Other, trivial command sets exist, but none are as important as the Hayes set. Almost all modems have the Hayes set, and you should avoid those that don't.

Error Checking

Say you (and your modem) live out in the boonies, and the quality of the phone lines is so bad that when you call Mom she asks you if the room's on fire. Or, say you live with several others, and right in the middle of an important online session, as a news article as being sent— an article you paid ten bucks to receive—someone picks up an extension phone.

In both cases, minor havoc results as your modem tries to make some sort of sense out of all the extraneous noise. At best, you see a screenful of garbage data; at worst, your modem hangs up. "Wouldn't it be swell," you say to yourself, "if these modems could figure out *for themselves* that something's gone bonkers and some data will have to be sent again?"

You think like I do, my friend, and as it happens like modem designers do. Many modems have insurance built-in, in the form of error-checking protocols. Independent of you, your Mac, or the software running thereupon, two modems that feature the same error-checking protocol can double-check the data being transmitted, and when data gets mangled during transmission, it is simply sent again.

The oversimplified version: Error control monitors certain information sent with each block of data. If the data received don't match properly, the receiving modem notifies the sending modem that an error has occurred and asks it to retransmit the block of data.

It's actually a lot more complicated than that but trust me, it works.

Currently there are only two standards for error checking: the old one and the new, more popular one:

- **MNP (Microcom Networking Protocol)**   MNP, developed by Microcom, was one of the first error-checking protocols. Every now and then, Microcom comes out with a new enhancement to the protocol, which is why you often hear of MNP Level 4 versus Level 5 versus Level 10. Microcom owns the protocol and licenses the scheme to other manufacturers. MNP Level 4 is the most advanced MNP error checking generally found in non-Microcom modems, because Microcom has released it into the public domain where anyone can use it for free. The best versions—Level 5 and above at this writing—are exclusive to Microcom hardware. Level 10 is currently the highest version.

- **V.42**   As the V implies, this is the internationally supported CCITT standard for error checking. V.42 includes MNP Levels 1 to 4.

They both do a fine job of trapping errors, but V.42 has an advantage: A modem manufacturer doesn't have to pay a dime in licensing fees to implement V.42, and it includes MNP Levels 1 to 4, so it's more popular. The sole advantage of MNP is that Microcom is constantly refining and improving the standard. For the CCITT to improve upon V.42, it'd have to go through a long bureaucratic process; enhancing MNP means little more than Microcom engineers earning their pay. Buying a modem with the latest version of the MNP protocol will set you back a pretty penny, but is of value only when communicating with modems containing that same level of MNP. In other words, V.42 is the more attractive standard.

Data Compression

Say you're taking out a classified ad. You're allotted two lines of forty characters each. You begin to write out "1982 Brown Plymouth Gran Fury, in perfect condition, with air conditioning" when you run out of space. "Aha!" you exclaim, "I see a way of transmitting exactly the same info in far less space!" And so you write instead "82 Br. Ply. Grafur, Perf Cond, w/AC." That's data compression.

Two modems with data compression features can transmit data in as little as a quarter of the time it would take without data compression. Without any direction or intervention from you, your Mac, or your telecom program, your modem takes the data fed to it by your Mac, compresses it, and sends that compressed data to the receiving modem. The receiver gets that pile of numbers, decompresses it back to its original form, and sends it to the computer connected to it.

Thus, neither computer detects that data compression has ever taken place; the data that goes into the modem at one end is the exact same data that comes out of the modem at the other end. So a text file that might have taken ten minutes to transmit can arrive in as little as two and a half minutes under data compression. If it's a 9600 bps modem, it's still transmitting data at 9600 bps; it's not working harder, it's working *smarter*.

Data compression is wonderful in that it's a cheap way to get great performance from a modem. The best part is that data compression works on *everything* that goes through the modem, not just files. Messages and information text also come through at a speedier rate.

There are two data compression standards:

- **MNP Level 5 (and above)** Microcom implements data compression along with error checking.

- **V.42bis** The CCITT standard version.

The same advantages and disadvantages apply here as applied to error checking: V.42bis is in the public domain, but Microcom updates MNP regularly. The V.42bis standard has a performance advantage, though. As you'll see in Chapter 5, some files are already compressed by your Mac *before* they go through the modem. As the data's already been scrunched down as much as possible, any attempt to cram them down more only costs time. V.42bis leaves such data alone, but MNP 5 wastes time trying to shave off a byte here and there.

What data compression and error checking have in common is that they don't rely on any special feature: They exist solely as programs that run as needed on the computer inside your modem.

Software in ROM

Besides the features and standards detailed at length previously, different manufacturers can include a cornucopia of functions within the modem's software (actually, since it's burned into the modem's ROM, it's called *firmware*). When you're buying your modem, try to look at the manuals and check for features like additional dialing commands, extended result codes, built-in help, and diagnostics.

Additional Dialing Commands Every modem can dial a number you give it, but many costlier modems expand that idea wonderfully. You can store a phone book of numbers in the modem's memory and have the modem automatically redial a number until a connection is made. Some modems can even deal with letters of the alphabet when dialing (give it PIN–HEAD and it dials 746-4323). Many of these functions may be duplicated by your Mac's telecom software, but they're handy features nonetheless.

Extended Result Codes All modems let you know what's going on, but the better ones have a much better vocabulary. Rather than telling you that it didn't connect, a good modem can tell you why (busy, no dial tone, and so on), and also tell you everything about the kind of connection it managed to establish (Speed? Error checking? Data compression?).

Built-in Help Type one simple command and the modem outputs a list of all modem commands and what they do. Essential when traveling without a manual!

Diagnostics Another command outputs a list of all the current modem settings, the last number dialed, why the modem hung up, and other info essential in figuring out why things aren't working right.

To look for conveniences like these, you have to talk to a technical-support person at the manufacturer. Many modem manufacturers will send you a copy of the manual upon request. When you're spending more than $200 on a modem, it can help you to make an informed decision.

Security Features

For most people, a modem's security features don't make a modem even a tiny bit more useful, but do drive up the price. So skip ahead to the next section if you want to.

If you need to set up a secure communications network, however, you should look for one or two things.

A simple feature is password verification. Normally, a BBS program running on a computer asks for a password from a user, but when this feature is built into a modem, it allows that same security to take place before the computer knows that a call has come in. If the user's password is verified by the modem, then the computer is notified that a call has come in and the connection continues as usual.

But more secure than this is ringback security. The modem keeps a list of authorized users *and their phone numbers*. When someone calls in and provides an authorized user name, the modem immediately *hangs up*, and *dials that person's phone number* to establish the connection! This guarantees that only authorized users can have electronic access to your system; even if someone swipes a user name, the best the miscreant can do is get your modem to call the legal user's modem and shriek in his or her ear a bit. It's also useful (or unattractive, depending on how you look at it) in that a salesperson or field rep can call from across the country and be charged only for the minute it takes to give your modem his or her name. The rest of the session is billed to your phone bill; your modem placed the (long-distance?) call.

Making a Buying Decision

What features make a difference in your life? Backward compatibility ensures that you'll never go wrong by buying the best modem you can afford. But you certainly don't need to spend a lot to cover all the features you'll need. Four common sets of features cover every budget.

One last thing (and I'll repeat it again and again): It's best to buy from vendors who provide a thirty-day money-back guarantee. You need to try this stuff out in your own environment—what works in the dealer's showroom (or is promised to work in a mail-order ad) doesn't always work when you plug it into your Mac at home. A money-back guarantee ensures that if you get it home and are dissatisfied in any way, you can get your money back and try a different brand or model.

Also note that the models mentioned are merely examples; dozens of similar products are available from a variety of manufacturers.

Bleacher Seats

This is a plain, entry-level Hayes-compatible modem with only the basic features required for telecom. For about a hundred bucks, you can get a small, plastic modem that runs at 2400 bps without error checking or data compression. Generally it has a built-in speaker and a full bank of indicator lights, but at this price you don't find many frills. On the other hand, it's great for people just getting started: it's simple to set up (just plug it in and go), and it costs a great deal less than most software programs on the market.

Examples: the Zoom Telephonics 2400 (Figure 2–5) or Prometheus Promodem 2400 Mini.

Figure 2–5: The "no frills" Zoom Telephonics 2400

Box Seats

This is a 2400 bps modem with a lot of the trimmings. Instead of a plastic case, it has a metal or well-vented plastic enclosure so it's not as likely to burn out as a Bleacher model. It's decked out with V.42 error checking and V.42bis data compression, and may feature some advanced diagnostics in ROM.

Choose this for your entry-level modem if you can spend just a bit more; at $150–$300, it may be well worth the money. Remember that V.42 and V.42bis can edge performance way up. If you can spend more than $300, though, it makes more sense to start looking at 9600 bps V.32 modems.

Examples: the Zoom Telephonics V.42bis, Emac 2400, SupraFaxModem Plus (Figure 2–6).

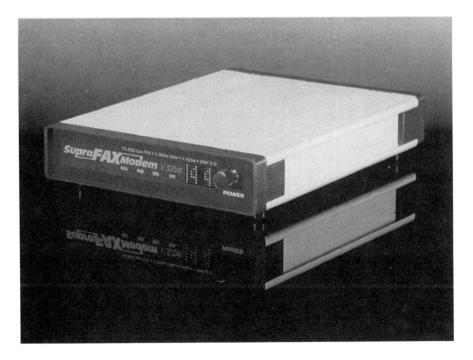

Figure 2–6: The SupraFaxModem Plus includes most of the trimmings

Skybox Seats

Now you're talking fast. An entry-level V.32 modem that communicates at 9600 bps. It's hard to believe the value of such a speed increase until you witness a high-speed telecom session; do you really want to stay on-line four times longer then absolutely necessary?

There's a serious jump in price, of course: you're talking $400 at the low end. At that price you're liable to get a cheap enclosure and not a lot of extra features, though V.42 and V.42bis are becoming almost a given with V.32 hardware.

Examples: the Zoom Telephonics V.32 (a great deal, by the way) shown in Figure 2–7, Practical Peripherals PM9600SA, Hayes Optima 9600.

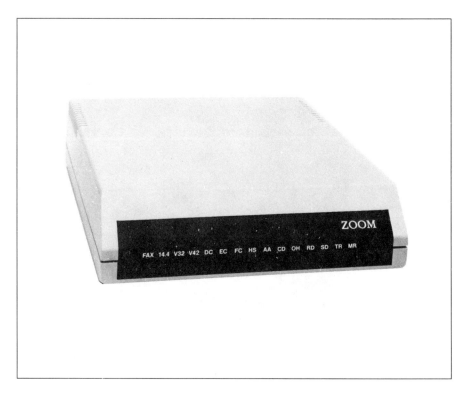

Figure 2–7: The Zoom Telephonics V.32 is feature-packed

Commissioner's Box

Edging toward the stratosphere in both features and price, this kind of modem has every single feature, and it is usually designed to be good enough for a BBS modem. It's also designed for the folks who spend thirteen hours a day with their modems, living vampire hours (working only during the night).

They can be expensive, starting at about $700 and soaring into four figures, but if you're dedicated to telecom, you'll be happy with no less. All speeds and data compression/verification standards are supported, the unit could be left on continuously for years without burning up, and so on. I don't recommend this pro-quality modem for someone just starting out; it takes a while to begin to appreciate its features, and some of them can take time to set up and configure properly. But once you get it working, it'll fly. It'll *ruin* you for all other modems.

Examples: the USRobotics Courier HST Dual Standard shown in Figure 2–8 (this is the modem both of us use—it's great and worth every penny when you get serious about telecom), Hayes Ultra 9600, Telebit T2500.

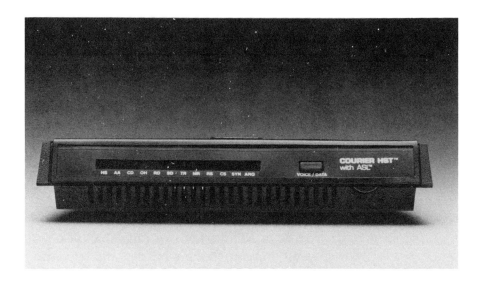

Figure 2–8: The USRobotics Courier HST is about as good as it gets

Specialty Modems

Until now, we've been talking about the most common type of modem: the non-Mac-specific kind that plugs into a serial port, and is used for communicating with other modems. But alternatives are available to suit various special circumstances.

Pocket Modems

The proliferation of notebook MS-DOS computers has engendered a proliferation of equally portable modems for telecom on the road. In theory they're not different from any other modem that connects through a serial port, but they come in a more compact size.

Mac owners should be careful before buying these modems, though, because some factors can render them unusable with Macs. Many of them get their power directly from the computer's serial port, and some of these don't work with the Mac. Many of them also require special cabling, unavailable for the Mac.

You'll pay a premium for tiny size, and unless you're desperate for space, avoid these generic pocket modems.

Internal Modems

Some people are vaguely offended by the concept of having to put a new box on their desk every time they want to do something new. Internal modems are just the ticket. These modems install inside an open Mac (Mac II series, Quadra) or Portable or PowerBook, leaving nothing extra on your desk but a phone line that plugs into a phone jack on the back of your Mac.

Personally, I'm prejudiced against these internal modems. First, they tend to be more expensive than a similarly configured external modem; second, you can't simply unplug an internal modem and use it with a Mac Classic or even an IBM, as can be done with an external; and third, you have no hands-on access to the thing at all—no indicator lights, no nothing.

If you have a PowerBook or Luggable (yes, that's a swipe at the Macintosh Portable), though, internal modems can be a tremendous convenience. When you have to cram all your paraphernalia into an overhead compartment and an underseat bag, every bit of space helps.

It also helps to know that you'll never find yourself in Nashua, New Hampshire, without a modem cord and thirty minutes away from a deadline! These internal modems plug into slots waiting inside your portable Macs. Installation in a Mac Portable is trivial, but you may have to refer PowerBook installation to a qualified technician. Space is cramped, so fitting the new circuit board properly requires precision. No matter which portable Mac you own, though, expect to pay more for an internal modem than you would for a comparable external model.

ADB Modems

If you don't mind a little fob dangling off your portable, you may want to consider an ADB modem. Normally you plug a modem into a serial port. But someone at Global Village Communications decided that it'd be much niftier to be able to plug a modem into an Apple Desktop Bus (ADB) port, normally used for mice, keyboards, and trackballs!

There is a method to the madness: By plugging a modem into an ADB connector instead of a serial port, you free up a port for other things; without one of Global Village's TelePort modems, it's difficult to have an AppleTalk connector and a StyleWriter printer installed along with a modem without a lot of cable switching. The TelePort works beautifully; it comes with special software that allows you to use the modem and printer ports for anything you like, while the TelePort uses the ADB port. Since the modem itself is small—slightly bigger than a deck of cards—and designed so it can be mounted on a wall, outlet, Mac, or monitor, the software installs faux modem lights right in your menu bar, as shown in Figure 2–9.

Figure 2–9: TelePort software puts "modem lights" in your menu bar and provides serial port emulation

Is it a good substitute for a regular serial modem? Probably. If you're short of free serial ports, the TelePort is invaluable. Folks with portable Macs will find it a convenient, cheaper substitute for an internal modem. And if you intend to buy a modem with fax capabilities (more on these in a moment), Global Village's fax software is about as good as it gets.

But all other things equal, most telecom beginners are better off with a more traditional serial modem. They require no special CDEVs (Control Panels) to work, and besides when you outgrow them, you can sell or give them to just about anyone; a TelePort can be used only with Macs.

Global Village makes some wicked hardware regardless, and it's reasonably priced, too. I've had excellent results with both the TelePort connected to my desktop IIci, and the PowerPort I just installed in my PowerBook.

Network Modems

Say you manage a network of a dozen Macs or so. Every now and then, any one of them may need to be able to dial into a remote database to download mail and other business data. Three solutions come to mind: You can buy a dozen modems, one for each Mac. Or you can buy one modem and set aside a Mac for telecom use. The best solution, however, may be to buy a NetModem.

The NetModem, made by Shiva, is a modem that can be shared across an AppleTalk network just like a laser printer. Once it's installed, any user can go to the Chooser and select the NetModem. From there, special software tricks your Mac and any telecom software into thinking that faraway modem is hooked into the modem port.

Shiva makes a basic 2400 bps model as well as a V.32 version. For even greater flexibility, try Shiva's NetSerial, which offers network availability to *any* serial device you plug into it. This allows you to plug in a V.32bis/V.42bis modem, making it available to dozens of people.

Fax Modems

A modem is a device that takes numerical data and sends it across a phone line to a receiving machine. A fax machine is a device that takes an image, converts it to numerical data, and sends it across a phone line to a receiving machine. It wasn't long before it occurred to someone that a computer modem could handle both functions: talk to both modems and fax machines.

It's a slick concept. Modem functions work as they do on any other modem, but the device includes extra software and hardware for handling fax. Typically, you get a Chooser-level printer driver and a stand-alone application or desk accessory for managing the device's fax processes. When you've finished typing a document in your favorite word processor, spreadsheet, or graphics program, you select your fax modem from the Chooser as you would any printer, give the Print command from that word processor, and specify the phone number of the receiving fax machine (as well as other pertinent data) in the print dialog box that follows. Just as your Mac would when printing to an actual printer, the letters, symbols, and images of that document are converted into dots. Instead of going to a printer, however, the dots go out the fax modem as a standard, outgoing fax—receivable by any standard fax machine. And in most cases, faxes that originate on your Mac look better than pages fed through a stand-alone fax machine.

Incoming faxes are handled by the software; when a fax comes in, the fax application takes the image and saves it as a PICT or TIFF file, which can be viewed on the screen or printed at your leisure.

The only catch here is in sending images from hard copy. If your Mac doesn't have a scanner attached, you can transmit only those documents generated by Macintosh programs. A smaller catch is that incoming faxes can take several hundred kilobytes of disk space each. Depending on your incoming fax volume, and whether you keep incoming faxes indefinitely, you may want some additional disk space to go with your fax modem. A trivial catch—which could be perceived as a bonus if you like to read your faxes on the Mac's screen—is that once your fax is received, you have to print it if you want hard copy.

Fax modems are getting cheaper and cheaper, so much so that some modem manufacturers (like Zoom Telephonics) throw in fax features with even their cheapest entry-level modem. The bargain-basement modems may only be capable of sending faxes and not receiving them; be sure to check feature lists carefully. The single most important component of a fax modem is the software that comes with it. QuickLink II/Fax, for instance, which ships with many of the less expensive units, has been almost universally condemned as, at best, a barely functional fax program, lacking many of the bells and whistles of a commercial package. The pity is that, whereas a data modem sticks to a well-defined, standardized command set and as such can be operated by any telecom program, no such standards exist for fax modems (though one is currently under deliberation). Therefore, you're stuck with the software that ships with the modem, or a limited selection of third-party solutions.

If you send and receive a lot of faxes each day, you'll probably be better served by a stand-alone fax machine. While it's receiving an incoming fax, your Mac can be almost-normal to virtually unusable. In other words, it'll probably slow down work in your foreground application, perhaps a lot. Variables are the speed of your Mac (faster processors mean less disturbance), and which software came with your fax modem.

Global Village's TelePort fax modems (discussed previously under "ADB Modems") are about the best. The software is elegant and easy to use, and it works reliably. (Figure 2–10 shows a typical TelePort/Fax screen.)

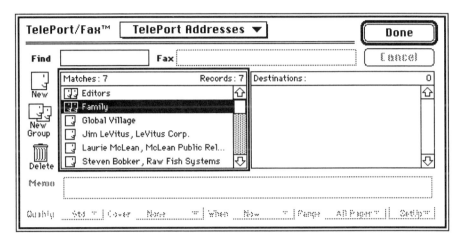

Figure 2–10: Global Village's TelePort FAX modems have slick software.

Fax modems are nice, but a real fax machine may serve your needs better than a fax modem. Or, if you want the best of both worlds, use both a fax modem and a stand-alone fax machine, like I do.

I use a Global Village fax modem for sending documents that originated as Mac files—letters typed in Microsoft Word, pictures drawn in Canvas, and so on. They always arrive looking much better than if I printed them on the laser printer and sent them using my stand-alone fax machine.

I also use my stand-alone fax machine every day. It's best for receiving faxes and sending any faxes that originated as hard copy— magazine articles, photos, finger paintings, and so on.

Even if you have a scanner (I do), it's easier to feed a sheet of paper into a stand-alone fax machine than it is to scan it, save it, and send it using a fax modem.

If you decide to try a fax modem, make sure it comes with a money-back guarantee.

Snake Oil

Unfortunately, some companies are less than honest and straightforward when it comes to marketing their products. It'd be irresponsible of me to suggest that *every* corporation that tries the following scams on you is stuffed to the gills with thieving weasels; I'm just saying that you can find some popular, misleading statements in modem ads. Such as:

- **Speed lie #1** Throughput. As I said before, V.42bis is neat; with on-the-fly data compression, data can be transmitted in a quarter of the time it'd take without compression. Unfortunately, some copywriters use this info to bamboozle you into thinking that you're getting a great deal on a 9600 bps modem. When you see in big bold type "9600 bps throughput modem!" generally they mean "This is only a 2400 bps modem, but when you use data compression it can work as fast as a 9600 bps model." Remember that unless you see V.32 listed among the modem's features, that modem is *not* a 9600 bps modem.

- **Speed lie #2** Fax transmission. With most fax modems, fax data gets sent at 9600 bps. So again you'll see, in big bold type "9600 bps modem!" Technically, it's true. They just don't mention that when used as a plain old computer modem, its maximum speed is 2400 bps. Again, if it doesn't say V.32, it isn't a 9600 bps modem.

- **Package scams** The best way to make a huge profit on a $100 modem is to sell it as part of a $300 software package. Often, the "$200 Retail Value Communications Package!" is actually an obsolete copy of an old telecom program that the marketer bought as salvage for ten bucks. Not all package deals are fishy—some are excellent values—but make sure that the software included is up to date, and that you *want* the software to begin with. As you'll see in Chapter 3, shareware software that sets you back only 30 bucks can be far more useful than commercial software.

Parting Shots

By now, you should understand the basics of modem hardware and be well equipped to go out and shop for the modem of your dreams. In a nutshell, these are the essentials :

- It's unlikely that you'll need a special type of phone line for your modem—the one in your home or office will work fine. You may want to install a separate line for your modem later, but it's not required.

- Differentiating factors include switched phone jacks, built-in speaker, indicator lights, imperviousness to heat, speed, error checking, and data compression.

- Get the fastest modem you can afford.

- Make sure you get a money-back guarantee.

- Fax modems are nifty but have certain drawbacks.

- Don't be fooled by marketing hype.

3

The Software End

Selecting the software that best suits your needs

In Chapter 2, we told you what to look for in modem hardware. When you buy a modem, at least you've got a shiny metal box with buttons and lights on it. No such luck when you buy software. Although it usually costs less than hardware, all you get is three diskettes and a 230-page user manual—not much to look at. That's usually the second thing a new computer user learns. (The first, of course, is Murphy's law of computer ownership: "Anything that can go wrong will go wrong, and always at the worst possible moment.")

The good news is that shopping for software can be much simpler than making a hardware purchase. You're choosing the program that you'll be firing up every time you want to get on line, so you can make decisions based on gut-level "I like the way this program works" responses rather than comparing lots of technical options.

You can indeed spend a few hundred dollars for a telecom program, but as you'll learn in this chapter, the best telecom software to start with is a shareware program with a $30 registration fee—ZTerm. Even if your modem came with software, ZTerm is worth checking out.

A word of warning: there's a basic problem in discussing the various features of telecom software early in this book. Does it make any sense to write "Make sure your telecom program supports Foobar commands" when you won't know what good Foobar is for another hundred pages? We decided unanimously to discuss what software to buy *before* talking about how to use it. Feel free to skip ahead to pertinent chapters or glossary entries if you get confused.

Choosing Software

Different people are going to expect different things from telecom software. Contentious on-line discussions about the best telecom program are common.

> After reading another chapter or two, when you feel qualified, log onto an on-line service or BBS (I suggest CompuServe's Communications forum [go MACCOM] or America Online's Business forum [keyword: MacBiz]) and post a public message. Title the message "Which telecom software should I buy?" In the body of the message, describe your situation and level of expertise. I promise you the dozens of responses you'll receive will be worth the time and expense it takes to collect them, and a wonderful complement to what you are about to read.
>
> To log on and leave a message if you don't have any telecom software yet, try one of the following solutions:
>
> • Beg or borrow a copy of a shareware telecom program (we like ZTerm, as you'll find out in a few pages) to use in your research.
>
> • Subscribe to America Online (see Chapter 7), an on-line service that provides a free copy of its proprietary software (which can be used only to access America Online) when you sign up.

At some point you'll have to evaluate software by the opinions in the book, those you've gathered on line (assuming you elected to perform the exercise described earlier), and the judgment of friends, acquaintances, and user group members, or experiment until you find a package that best suits your taste and style.

The Macintosh Communications Toolbox

"Supports the Comm Toolbox" is the current catchphrase in software advertising. Every software publisher wants you to know that their telecom program uses of one of the latest additions to the standard Macintosh System software without telling you what those advantages actually are. Advertisers are funny that way.

Communications has always been slighted in terms of the standard Macintosh user interface. In any word processor, you print a document by selecting Print from the File menu. To make a word processor work with a new printer, you simply put the proper printer driver in the System Folder, where any Mac program can find it and therefore print using it.

But how do you establish a connection to a remote computer? Five different telecom programs can handle it five different ways.

So Apple developed the Macintosh Communications Toolbox (CTB hereafter), a set of standard System routines available to communications programs that attempts to bring modularity and a consistent user interface to communications. File-transfer protocols, methods of connecting to a remote service, and various terminal emulations can be distributed as stand-alone tools; if you want your telecom program to use a specific file-transfer protocol, you can put the appropriate tool in your System Folder. Magically, your telecom program (and all other programs that are compatible with the Comm Toolbox) will now support that particular protocol.

Comm Toolbox support is a desirable feature in a communications program, but beware: some programs rely too heavily on it, at the expense of interactivity. The Comm Toolbox can sometimes act like another layer between you and the modem. You give commands to your telecom program, the telecom program gives commands to the

Comm Toolbox, then the Comm Toolbox gives its orders to the modem. The best programs *support* the Communications Toolbox, but don't force you to use it directly if you don't want to.

For a more detailed rundown on the Comm Toolbox, see Appendix C.

Common Interface Elements of Telecom Software

In this section, you'll learn what to expect from a telecom program. Though dozens of programs exist, they have many common elements.

Terminal Window

The terminal window is the most fundamental thing on the screen. It's your eyes and ears. Figure 3–1 shows ZTerm's terminal window.

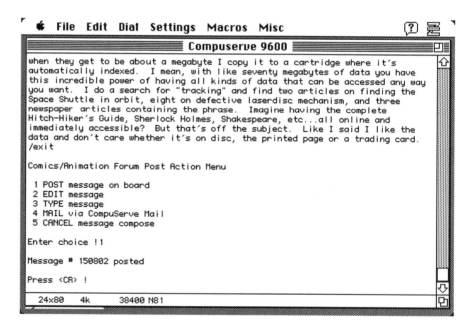

Figure 3–1: ZTerm's terminal window

The terminal window shows you both the text you've transmitted to the on-line service you're connected to and what the service has transmitted back. The terminal window is like the window in your word processor, except that you're not the only one entering text.

Notice the scroll bar to the right of the screen. As new text comes in at the bottom of the window, the old information scrolls off the top. Any decent telecom program remembers all the text that's passed through the terminal window and allows you to scroll back to see something you may have missed. The old lines of text go into the *scrollback buffer*. Since you can scroll back, you don't have to waste time asking for file listings or help summaries from a BBS more than once; to see something again, just click in the scroll bar.

Some telecom programs (usually ones based on the Comm Toolbox) put all the scrolled-off data into a second window, apart from the terminal window. Although it works just as well, it's less convenient. Also, some software limits the size of the scrollback buffer; once you've exceeded the limit, you lose old information The best programs have scrollback buffers limited only by available disk space. If you stay on line for an hour or two, this is a useful feature.

Status Line

A status line gives you such information as what the current communication settings are, what service you're currently connected to, and how long you've been on line. Usually, the status line appears in the terminal window; it's at the top of White Knight's main window in Figure 3–2, and you can also see it at the bottom of ZTerm's window in Figure 3–1. White Knight's status line also puts some handy features out in the open, including buttons for archiving data in the terminal window to a printer or a text file on disk.

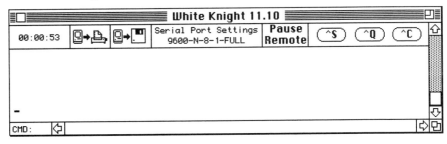

Figure 3–2: White Knight's status line

Think of the status line as a detailed set of dashboard gauges. A good status line is very useful. If garbled text starts spewing into the terminal window, you can verify at a glance that your communications settings are correct without having to check each menu.

Some telecom programs let you enter how much a particular service charges per hour of connection time. A status line that says you've been on line for over two hours has only a fraction of the impact of looking up and seeing $28.92.

Button Palettes

Apple's guide to how the Mac user interface should look (*Human Interface Guidelines: The Apple Desktop Interface;* Addison-Wesley) advises programmers to use buttons liberally. Thus, many telecom programs use buttons. For example, Smartcom II has a row of buttons right at the bottom of the terminal window (Figure 3–3).

Figure 3–3: Smartcom II's buttons

To dial the phone, click on the phone. To send a file, click on the Send icon. Another common use of buttons is found in MicroPhone II (Figure 3–4).

Figure 3–4: MicroPhone II's button palette

Here, the user defines the buttons. I created the buttons in Figure 3–4 for logging onto two on-line services. Once I've connected to a service, those buttons disappear and different ones take their place— buttons I've created for performing functions I need while logged onto that service.

Features Under the Hood

So much for surface characteristics. Buttons and indicators are great, but there's more to telecommunications software than that. This section describes behind-the scenes features common to most telecom programs on most platforms.

File-Transfer Protocols

Make sure your telecom program doesn't skimp in the quality and variety of its file-transfer protocols.

A *file-transfer protocol* is a method of taking a file on one computer, chopping it into tiny, easily managed blocks of data, sending it to another computer, and then reassembling all those electronic blocks back into an exact copy of the original file with no errors in transmission.

There are many, many file-transfer protocols. The more file transfer protocols your telecom program supports, the better prepared you'll be. Here's a quick rundown of popular protocols (a more comprehensive explanation of each protocol appears in Chapter 5):

- **ZMODEM** The best, fastest, and most popular protocol in common use. If a telecom program lacks this protocol, it's *sorely* lacking. ZMODEM suspends error checking automatically if it senses an error-checking modem.

- **XMODEM** A basic, slow but adequate protocol. It's one of the oldest file transfer protocols, and one of the simplest, so nearly every telecom program and BBS supports it. Use it as a last resort. Many telecom packages also include XMODEM CRC, which stands for Cyclical Redundancy Checking, a method of error-checking that's a bit more effective than plain-vanilla XMODEM (sometimes referred to as XMODEM Checksum to differentiate it from XMODEM CRC). While the two flavors are sometimes segregated as different protocols on a BBS, in most Mac telecom software CRC and Checksum are part of the same XMODEM protocol.

- **XMODEM 1K** A faster variant of XMODEM. It breaks the file to be transmitted into bigger chunks than XMODEM, so it stops less often to ask "Hey, Bud, that block come through okay?"

- **YMODEM** Faster and a bit more flexible than XMODEM, but still not as good as ZMODEM.

- **YMODEM-G** YMODEM without error checking. You'd use this protocol with a V.42 modem, which does the error checking.

- **CompuServe B and Quick B** CompuServe-specific protocols. An attempt by CompuServe to make up for the fact that they don't support ZMODEM.

At the very least, you want software that supports ZMODEM and the XMODEM variants.

Terminal Emulation

Terminal emulation features are either crucial or irrelevant. *Terminal emulation* defines how the host computer (the BBS) controls what appears in your terminal window. Most of the time, of course, the text scrolls continuously across your screen. Some services prefer to draw text anywhere on your screen, highlight certain text, draw lines and boxes, even draw color graphics on your screen.

Some folks use *dumb terminals*, which are nothing more than a keyboard and a monitor with no computing power built into them, to talk to their host computers. The half-dozen or so popular brands of these dumb terminals have different features. Your Mac can operate like a dumb terminal (displaying complex text and graphics) if your telecom software has the proper terminal emulators. You only need terminal emulation if you plan to connect to another computer that expects you to be using a dumb terminal. Here's a rundown of the most popular ones:

- **TTY** The simplest form of terminal emulation; stands for *Teletype*.

- **VT52/VT100/VT102** The most popular standard in telecom software. The host computer has direct control over the placement of text, allowing fully interactive displays and therefore a nicer user interface.

- **Tektronix** Denotes a family of graphics monitors. You'd want this terminal emulator only if you were hard-wired directly into a mainframe computer, and needed to do wireframe graphics.

- **VT340** The most sophisticated and most widely compatible emulation. Of use only if you're using a Mac to replace a VT340 terminal.

The bottom line: TTY and VT52/VT100/VT102 are all you realistically need. If you're using your Mac to take the place of a dumb terminal connected to a computer at school or in an office, though, better double-check with the system managers of that computer to find out if you need Tektronix or VT340 emulation.

Scripting

As you become a regular BBS user, you'll quickly realize that you have to perform a lot of procedures, exactly the same way every time. You have to dial a phone, then enter your name and a password, or you have to navigate from one area of a BBS to another through a repetitious sequence of commands, and so on. You could get a trained *monkey* to do the job for you, it's so repetitive.

Such a monkey is built into every telecom program that allows you to create *scripts*. A script can do something as simple as dial the phone and transmit your name and password when connected, or something as complex as wait until 3 A.M. when the phone rates are lowest, connect to five on-line services, download all new files and read all new messages, and automatically send out a stack of messages you wrote the night before.

Most telecom programs offer *some* scripting, but vary in how robust the scripting language is. A rudimentary language would be limited to simple tasks such as connecting to a service, waiting for the service to send a specific string (like *Please enter your password:*) and then sending something back in reply. With more sophisticated scripting languages, you can practically write your own telecom program from scratch, with customized windows, buttons, menus, dialog boxes, sounds, and more.

You could do without scripting, but you'll work much harder. No question.

Dialing Features

I'm amazed at how differently all the Mac telecom programs handle something as simple as dialing a phone number. Some maintain the list as a phone book, others as a menu, and worse still, some keep one settings file for each of your on-line services.

No matter how the settings are stored, be careful how you use software that allows you to store a password and user ID along with the service name and phone number. Typically, the passwords are stored as special keyboard macros, which allow you to press Command-1 instead of typing your password. Unfortunately, this convenience represents a possible security risk if you share your Mac with others.

> Security Warning: It's relatively easy for an unscrupulous person to discover your password by reading your settings file with a standard text editor or using the program's built-in scripting function to learn it. They could even take the whole program and run your macro to log on. This means someone could use your account to run up huge bills without your knowledge or permission. Be careful where you leave your passwords!

> If you create a macro or script that contains your password, be sure your Mac is never be used by anyone you can't trust. If your Mac is often used by others, consider writing your scripts so they pause and ask you to enter the password manually.

A fundamental dialing feature is conspicuously absent from many Mac telecom programs: round-robin (or queue) dialing. You give the program a list of services, and each one is dialed in turn, until you've connected to every one of them. Some programs force you to dial individually, or to write a script to perform the queue dialing for you.

Fortunately, all the telecom programs we know will redial until a connection is made if they receive a busy signal.

Hardware Control

Not all telecom software supports hardware flow control and hand-shaking—procedures your modem follows to make sure things go well (see Chapter 4). If your modem supports these features, and you want to use them, make sure your telecom software supports them.

Host Modes

Say a pal from New Zealand needs one of your spreadsheet files, and it's too late for Federal Express. You decide to send it to him electronically, but he doesn't belong to any commercial service or public BBS.

If your telecom software has a host mode, with two or three mouse clicks you can set up your Mac as a small, simple BBS. In most cases, it's as simple as giving the software your pal's name and assigning him a password, then saying which files he's allowed to download. When he calls in from New Zealand and logs in correctly, he can download that spreadsheet file (and *only* that spreadsheet file) while you sleep.

Tchochkes

Tchochke is a Yiddish word meaning "features that fit in none of the above categories." (I know this because renowned Yiddish expert Guy Kawasaki told me so.) These are, for the most part, bonus features, thrown in by software vendors to "add value." Whether they do is a matter of opinion.

Templates   Some of the most popular programs come with an assortment of prewritten scripts to automate your adventures on commercial on-line services like CompuServe. They're nifty bonuses: At the least, they're good practical examples of how the program's scripting language works; at best, they can be useful additions to your software library. MicroPhone II comes with an outstanding library of useful templates, including one that facilitates access to Dow Jones News/ Retrieval Service and another that turns your Mac into a mini-BBS (like a host mode only better), as well as several others.

Built-in Word Processors   Some packages include a simple text editor for writing scripts and composing replies to messages. A text editor is handy because it takes much less memory than a full-featured word processor. On the other hand, Apple's TeachText application works about as well as most of them, and it's free.

The Software Itself

As always, to make an informed software purchase you must go to software stores, user groups, and bulletin boards and listen to as many opinions as you can stand. Everyone who's owned a modem for more than three weeks has a fervent opinion about some program or another.

Here's a collection of opinions to get you started. They cover nearly all major Macintosh telecom software available at this writing. We'll say when a program is great, we'll howl with delight when we say a program is truly lousy, but in both cases we'll try to explain why we think the way we do.

Keep in mind that these are, largely, opinions. If you already have one of these programs and love it dearly, good for you. Enjoy!

MicroPhone II 4.0

MicroPhone II from Software Ventures, is one of the largest, most full-featured, and impressive telecom packages available for the Mac. And it's probably the only telecom package that has something for everybody. For novices, it has simple, nonthreatening menus. For telecom regulars, it has many advanced features and the most complete scripting language on any platform. The documentation is also quite good.

Figure 3–5 shows Loran, a set of MicroPhone scripts that automatically logs onto a service (such as CompuServe), grabs all your mail, and allows you to read and compose your replies off line. Notice the scrolling lists, the pop-up menus, the individual menus and buttons—all generated by MicroPhone II scripts.

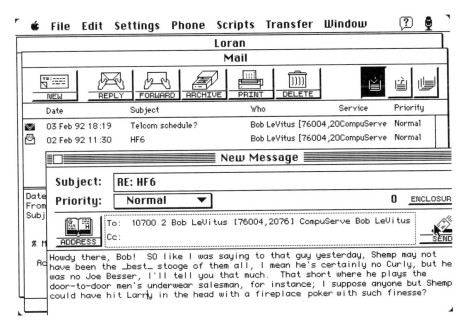

Figure 3–5: Using Loran, a set of MicroPhone II scripts, to log onto CompuServe

That's another great thing about MicroPhone II: It comes with lots of scripts, both ready-to-run telecom tools (one set of scripts turns MicroPhone II into a capable BBS program) and scripts set up as teaching examples. Finally, MicroPhone II has integrated the Communications Toolbox flawlessly; you get many of the advantages of independent communications tools without the distance the Comm Toolbox can sometimes place between you and the hardware.

The disadvantages of MicroPhone II are its high price (more than $200; not the best choice for a neophyte) and its slow speed compared to telecom programs like White Knight and ZTerm. MicroPhone II takes longer to establish a connection and download a file, and unless you're using a fast Macintosh, scripts execute kind of slowly. Also, MicroPhone II lacks certain features: no status bar, and it won't tell you how efficiently a file transfer went. It also has Command-key equivalents for most of the main functions (sending and receiving a file and stuff like that), but not for for other menu elements. (You can, however, use utilities such as QuicKeys and ResEdit to create Command-key shortcuts.)

Buy MicroPhone II if you want a great, heavy-duty telecom program, enjoy writing great-looking telecom scripts, or price is not a concern.

I use MicroPhone II and I like it a lot. Andy, on the other hand, thinks it's too slow and says, "you shouldn't have to load 200K of INITs to get a halfway decent set of keyboard shortcuts." Since I use QuicKeys, a fantastic keyboard enhancer and macro program from CE Software that uses about 200K of RAM, and it doesn't feel slow to me, I recommend it wholeheartedly.

Smartcom II 3.3 for the Mac

Smartcom II, from Hayes, is both easy to use and powerful, with limitations. It allows its users to establish connections and get to work with a minimum of mouse-clicking (see Figure 3–6: it has got to be the most friendly dialing screen on the market).

But for an easy-to-use telecom program, the menus are haphazardly laid out. Also, there's no simple way to deal with more than one service at a time.

Smartcom II tries to provide lots of power, with a modest scripting language, Communications Toolbox support, better-than-average on-line help, and sophisticated modem control. It doesn't give you a status bar, but you have to give it points for that soothing row of buttons at the bottom of the window, representing all the most common telecom functions. But for a powerful tool, its scripting language is somewhat skimpy.

On the whole, Smartcom II is an inexpensive program (under $100 by mail order) that delivers lots of features reliably, and it's simple enough that it won't intimidate anyone.

Buy Smartcom II if you want something simple enough for a beginner, powerful enough to rely on as you become more experienced, and reasonably priced.

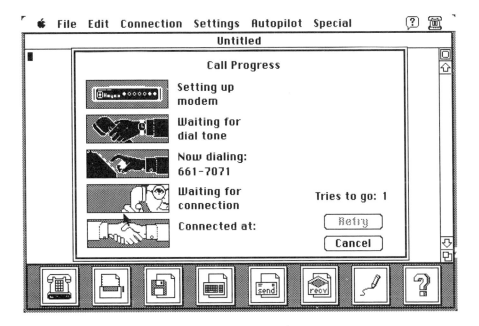

Figure 3–6: Smartcom II tries to simplify telecommunications

White Knight 11.12

There are only two schools of critical thought regarding White Knight (see Figure 3–7), from FreeSoft.

- **School 1: White Knight's the ultimate tool for the modem junkie** You're in control of every possible technical detail. If you want to control your modem directly, it doesn't get in your way. Its status line always reports on the status of the serial connection. And just about every feature can be accessed with a Command-key sequence. This is especially handy if you realize that the BBS is going to send you a file using a protocol different from what you expected; in White Knight, you can quickly press Command-R-Y to set the protocol to YMODEM before the BBS gives up. While its scripting language isn't as robust as MicroPhone II's, White Knight's scripts run fast. In fact, everything in White Knight works fast. It also has built-in host modes and user-configurable buttons.

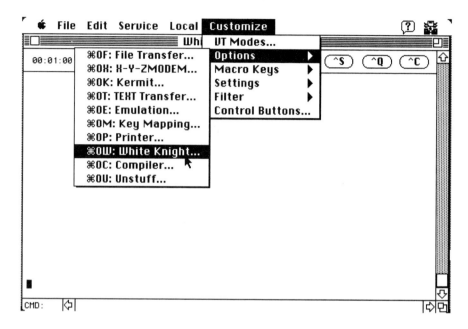

Figure 3–7: White Knight 11.12's user interface

- **School 2: White Knight's the most unintuitive, ugly, hard-to-use program** It wasn't designed to be especially pretty, or elegant, or easy to use (Command-R-Y? Who ever heard of a two-letter command key sequence? Figure 3–7). Working with it can be frustrating. Recently, I copied my White Knight folder from one hard drive to another, and discovered that when I ran White Knight from its new destination, it couldn't find any of my settings files or scripts; the program had recorded the files' location on the hard disk rather than within the White Knight folder. And unlike other telecom programs (ZTerm and MicroPhone, for instance) that can add lines into the scrollback buffer indefinitely, White Knight makes you specify how many screens of information it will remember.

White Knight is the brainchild of one person, Scott Watson, who has released about 20 versions over the past 4 years. He listens to his users; new versions are likely to incorporate features suggested by you. If you call for technical support, there's a good chance Scott will take the call.

White Knight is perhaps the best value in commercial telecom software; you're certainly not going to find more features for its price—well under a hundred bucks by mail order.

Buy White Knight if you want the fastest telecom program and the greatest level of control over your modem.

ZTerm 0.9

ZTerm is one of the best Mac telecom programs available. Its interface is simple and uncluttered, and you can master it within minutes. ZTerm has every important feature for users of any skill level. It supports all the important protocols, it's fast, it partially supports the Communications Toolbox, it allows you to have close contact with the modem if you prefer, it doesn't take up too much memory, and it's simple to use.

It's shareware, too. That means you can get a copy of it for free from any BBS or user group, then send $30 to the author only after you've decided to keep it.

Look at Figure 3–8. ZTerm is the best queue dialer on the Mac.

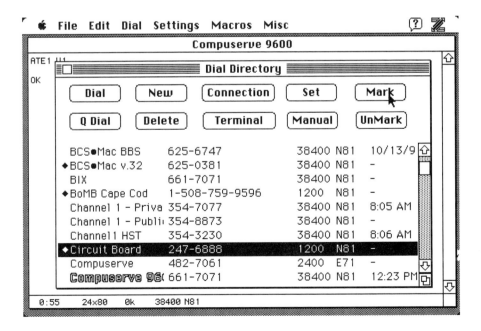

Figure 3–8: ZTerm, the Volkswagen of telecom programs

Disadvantages include its bare-bones scripting language, lack of a bound manual, and no staff of operators standing by 24 hours a day to provide technical support. ZTerm is the program Andy pulls out when he just wants to spend a leisurely evening on line. (I, on the other hand, use MicroPhone II for all my telecom needs, ignoring the speed penalty that seems to drive Andy nuts, and reveling in its elegant scripts and buttons.)

Who should get ZTerm: *everyone*. It's the perfect program for people just starting out, in that it's an elegant, full-featured, reliable program that can be had for free. *If* a month or two later you decide you'd rather have a commercial program, you've lost no money. So some of the best advice we can give you is to get a copy of ZTerm and try it for a while before you consider buying a more powerful (and more expensive) commercial program. It'll give you a chance to go on line at a very low cost, and you may even like it enough to adopt it permanently. (Though, as I said earlier, its scripting support is meager at best. When you become more addicted to telecom, you'll probably want MicroPhone II or White Knight, for their scripting capabilities if nothing else.)

PacerTerm 1.02

PacerTerm, from Pacer Software (under $200 by mail order) is based entirely on the Macintosh Communications Toolbox, and it's integrated and streamlined so well that every feature and function is where you expect it to be. You don't have to push a button to dial the phone or transfer files (though you can set up scripted buttons of your own).

Another slick feature: PacerTerm comes with advanced connectivity tools, which allows it to work nicely on UNIX systems, extended networks, and in other situations not generally covered by the most telecom programs. These connectivity tools alone (which will work with any telecom program supporting the Communications Toolbox) can justify the purchase of PacerTerm.

Finally, the program's scripting language is based entirely on HyperTalk (Figure 3–9)! It doesn't have the range of MicroPhone II, but the HyperTalk-based scripting (coupled with some simple commands for creating and manipulating dialogs and alerts) makes PacerTerm the easiest program to script for if you already know HyperTalk. You'll be up and running in seconds, and even if you don't know HyperTalk, you'll still find the English-like syntax agreeable.

Buy PacerTerm if you want UNIX connectivity and you need some top-notch scripting tools, or if you're well-versed in HyperCard's scripting language, HyperTalk, and you want to get started writing advanced scripts right away.

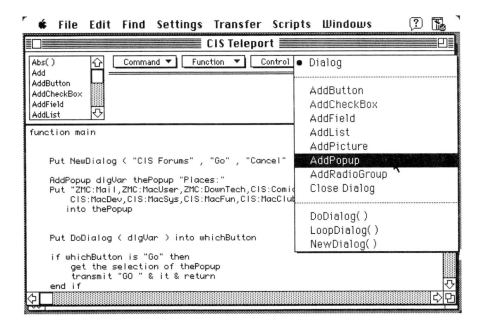

Figure 3–9: PacerTerm's scripting language is HyperTalk

QuickLink II

Avoid Smith Micro Software's QuickLink II. It's a hideous, flawed program, and it will cause you no end of frustration. Typically you get it free with a modem; if so, use it once, to connect to CompuServe, GEnie, or a local BBS, and download a copy of ZTerm. If you bought a fax modem, though, you might be stuck; chances are QuickLink II/ Fax is the only program that'll work with the modem for sending faxes. In that case, use QuickLink II for faxing *only* and use another telecom program for everything else.

MacKnowledge

MacKnowledge, by Prometheus, also comes free with some modems, but unlike QuickLink II, MacKnowledge is a capable program. It's still outclassed by ZTerm or just about any of the commercial programs, though.

VersaTerm Pro

Get VersaTerm Pro (around $200 by mail order), from Synergy, if you need terminal emulators that are a magnitude more complex than the VT52/VT100/VT102 found on most commercial software. If you need to work with mainframes or minicomputers, you probably need VersaTerm Pro. If neither of these conditions apply, you're best to leave VersaTerm alone.

Parting Shots

Your first telecom program should be ZTerm. It's one of the best telecom programs available, its features won't intimidate you, and it's shareware. You can get it for free from any Macintosh user group or BBS (to download a telecom program without having a telecom program, see the tip near the beginning of this chapter), and you pay only the $30 registration fee once you've convinced yourself it's worth it.

If you outgrow ZTerm, look into MicroPhone II, White Knight, or Smartcom II. Choose one of them based on your attitude toward telecom, after a few weeks or months with ZTerm:

- Get Smartcom II if you'd say: "Well, I sure do love it! But I sure wish things were easier," or "Look, my boss is forcing me to work with this computer. I hate it; just let me log on, log off, and get on with my life."

  Smartcom II has all the basic tools you need, it's easy on the pocketbook, and it's probably the most user-friendly telecom program of them all.

For the record, I hate the phrase *user-friendly*. It's one of those phrases like *Ecologically safe!* and *Cholesterol free!* that marketing hucksters slap on a product when they want to sell a lot more of whatever it is. The only marketing catchphrase I hate more is *sexy*, which in my humble opinion should only be applied to humanoid bipeds.

- Get MicroPhone II if you'd say: "Can't get enough of this telecom stuff. I'd love to start developing my own scripts, big time! Gimme windows! menus! dialogs! I don't mind spending a few extra dollars."

  I can't think of any other telecom program (for any computer) that can get someone so enthused about telecom scripting. Sure, you can't get those heavy duty scripts together without spending some days and weeks pounding away at the system, but it's a very rich and fulfilling experience.

  All you lack with MicroPhone II is a little speed.

- Get White Knight if you'd say: "Speed and control. That's my life. I want nothing between me and my modem. I want things as fast as it can be."

  White Knight was written for telecom enthusiasts who want raw power. When you want to interact with your modem directly, the software gets out of your way. When you want White Knight to *do* something for you, it does it fast. Its scripting language is robust, but parts of the user interface will take some time to get used to.

- Don't buy anything else if you'd say: "I like ZTerm just fine."

  Drop ZTerm only if you want great scripting, a slicker user interface, or if ZTerm is missing a single, key feature you need. For communicating with UNIX hosts, for example, VersaTerm and PacerTerm are better suited.

In the next chapter you'll learn everything you need to know to successfully complete your first session on line.

4

Your First Time

Hardware Setup, Software Setup, Your First On-Line
Session, and Other Decisions

This chapter has a simple goal: to help you set up your modem and
telecom software, and to wind up on line, with your local public
bulletin-board system.

We'll assume you have a phone line (go back and reread Chapter 2
if you don't).

Macintosh to Modem Connection

Let's start with something simple: the modem cable. Either the regular type or the hardware handshaking type work just fine. A hardware handshaking cable has a few extra connections that allow your telecommunications software to take advantage of hardware handshaking and flow control.

> Because modems and computers are high-speed devices, the modem may send data to your Mac when it's not ready to deal with it; similarly, your Mac may give your modem some data to transmit when the modem's too busy. To prevent the whole system from breaking down, the engineers have come up with a scheme so your Mac and your modem can tell when the other's ready to handle some data and when to lay off and wait for its partner to catch its breath. Any such scheme is a handshaking or flow control protocol.

There are two types of handshaking protocols. In software, special characters are sent down the stream of transmitted data to say "Whoa!" and "Giddyup!" to your modem; this is known as XON/XOFF (or software) handshaking. In hardware, special wires in the modem cable control handshaking. When there's current flowing in the "Giddyup!" wire, the device is ready to take on some data. Current in the "Whoa!" wire prevents data from being transmitted. This is known as hardware handshaking (if you like acronyms, the scheme supports DTR, CTS, and RTS).

Both protocols do a splendid job of preventing huge pileups of data in both directions, but XON/XOFF handshaking is just a bit less efficient. Because hardware handshaking takes place entirely outside the flow of data, it doesn't affect the speed of transmission. Another disadvantage of XON/XOFF is that sometimes data stops and goes when it shouldn't. The "Whoa!" and "Giddyup!" signals are just numbers being transmitted across that cable, after all, and remember your Mac and modem are always exchanging numbers. If part of that great arcade game you're downloading is misinterpreted as a "Whoa!" signal generated by your modem, the transfer of data halts and you'll have no idea why.

The point is that you should buy a hardware handshaking cable if you don't already have a cable. They only cost a dollar or two more (if that) than a nonhandshaking cable. If you go through the steps needed to turn hardware handshaking on, it results in a little higher performance. But even if you don't, it functions just like any nonhandshaking cable and you won't have lost anything. Allow me to dispel one myth before I drop the subject, though: No modem *requires* a hardware-handshaking cable. If a salesperson tries to tell you that you *must* buy a special cable to take advantage of a modem with built-in error checking or data compression, don't believe it.

Plugging In Your Modem

I know that almost all of you have looked at the back of your Macintoshes, seen the connector with the picture of a phone with data coming through it, and guessed that you plug the modem cable in right there. Let me mention a few alternatives, though.

First, the printer port right next door does just as good a job as the modem port. You can't use an AppleTalk network (all software looks for AppleTalk through the printer port and *only* through the printer port), and you probably have to explicitly tell all your telecom software that someone gave you this crazy idea not to use the modem port, but your modem works fine there nonetheless. It's generally the only way to have two modems (or one modem and a serial connection to another computer) up and running at the same time.

Unfortunately, if your two ports are already spoken for, your options are limited. If you have a Mac II series computer with NuBus slots, you can buy an expansion card with extra serial ports on it, such as Creative Solutions' Hurdler board or Applied Engineering's QuadraLink. Either of these gives you four extra serial ports (Creative Solutions also makes a two-port Hurdler) that come with special Control Panel software that bamboozles your Mac into thinking that one of the ports on the card is actually the modem or printer port. To use a modem plugged into one of those extra ports on the card, you open up the Control Panel, define that new port as the modem port, and get cracking. Whatever's plugged into the *real* modem port can't be used until you switch things back.

If you're using a telecom program that takes advantage of the Macintosh Communications Toolbox, though, everything's much simpler. Because the Comm Toolbox is much less fussy about communications devices (it only cares about *how* to find them rather than *where* they are physically) all the ports on the card as well as the modem and printer ports on your Mac can be active and working simultaneously. For more info on the Comm Toolbox, check out Appendix C.

There's another way. The TelePort ADB Modem (discussed in Chapter 2) can emulate a modem connected to the printer port while that port's in use for AppleTalk! Your Mac has three little pieces of code (device drivers): One controls the modem port, one controls the printer port, and one controls AppleTalk. If you have a local printer connected to the modem port and you are using AppleTalk on the printer port, the *software driver* for the printer port is sitting around idle! So through some clever programming, the people at Global Village wrote a Control Panel that gets that unused driver to work via their ADB modem rather than through the serial printer port it's usually associated with. Thus, when a telecommunications program looks for a device hooked up to the printer port, it ends up finding that TelePort modem on the ADB chain! Cool, huh?

Setting Up Your Modem (Part 1)

Now that you own everything you need, start setting things up. Plug one end of the modem cable into the modem port and the other end into the modem, plug a phone line into the modem where it says Line In (or something similar), and plug a telephone into the Phone Out jack (ditto).

Plug cables into your Mac only when the power's off. When volts and amps are seething through the hardware, there's always a slim chance that you'll inadvertently short something out (leading to an expensive motherboard replacement).

If you've already plugged everything in, remember that these things ought to be done only with the power off. You may get away with it most of the time, but one day it'll cost you. Trust us on this one.

Some modems also have an impressive row of tiny switches installed along the back. I'm not going to talk about those much, for some good reasons. First, their functions can vary from modem to modem, so any advice like "be sure the switch for X.25 default is off" would probably be of little use to most of you. The switches generally determine some of the fundamental operations of the modem, and usually they're all at the proper settings out of the box. Ignore them for now. If they become important, I'll point them out in turn (or you can always look in the manual as a last resort).

Now then. Take a deep breath, switch on the Mac and the modem (it doesn't make a difference which one first), and launch the communications software of your choice. After a second or so, the modem's bank of lights settles down to something like Figure 4–1.

Figure 4–1: A typical array of modem lights

Of course, different modems have different arrangements of lights, and perhaps different labels, but most modems have at least the core group of important lights shown in Figure 4–1.

Status Lights

In Chapter 2, I mentioned that a good bank of status lights is a necessity. Now you get practical proof. When I see that arrangement of lights, I can tell that everything's OK. It conveys a wealth of information:

- **HS**   High Speed. When lit, the modem is ready for high-speed communications. On early modems, this light meant "I'm going to try for a 1200 bps connection if possible" when lit, and "I'm going to limit myself to 300 bps" when not. Now that five or more speeds are possible, things are more complicated. Usually HS means "The highest speed I'm capable of," though some companies have fitted a tri-color LED into this slot: red means 2400, yellow means 9600, green means 14,400. Consult your manual for details.

- **AA** Automatically Answer. When lit, the modem is configured to automatically answer the phone whenever it rings and handle all incoming calls as if they were other computers trying to dial in.

- **CD** Carrier Detect. When lit, the modem has found another modem or data device at the other end of the phone line.

- **OH** Off Hook. When lit, the modem has the telephone "receiver" off the hook. The modem could be doing anything when this light is on—preparing to dial, dialing, connecting to another computer, patiently listening to a busy signal, and so on.

- **RD** Received Data. Every time the modem receives one bit of data from whatever remote computer it's connected to and passes it along to your Mac, the RD light flashes once. As data consists of thousands of bits, usually this light appears to flicker at 2400 bps and looks like it's always on at 9600 bps when information is being received.

- **SD** Sent Data. Like RD, only in reverse: It flashes when the modem transmits data to the remote computer.

- **TR** Terminal Ready. When lit, the modem thinks your Mac is all set to communicate with it. If the TR light is off, it probably means the Mac can't communicate with the modem—or the Macintosh hasn't been turned on yet! (Many Mac cables don't have TR wired properly, in which case the light will never go on! If your light doesn't go on, don't panic.)

- **MR** Modem Ready. When lit, the modem is ready to go. It's usually off only for brief periods, such as when the modem's switched off, it's going through a self-test, or new settings are being written to its memory.

At a glance you can look at Figure 4–1 and see that everything's as it should be. Here's specifically what the lights tell you:

- **HS on**   The modem will try to connect at the highest speed possible.

- **AA off**   If a phone call comes in, the modem will not answer it.

- **CD and OH off**   The handset is on the cradle and we're not connected to another remote computer.

- **RD and SD off**   Since we're not connected, no data will be sent or received.

- **TR and MR on**   The modem's working fine, and it's satisfied that the Mac's ready to send it data.

Problems with Status Lights

At this point, only one thing can have gone wrong: The TR and MR lights remain unlit. Unless this has happened to you, skip ahead to the next section.

Problem 1: MR Light Didn't Come On   Make sure the modem is plugged in and turned on. Switch it off, then on again. The light should come on within a few seconds of powering up the modem. If it doesn't come on, the best solution is to call up the company that made the modem and ask why.

> The MR light is like the power light on any appliance. If it's on, great; if it's not, there's not a whole lot you can do except yell at the manufacturer.

Problem 2: TR Light Didn't Come On   This problem is usually easily solved. When the TR light stays off, it means that the modem does not detect the DTR signal on the modem cable. Possible causes:

- The Macintosh is off. No power, so no DTR (Data Terminal Ready—a hardware signal generated by a modem or computer that says it's ready to communicate) signal. Figure out the solution to this one yourself.

- You haven't launched your communications program. The DTR signal is activated by the serial port, and if the port isn't currently in use by any program, it does nothing. Launch a communications program.

- You're not using a hardware handshaking cable. A regular cable has no wires for transmitting DTR, therefore the TR light will stay off. If you bought a regular cable, you can simply flip a switch on or inside your modem. The other alternative is to go out and buy a handshaking cable. You may want to reread the "Macintosh to Modem Connection" section at the beginning of the chapter.

Specifically, you should look for a switch called DTR operations or DTR override and set it to DTR override/DTR always ready. Check your manual for all the details. If there's no switch like that, you can send the modem a command (AT&D0) that does the same thing. (You'll have to perform this step if you want to use hardware handshake flow control.) You'll learn more about that command in the "Handshaking" section under "Advanced Modem Setups" later in this chapter. Flipping a switch is preferable.

> **Very Important:** Before you start flipping switches, be *sure* to jot down their current factory settings. Usually the switches control some esoteric functions, and if you have no idea what's been changed and what hasn't, you'll be in deep yogurt. It's only prudent to leave yourself the possibility of restoring the bank to its original configuration.

If none of this has lit the lights, there's something wrong with either your cable, your Mac, or your modem. To find out what the problem is, borrow a pal's modem and cable and replace your components one by one until you find out what's broken.

Setting Up Your Modem (Part 2)

Getting your hardware to work isn't all that great a challenge. You do have to properly assign some settings and parameters for communications, but most of the work has already been done for you at the factory. Most modems work just fine, right out of the box—even the inexpensive ones.

If you have a full-featured V.32bis, V.42bis high-performance modem, you have a little more work ahead of you. Although your modem works fine out of the box, a little time invested in determining proper function settings for your hardware can result in much greater speed.

Throughout this chapter, I use Dave Alverson's excellent shareware communications program ZTerm (version 0.9) for all examples and most screen shots. Reason #1: Because it's shareware, you can get it for free if you know someone with a copy, or for a nominal fee from a user group or shareware catalog. (Don't forget to pay the $30 registration fee after you've convinced yourself that ZTerm is a fabulous program.) Reason #2: ZTerm is a fabulous telecommunications program. Go back to Chapter 3 for the full rave concerning the program, but trust me: it's great.

Now you can take the first glorious step toward logging on. First make sure your telecom program can communicate properly with the modem. Then, as this is the first time you've taken your new modem out of the box, configure it so you can squeeze maximum performance out of it. Next, you set the communication parameters for your first logon session. Finally, you log onto a BBS!

Choose a Port

Let's start with a simple task: to tell your telecommunications program whether your modem's hooked up via the modem port or the printer port. Almost all Mac software assumes that a modem is connected to your Mac's modem port. If you plugged it into the printer port, you have to let the program know that.

In ZTerm, you change ports by selecting Modem Preferences under the Settings menu, then clicking on the proper port in the pop-up menu; in MicroPhone II, you choose Communications from the Settings menu, then click on the proper port's icon (see Figure 4–2). You don't need to adjust any other settings at this point.

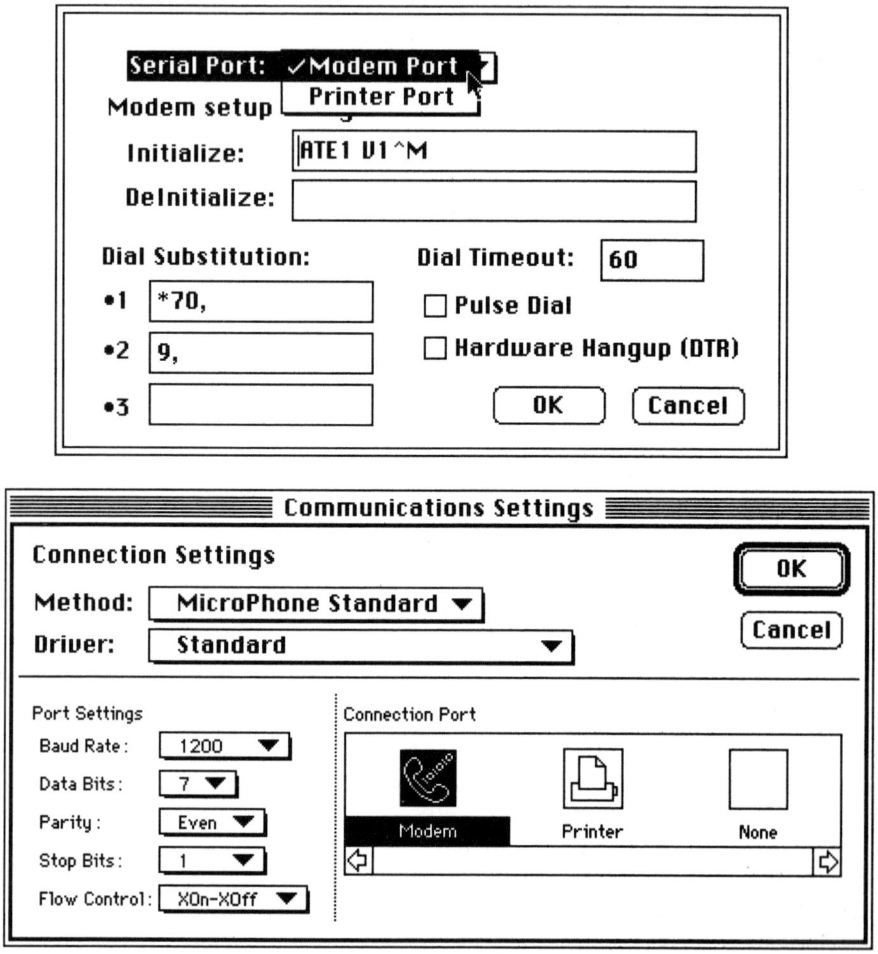

Serial Port: ✓Modem Port
Modem setup   Printer Port

Initialize: ATE1 U1^M

DeInitialize:

Dial Substitution: **Dial Timeout:**   60

•1   *70,   ☐ Pulse Dial

•2   9,   ☐ Hardware Hangup (DTR)

•3   (OK)   (Cancel)

═══════════════ **Communications Settings** ═══════════════

Connection Settings   (OK)

Method: [MicroPhone Standard ▼]   (Cancel)

Driver: [Standard   ▼]

Port Settings   Connection Port

Baud Rate :   [1200   ▼]

Data Bits :   [7   ▼]

Parity :   [Even   ▼]   Modem   Printer   None

Stop Bits :   [1   ▼]

Flow Control : [XOn-XOff ▼]

Figure 4–2: Choosing the modem port in ZTerm's Modem Preferences dialog box (top) and MicroPhone II's Communications Settings dialog box (bottom)

Sending Your First Commands to the Modem

Once you've chosen your port, you'll see a terminal window like the one shown in Figure 4–3.

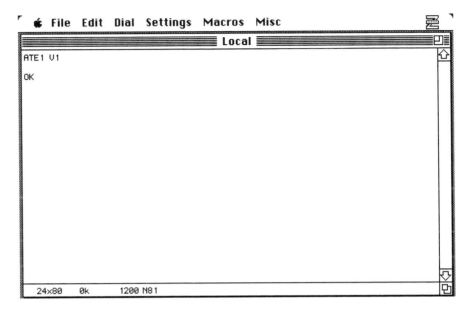

Figure 4–3: ZTerm, getting ready for a session

In every telecom program, the terminal window gives you a view of all the text that's passed from Mac to modem (and thence to the BBS), and from the BBS to your Mac. Because you're not yet connected to another computer, the window shows you the interaction between Mac and modem for now.

Remember how in Chapter 2 I tried to convince you that a modem is actually a computer all on its own? Now you can see for yourself. Type

AT

What you type appears in the terminal window. When you press the Return key you should see

OK

in the terminal window underneath the letters AT.

Seems trivial so far? In fact, you've just set into motion a complex and wonderful chain of events that deserves some explanation.

You typed some letters into the terminal window. Your communications program transmitted those characters to the modem, and to let you see what you were typing, the modem transmitted those same characters right back. Thus, the characters you see on the screen aren't what you typed (as would be the case if you were using a word processor), but the letters the modem sent back through the serial cable.

Want proof? Type some more—it doesn't matter what—and keep an eye on the SD and RD lights on your modem. Every time you hit a key, you can see them light up, seemingly simultaneously. The SD light blinks once as the character goes into the modem, and the RD light blinks as the modem sends it right back to the Mac.

When you press Return, the modem looks at what you've just typed and checks to see if you issued a command. AT is the simplest modem command; basically it means "Do nothing." So the modem complies, then reports back with a cheery OK.

Actually, this is only the second command the modem's received since you launched your communications program. If you look at the top of the terminal window in Figure 4–3, you can see a modem command that ZTerm has sent. This is called an *initialization string*— a command the program always sends at startup to make sure that certain modem features have been enabled. (If your telecom program doesn't send one, don't worry.)

Congratulations! You've successfully interacted with your modem, and you didn't even have to set any parameters. Right out of the box, modems are programmed to sense most of those communications parameters and adapt themselves accordingly. The only limitation here is data speed. If your telecom program assumes you're using a 2400 bps modem but yours is a 9600, the modem slows itself down to the lower speed.

Troubleshooting

Don't read this section if you completed the last section successfully. But, if you tap on the keyboard and nothing appears in the terminal window, type a few characters while you look at the modem's SD and RD lights to make sure data's being exchanged between Mac and modem. If they're flashing, then you know the software is sending its data through the proper port, you know the cable isn't defective, and best of all you know the hardware is in proper working order.

If they don't flash, double-check that you've selected the correct port and make sure the cable's plugged in nice and tight at both ends. If this doesn't fix things, I can think of two possible problems. One: You have a Mac to ImageWriter I printer cable—which is wired wrong for modems—instead of a modem cable, although it looks about the same as a modem cable. If that's the case, get a modem cable. Two: Either your serial port or your modem is broken. Phone your dealer.

A rather unlikely third possibility: The last person to use this Mac may have installed a port-swapping control panel, like the one that ships with the TelePort ADB modem. With that control panel diverting data from the real modem port, all kinds of anarchy can ensue. Check your System Folder (or Control Panels folder if you're using System 7, which we recommend highly) for anything untoward, usually a control panel called TelePort.

If the lights flash but you see gibberish in the terminal window, then your communications program is probably zipping data out the serial port much faster than your modem can handle. Skip ahead to the data rate discussion in the "Configuring Your Telecom Program" section later in this chapter, and set your telecom program's speed to the maximum speed of your modem.

Usually, this isn't a problem,. Almost all telecom programs assume a low speed as a default—typically 2400 bps, but ZTerm assumes 1200 bps—so this shouldn't concern you.

If what you type is printed twice on the screen (AATT when you type AT), then your communications program has turned on its Local Echo command. When Local Echo is enabled, the Mac echoes to the terminal window whatever you type. Because the modem sends what you type back through the serial port anyway, each letter you type comes out twice. Whatever your telecom program, make sure Local Echo is off; you'll need it only when you've wired your Mac directly into another computer with a serial cable or when connecting to one of the few services which require it (such as GEnie). In ZTerm, you can turn off Local Echo by unchecking that option in the Connection dialog box; it's at least that easy to turn off in most other communications programs.

If the opposite happens—you see lights flash but nothing appears in the terminal window—it's possible that your modem doesn't echo characters automatically. Turn on this feature by typing

```
ATE1
```

followed by a carriage return. This is the modem command that makes the modem repeat all characters you type back to the terminal window.

> If the letters appear on the screen but nothing happens after you press Return, try typing the command in capital letters. Some modems ignore modem commands if they're in lowercase.

More Modem Commands

As you may guess, AT at the beginning of a line tells the modem "What follows is a modem command." It's short for Attention. Many AT commands exist; I'll limit this discussion to the most important ones. No matter how much or how little you spend on your modem, no matter how complex or simple your hardware, you should be familiar with all of these commands.

To use any of these commands, type it into the terminal window and press Return.

- **ATD**   Dials the phone. You follow the D with either a T for touch-tone dialing or P for pulse (rotary) dialing, then insert the phone number. To dial 391–2298 using a touch-tone phone, you'd type

```
ATDT  391-2298
```

    If you type phone numbers with hyphens or parentheses in them, don't worry—the modem ignores them.

- **ATH**   Hangs up the phone, losing any connection that may be active.

- **ATZ** Clears the modem of any changes you've made to its default settings. Very handy—use this command when you've been changing modem settings and you now want the modem to act the way it did when it first came out of the box.

- **ATM***n* Controls the internal speaker, where *n* stands for a number telling the speaker how to behave; M0 means "Turn the speaker off and leave it off," and M1 means "Leave the speaker on while dialing, until you connect" (this is the usual default). Use M2 to leave the speaker on at all times.

- **ATA** Answers an incoming phone call. You'd use this command if the phone was ringing, and you knew it was a pal phoning in with her modem so you could send her that important spreadsheet. ATA causes the modem to connect to your friend's computer.

In addition to these commands, there are two other basic commands that don't have to be preceded by AT:

- **+++** Normally, once it's made a connection with another computer, your modem doesn't analyze incoming or outgoing data for modem commands. If you need to send a command while you're on line, you can make the modem go back into command mode by typing **+++** once, rapidly. If no data is transmitted for a few seconds before you start typing and no data is transmitted for a few seconds after, the modem responds with an OK. You'll still be connected to that remote computer, but the modem won't be sending out what you type. To break out of command mode and resume talking to the remote computer, type **ATC** (C for connect), or **ATO** (O for on line). Consult your modem manual to find out which to use with *your* modem.

- **A/** Repeats the last command. Most often, you'd use this command if you attempted to dial the phone but got a busy signal, and wanted to redial. Though just about all telecom programs redial for you, it's still useful.

Again, these are only the basics. I urge you to consult your modem's manual and look for more cool commands to make your on-line existence so much nicer.

Advanced Modem Setups

The wonders of high-end modems come at a price. If you skip this section, your modem will certainly work fine. But since you'll pay five or ten bucks an hour to connect to a commercial on-line service, wouldn't you like to shave 20 percent off your bill by configuring your modem for the greatest speed?

For each feature covered in this section, first check your modem manual to see if its operation can be determined by a DIP switch at the back of the modem. It's an easier way to set features. Most modems use the switch settings as the power-on defaults, which can usually be changed with typed-in commands.

Otherwise, you can make all necessary preparations by issuing the proper AT commands while off line.

Handshaking

Whether you're using hardware handshaking or doing it via software, you must make sure your modem knows how handshaking and data flow control are handled.

AT&Dn is the AT command that deals with handshaking, ensuring that the DTR signal is happy at all times. Assuming there isn't a DIP switch at the back of your modem you can flip to access handshaking features, here are the common variants and when to use them (be sure to add the AT prefix before each command):

- **&D0** Ignores DTR completely; assumes DTR is always on. You'd enter this command (AT&D0) if you wanted to use software handshaking.

- **&D2** Pays attention to DTR. Use this command if you want to use hardware handshaking.

Next feature: flow control (those "Giddyup!" and "Whoa!" signals we beat to death earlier), which uses the AT&H*n* commands:

- **&H0** Doesn't use any flow control at all. Some systems go wonky no matter what flow control method is used; otherwise, avoid using this setting.

- **&H1** Uses hardware flow control exclusively. Use this command only if you're sure you have a hardware handshaking cable! If you use a nonhandshaking cable with this setting, things may come to a quick crashing halt.

- **&H2** Uses software flow control (XON/XOFF) exclusively. Use this command if you don't have a handshaking cable, though it works properly with either cable.

- **&H3** Uses both methods. This is the safest command to use—in the sense that you have all the bases covered—but keep in mind that you still have the drawback of XON/XOFF: the flow of data can be impeded by the presence of those special XON/XOFF characters in a file you're downloading.

Remember it's important to match whatever flow-control scheme you've enabled in hardware with the proper setting in your telecommunications program. But beware: Hardware handshaking and flow control are harder to configure properly than software control.

Here's a handy guide to choosing your protocol:

- "I want to use hardware handshaking and flow control, and I have the proper cable." Use the commands AT&D2 and AT&H1 to enable DTR and hardware flow control.

- "I don't have the proper cable, so I want to avoid DTR problems and I want to use XON/XOFF." Or "I have the right cable but I'm going to take the safe way out." Use AT&D0 and AT&H2.

> You can concatenate AT commands: AT&D0&H2 will achieve the same thing as the separate commands AT&D0 and AT&H2. All AT commands can be concatenated this way.

Data Compression

If your modem has V.42bis, you *must* read this section; if you don't, you will reap *none* of the benefits of data compression.

Conceptual exercise: You have a 9600 bps V.42bis modem. It's hooked up, and you've told your terminal program to communicate at 9600 bps. Logical: You're hooked up to a computer with a 9600 bps modem, it sends its data at 9600 bps, and your modem in turn sends it at 9600 bps to your Mac.

Now let's think about data compression. Remember, with V.42bis modems the computer you're connected to is going to compress the data its computer gives it on the fly, and transmit it to your modem at 9600 bps. That chunk of data the modem's just received contains as much data as can be sent in at 9600 bps, but it's *compressed*! So, it contains *more* data than could've been sent at 9600 bps! To take advantage of the time saved by compressing the data, the modem will have to send it to the Mac at a speed *faster* than 9600 bps!

So your modem *must* be able to get data into your Macintosh *faster* than it's getting the data from the phone line. The data being transmitted along the phone line is compressed; the data being transmitted along the serial cable is *not*.

To take advantage of on-the-fly data compression provided by V.42bis and MNP Level 5, you have to set up your modem so that it's always communicating with your Mac at a fixed speed. Normally, your modem changes the speed at which it communicates with the Mac to match the rate at which it's talking to the remote computer. If you connect to another computer at 2400 bps, the modem to Mac speed will be 2400. If you make another call and the remote modem is 9600 bps, your modem/Mac speed becomes 9600. You want your modem to always be able to send data to your Mac faster than it's receiving it from the remote system, so you have to tell the modem to never change the Mac/modem transmission speed.

Technically, this is known as fixed modem/DTE rate (DTE stands for data terminal equipment—your Mac, in this case). The speed you select for Mac/modem communications should be four times the maximum speed of your modem. When V.42bis is working at maximum efficiency, it can send data in one-fourth the time it would take without V.42bis, so four times the modem's highest speed is certain to be adequate. If you own a 2400 bps modem, have your telecom program communicate at 9600 baud. If you have a V.32 modem, (maximum speed 9600), select 38,400. For V.32bis (14,400 max) select 57,600 bps. You must be using hardware handshaking if you want to use fixed modem/DTE.

You don't have to specify a rate to the modem, because it always matches the Mac's data rate when you're off line. You do have to tell it *not* to change this rate unless you change it from your telecom program, though. To lock down the modem/DTE rate, enter **AT&B1**.

Making Settings Stick

One final task remains. When you change settings, the new settings are in effect for the remainder of the session only; when you come back to your modem tomorrow, you have to enter all those commands again.

Once you're satisfied with your setup, enter **AT&W**. This command retains these settings as long as the unit's plugged in or has juice flowing in a small internal rechargeable battery, or until you change them again, depending on your modem.

Once you've set parameters on the modem, you can leave them alone.

Configuring Your Telecom Program

So far, you've fiddled with controls on the modem. In this section, your telecom program is the sole target of fiddling.

Setting Communications Parameters

The constant in all serial communications, modems included, is a small set of communication parameters that have to be set for things to work properly. It's not enough to say how fast you want data to be sent; you must also specify details about how the transmission is to function!

Confounding this problem is the fact that a remote BBS isn't as polite as a modem. When you use a parity setting different from what the modem expects, it just adapts itself to work with your settings anyway. A BBS, on the other hand, knows what it wants and settles for nothing else. Still, you need not know the technical details. In fact, this entire section can be summed up thusly: 8/1/N or 7/1/E (which stand for 8 data bits/1 stop bit/no parity or 7 data bits/1 stop bit/even parity).

In a nutshell, the four major parameters that must be set for each BBS you call are data rate (bps), data bits, stop bits, and parity.

Data Rate   The data rate is how fast the target BBS's modems are. Most of the smaller BBSs run at 2400 bps, while 9600 is the norm among larger services and some public services.

If you have a V.42bis modem, I hope you've read the "Data Compression" section of this chapter. If you have, you know it's important to select a data rate four times faster than the top speed of your modem, no matter how slow the BBS's modems are.

Data Bits: 7 or 8   How "wide" should the transmitted information be? Older systems and large central computers (like those at universities and some major on-line services) use 7 data bits; everyone else uses 8.

Computers think of numbers as a series of ones and zeroes, or bits of information. A 7-bit number can go from 0 to 127, and so covers all ASCII text, and 8 bits (0 to 255) is how computers generally handle numbers, whether in memory or on disk. Using 8 data bits is more flexible than 7 because it can be used to transmit data files (software and the like) as well as straight text; if you try to download a file while connected with a setting of 7 data bits, all protocols except Kermit allow the two computers to switch to 8 for the duration of the download without your involvement.

Stop Bits: 1, 1.5, or 2   The stop bits are placed between transmitted characters so the hardware can tell where a single character begins and ends. The stop bits should almost always be set to 1.

Parity: Even, Odd, or None   Parity checks for transmission errors. Under this scheme, the hardware determines whether the bitstream has an even or an odd number of 1s (the sequence of 1s and 0s zinging along the phone lines that make up your data), and if there was supposed to be an even number but there was an odd number, then you'd know there was trouble.

But that was in the old days. Today, almost all systems use no parity checking, and the rest use even parity.

Common Settings   Almost all BBSs you connect to use 8 data bits, 1 stop bit, and no parity; those that don't use 7 data bits, 1 stop bit, and even parity. It's that simple; one or the other.

In ZTerm, all these settings are available in the Connection dialog box under the Settings menu. In other telecom programs, they may be hidden in dialog boxes, as in White Knight (Figure 4–4).

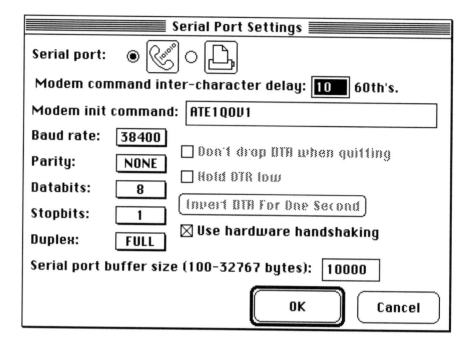

Figure 4–4: White Knight's Serial Port Settings dialog box

Your First On-line Session

Congratulations. You've made it this far; you're only minutes away from your first on-line session! At this point, all you need is the number of a good BBS to call.

How to Find the Number of a Local BBS

Darn good question. It's a lot like I imagine you'd have gone about finding a good speakeasy back during Prohibition. You find one, the people there can tell you of a couple others in the neighborhood, and the patrons of *those* establishments tell you of others, and so on.

The problem is finding that first speakeasy. The first place to call is your local Macintosh user group. Most user groups have their own BBS up and running, to help them keep in touch with their members. Even if they don't, the person who answers the phone is liable to know the number of a good BBS or two. If you don't know where your closest local user group is, call Apple's User Group Connection at (800) 538–9696, extension 500. It's not a BBS, but the people who answer the phone can tell you what Macintosh user groups are nearby.

If there's no local user group with a BBS, call your local computer store and ask (computer stores located on college campuses are good bets). And if *that* falls through, make a long-distance call to the BBS of one of the largest Macintosh user groups in the country, the Boston Computer Society Macintosh User Group BBS, at (617) 864–0712. There's also a second line for high-speed modems, (617) 864–2293. If you're on the West Coast, try the BMUG (Berkeley Macintosh Users Group) BBS at (510) 849–BMUG (that's 849-2684). We use the BCS•Mac BBS for our first logon in the example that follows.

By the way, although both the BMUG and BCS•Mac bulletin boards have a multitude of incoming phone lines, they are extremely popular. This means you'll probably get a lot of busy signals before you are finally able to connect.

First, Check the Number

How would you like to groggily answer a ringing phone at midnight, and hear a monstrous high-pitched whine when you bring the handset to your ear? Neither would anyone else. No matter where you get the number of an alleged BBS, always dial it yourself using a regular telephone during a reasonable hour of the day or night on the off chance that the number belongs to a human being and not a computer! If you hear a high-pitched whine, you can safely assume the number belongs to a BBS.

It's just common courtesy. Unfortunately, BBS numbers tend to change on occasion; phone lines get upgraded, system operators move to new houses, and so on. Again, *be sure* to double-check all BBS numbers with a regular phone call before letting your modem out of its cage. If the politeness factor doesn't entice you, consider that many homes now have Caller ID on their phones, so they'll have *your* number.

Once you have a valid BBS number, it's time to dial it and get on line. But first, double-check to make sure you've set your communications parameters correctly. Remember, normally you'd assume a BBS runs at 8 data bits, 1 stop bit, no parity, and change to 7/1/E if that didn't work. As it happens, I know that the BCS•Mac BBS uses 8/1/N.

Dialing Manually

You can either send the modem's dialing command yourself (ATD followed by the phone number), or you can have your telecom program send the command for you, via its buttons or dialog boxes.

Let's try the do-it-yourself method first. To connect at 2400 bps to the BCS•Mac BBS, type

```
ATDT   1-617-864-0712
```

into the terminal window. This command dials the number using touch-tone dialing. If your phone system cannot handle touch-tone dialing, the modem can mimic a rotary telephone if you specify pulse dialing. Use ATDP instead of ATDT to dial the number.

You give the dialing command all the numbers you'd normally push on your telephone. That can include dialing a 1 to get long distance, a 9 to get an outside line, even a string of digits to reach your long-distance provider and the account number the call should be billed to. You may run into trouble, depending on how good your phone system is.

If you're used to having to wait a second or two to get an outside line, another second to get long distance, and even longer for your long-distance company to put the call through, you may want to insert some pause and wait commands into the strings. A comma anywhere in the dialing string causes the modem to pause for two seconds before proceeding, and a W makes the modem pause until it hears a second dial tone. If your phone system is configured so that you have to dial 9 to connect to an outside line, wait for another dial tone, enter a number so the company knows who to charge the call to (666), then enter the phone number about a second later, your dial command looks like this:

```
ATDT   9W666,1-617-864-0712
```

You can also insert modem commands within the dialing command, for settings you want to use only for the duration of the call. If you keep the Mac in your bedroom, and you're worried that the modem will awaken your spouse, you can turn off the internal speaker for the duration of the call by inserting the M0 command, as in

```
ATM0DT  1-617-864-0712
```

Dialing with your Telecom Program

You can use all the dialing information you learned in the preceding section in your telecom program's dialog box, too; the program gets the phone number out of the dialog, puts an ATDT in front of it, and sends it to the modem.

The dialog box you use to dial numbers in White Knight is shown in Figure 4–5. Whatever you enter in the Number to Dial box is sent out the modem port, so you can imbed extra commands (such as waits and pauses) as necessary.

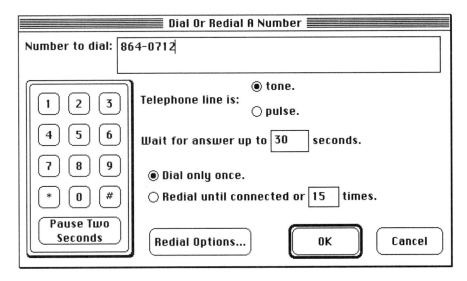

Figure 4–5: White Knight's Dial Or Redial A Number dialog box

Generally, the only other information you need to tell your telecom program is how long it's supposed to wait for the other modem to answer the phone before giving up. Some bulletin boards answer your call on the first ring, others only after several seconds. Allow about thirty seconds. If the telecom program can't detect another modem answering in thirty seconds, usually it means the line's busy or something else has gone wrong.

A standard feature of all telecom programs is automatically redialing a phone number until the modem can connect successfully. A sign of a good BBS is a phone line that's busy almost all the time. Turning on automatic redial ensures that you can go to the kitchen and make a sandwich instead of babysitting your computer. When the modem finally manages to connect, you'll hear the high-pitched whine and (with most telecom software) several beeps.

Creating Services

If you become nuts about telecom, you'll probably wind up using a half a dozen on-line services or more. That's a lot of phone numbers to memorize! Fortunately, most telecom programs can organize your BBS numbers into phone books of services, so dialing the BCS•Mac BBS becomes as simple as selecting its name from a menu, as in ZTerm (Figure 4–6).

Figure 4–6: A well-stocked ZTerm Dial menu

In most communications programs, defining a new service involves setting the correct communications parameters for that service, and providing the program with a name and a phone number. In ZTerm, you would choose Directory from the Dial menu, click on the New button, then fill in the name and phone number (Figure 4–7).

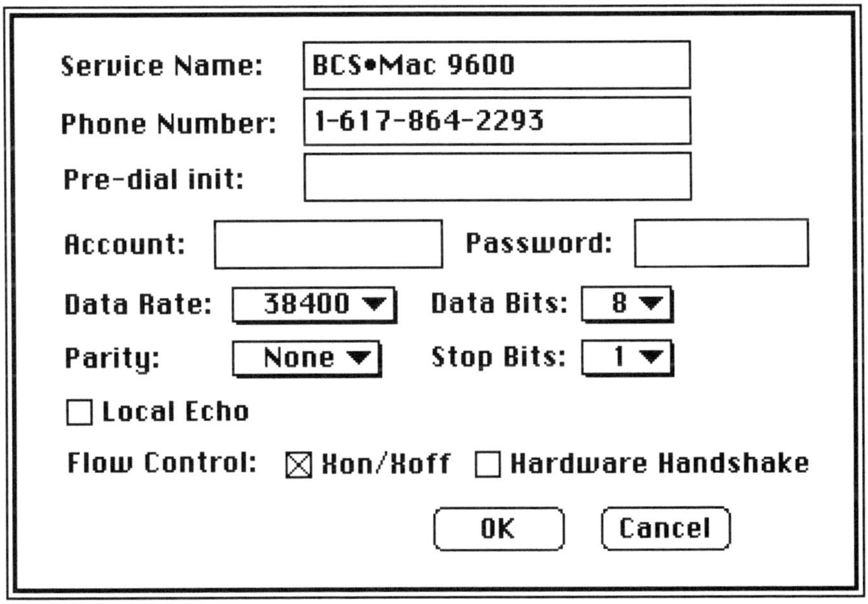

```
┌─────────────────────────────────────────────────────────┐
│  ┌───────────────────────────────────────────────────┐  │
│  │  Service Name:   │ BCS•Mac 9600              │      │  │
│  │                                                     │  │
│  │  Phone Number:   │ 1-617-864-2293           │      │  │
│  │                                                     │  │
│  │  Pre-dial init:  │                          │      │  │
│  │                                                     │  │
│  │  Account:   │              │   Password:  │      │ │  │
│  │                                                     │  │
│  │  Data Rate:  │ 38400 ▼ │   Data Bits:  │ 8 ▼ │    │  │
│  │                                                     │  │
│  │  Parity:     │ None ▼  │   Stop Bits:  │ 1 ▼ │    │  │
│  │                                                     │  │
│  │  ☐ Local Echo                                       │  │
│  │                                                     │  │
│  │  Flow Control:  ☒ Xon/Xoff  ☐ Hardware Handshake    │  │
│  │                         ( OK )   ( Cancel )         │  │
│  └───────────────────────────────────────────────────┘  │
└─────────────────────────────────────────────────────────┘
```

Figure 4–7: Defining a new service in ZTerm

Call Waiting

If you have Call Waiting, the benign-sounding "click" that signals another call coming in is death to telecom sessions. For whatever reason, that click causes almost all modems to hang up immediately (always at the worst time).

If you want to keep Call Waiting *and* use your modem, you must guard against that click by turning off your Call Waiting before you dial. Whether you're talking to a human or another computer, Call Waiting is turned off for the duration of a phone call if you precede the phone number with *70 (touch tone) or 1170 (pulse) when dialing, like this:

```
ATDT  *70,1-617-864-0712
```

This technique works with most phone lines in most parts of the country. If it doesn't work for you (try it once to find out), call your telephone service provider and ask how to suspend Call Waiting temporarily.

Actual Dialing

It's time to dial the service now. Whichever method of dialing you've chosen—manually or with your telecom program's dialing feature—do it now.

For the next half-minute or so, everything's out of your hands as your modem tries to establish a connection to the remote BBS. The exciting play-by-play follows.

Unless you entered the command manually, your telecom program first puts a dialog box on the screen like the one in Figure 4–8.

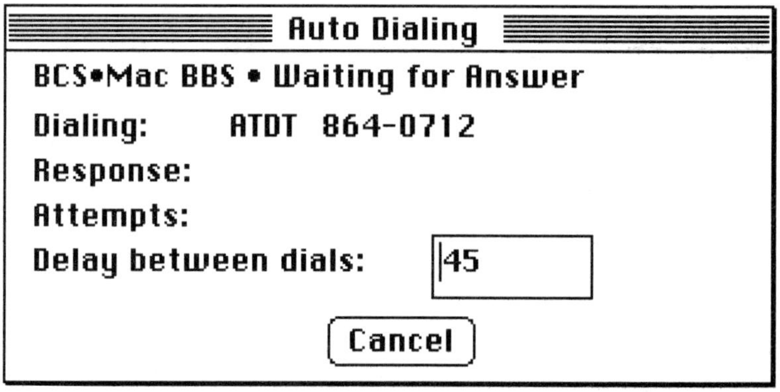

```
╔═══════════════ Auto Dialing ═══════════════╗
║ BCS•Mac BBS • Waiting for Answer           ║
║ Dialing:      ATDT  864-0712               ║
║ Response:                                  ║
║ Attempts:                                  ║
║ Delay between dials:    ┌─────────┐        ║
║                         │45       │        ║
║                         └─────────┘        ║
║                    ┌──────────┐            ║
║                    │  Cancel  │            ║
║                    └──────────┘            ║
╚════════════════════════════════════════════╝
```

Figure 4–8: Waiting to connect

The modem then receives the dialing command (you can see its SD light flicker briefly), and you hear a dial tone through the modem's speaker. The modem's OH (off hook) light comes on.

Next, the modem dials the number. If its speaker is on, you hear a dial tone, then the digits of the phone number.

If you hear a busy signal at this point:

- If you've enabled your communications program's autodialer, it waits the required number of seconds and then keeps trying.

- If you dialed manually, press the Return key. The modem gives up and returns to you for further instructions, reporting back with

```
NO CARRIER
```

The modem was listening for that high-pitched whine you heard when you first double-checked the number by dialing from a regular phone. That signal announces that it is indeed a modem. If the modem doesn't hear a carrier, it can't connect; NO CARRIER means "Sorry, no connection" and nothing more.

> Some of the more expensive modems are savvier; they can detect any number of frustrating situations (line busy, no dial tone, someone answered but it wasn't a modem) and tell you precisely what happened. If you have one of the less expensive models, you'll have to make do with a plain old NO CARRIER.

It's also possible that the phone keeps ringing and ringing without being answered. Maybe you got the number wrong, but the BBS may be "down" (inactive) so the folks who run it can perform some maintenance. Try calling back in a few hours.

But let's say a modem answers! First, you'll hear a click as a modem picks up the phone, then the carrier signal. Again this whine of the remote modem more or less says to other modems, "Let's get together and talk modem talk."

You next hear a mix of other noises as your modem generates tones of its own to tell the other modem a bit about itself. In a three-second burst that sounds like several cats hissing and screeching simultaneously, the modems discuss how fast they are and what advanced error-control or data-compression features they have. Once a consensus is reached concerning what features each can reliably use, you're connected and on line!

The mark of a true telecom freak is a keen ear and sharp attention to all those noises. Someone who's been using modems for a long time can tell you at once whether the modem you're connecting to is running at 1200, 2400, or 9600 bps, whether you can use V.42bis data compression, and if you can break the 9600 bps barrier in this session. After listening to that racket time and time again, you too may acquire this same skill.

If you're using your telecom program's automatic dialer, the program probably alerts you that a connection has been established by flashing the screen or making your Mac beep at you a few times. By the time you scramble to the keyboard, the dialing dialog box will have disappeared and you see the terminal screen.

As soon as the connection's established, the modem takes a split second to send your Mac a description (called a result code) of the kind of connection that's been established. It should look something like this:

```
CONNECT 2400
```

This means a connection has been established at 2400 baud. If you have a high-speed modem with tons of features, the message might look something like this:

```
CONNECT 9600/ARQ/V32/LAPM/V42bis
```

Now there's a real wealth of information. Here I can tell that I've connected at 9600 bps under V.32 (not V.32bis), and both V.42 error checking (sometimes called LAPM) and V.42bis data compression is active.

Some modems send a number as the result code, instead of a nice phrase like that. Try entering **ATV1** the next time you're off line; that's the standard modem command for "Use words instead of numbers, please!"

Connection Problems

Probably the most frustrating situation in telecommunications is when you hear the BBS's modem answer, you hear it emit its piercing cry, and your modem sits there, doing nothing. The carrier signal continues for five or ten seconds until, unanswered, the BBS hangs up in disgust.

The most common cause of this scenario is a modem with a low tolerance for line noise; that faint background static may be too thick for the modem to detect the BBS's carrier signal, and so it won't answer.

In your telecom program, adjust the communication speed down one notch at a time (9600 bps to 2400, to 1200, to 300). You can usually do this in your telecom program without logging off. Just change the setting, then press Return a couple of times. If the next lowest speed doesn't work either, try an even lower one, until you connect successfully. If you get disconnected while you're changing the settings, dial the service again. As lower baud rates engender greater margins of error, eventually you'll probably manage to connect. If you still can't, you'll have to gripe at the modem manufacturer.

Another possibility is that the two modems are having difficulties in link negotiation, where each knows that the other is a modem, and they're haggling over whether to use V.32, V.32bis, V.42, or V.42bis. These negotiations can go on ad infinitum.

Unfortunately, the solution to this problem is uncertain. You have to turn off these features one by one (see previous sections in this chapter or consult your manuals), and tell your modem not to negotiate for these features. With luck, you'll eventually find the feature that's causing trouble.

Garbled Talks!

Now that you've established the connection, the modem stops looking for commands in the terminal window and merely acts as a silent conduit between you and the BBS. The modem lights probably look like Figure 4–9.

Figure 4–9: Modem lights after connection has been established

The CD and OH lights tell you that the modem is currently using the phone line and you're connected to another modem!

The first thing to do after you see the CONNECT message in the terminal window is to press the Return key a couple of times. If everything is working, your terminal window fills with a welcoming message from the BBS, like the one shown in Figure 4–10:

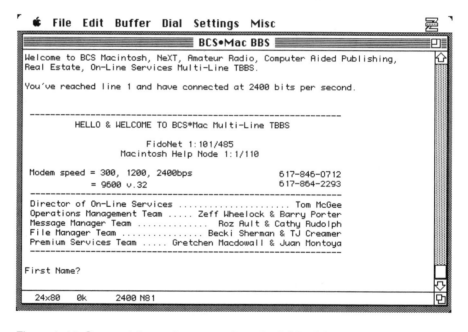

Figure 4–10: Success! A greeting screen from the BCS BBS

If this is what you're looking at, pop a cork and let the champagne flow…you're on line!

Of course, some of you can only dream of Figure 4–10, because the fruit of your labors is unintelligible garbage across the screen as in Figures 4–11 or 4–12.

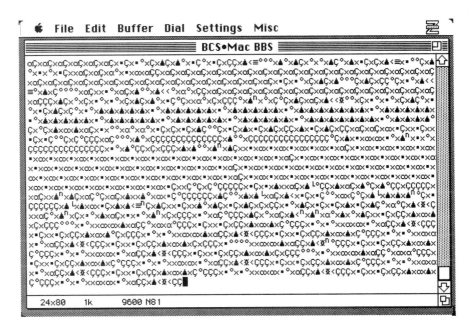

Figure 4–11: Typical screenful of garbage—this is not good

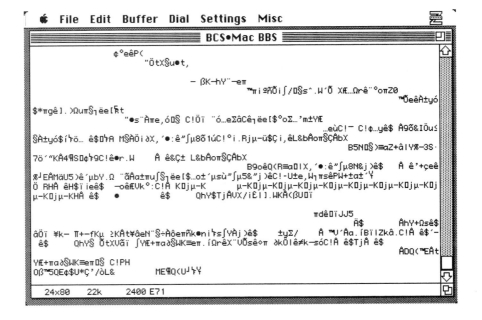

Figure 4–12: Another screenful of garbage—not good either

If you see something like Figure 4–11—a more or less solid block of garbage, consisting of similar characters repeated—it looks like the BBS's modems are much slower than the speed setting you gave your communications program. Try a lower speed, as described a minute ago. Keep trying lower speeds until you see something more like Figure 4–10.

If you see something like Figure 4–12—a hodgepodge of trash with frequent line breaks—then you should be using 7/1/E instead of 8 data bits, 1 stop bit, no parity, or vice versa. You should be able to make this switch without logging off. Change your telecom program's settings, press Return once or twice, and clear text should start to flow through.

These are trivial adjustments. They're such minor trouble that you shouldn't need to hang up and redial; your Mac hardware and software can almost always adapt.

Parting Shots

You've just made your way through what are clearly the most difficult procedures in telecom. Configuring your hardware and software can be a hassle, and surely account for most of the unused modems in closets and storerooms. But you did it. Congratulations! Now you can forget all about it and enjoy life on line to the fullest.

Now that you're able to connect to a BBS, the next two chapters will teach you all the cool stuff you can do while you're there, things like reading messages and electronic mail, downloading files, and posting messages of your own.

5

Reading and Sending Messages

Acquiring accounts, mangling messages, finagling files, and other stuff you do after you "CONNECT."

This is where the fun starts. In the past four chapters, you've learned the fundamentals and outfitted yourself with all the tools you'll need for on-line escapading. In this chapter, you'll learn how to gain access to local boards and weave your way through the public and private messaging systems.

If the commands and menus you see here don't match up precisely with those you find on your favorite on-line service, don't worry. Each BBS or on-line service is set up according to the likes and dislikes of its sysops, so no two operate in *precisely* the same way.

Setting Up an Account and Logging In

Let's start at the top: signing onto an on-line service. At the end of
Chapter 4 you dialed up a local BBS, established a connection, and got
to see the board's welcome screen once the BBS answered the phone:

```
CONNECT 2400/ARQ/LAPM/V42BIS BCS•Mac BBS

Welcome to BCSXT, Amateur Radio, Computer Aided Publishing, Real
Estate, On-Line Services Multiline TBBS.  You've reached line 9 and have
connected at 2400 bits per second.
```

```
               HELLO & WELCOME TO BCS*Mac Multiline TBBS

                         FidoNet 1:101/485
                     Macintosh Help Node 1:1/110

Modem speed = 300, 1200, 2400bps                   617-864-0712
            = 9600 v.32                            617-864-2293

Director of On-Line Services ..................... Tom McGee
Operations Management Team ..... Zeff Wheelock & Barry Porter
Message Manager Team .............. Roz Ault & Cathy Rudolph
File Manager Team ............... Becki Sherman & TJ Creamer
Premium Services Team ..... Gretchen Macdowall & Juan Montoya


First Name?
```

Reminder: *CONNECT 2400/ARQ/LAPM/V42BIS BCS•Mac BBS* isn't
part of the BBS's opening screen; this is a message sent by your
modem to let you know what sort of a connection was made. Here you
know you've connected at 2400 bps, and automatic data correction
and data compression are in use. Most modems give that info in plain
English as above, but some can send only numeric codes. Check
Appendix B and/or your modem's user manual for details.

The BCS•Mac BBS part came from the telecom program I'm using,
ZTerm. Yet another reason to like the program: If you save all the text to
disk as a permanent record of your on-line session, you'll know which
service you were on.

An opening screen is like the title page of a book; it's one screenful of info telling you where you are and what this board's all about. Usually, there's also room to credit the fine folks who keep the board up and running, as well as for additional access numbers. Dialing 864–0712 logs you on using any one of the board's dozen modems, but if you have a more expensive V.32 modem and you want to make sure you connect at high speed, dialing 864–2293 ensures either a high-speed connection or none at all.

Other than looking at the opening screen, there's not much you can do on a BBS before you *log on*. BBSs are one of the most open methods of communications, but before the BBS's gates open for you, the board has to know who you are and figure out whether you have the right to use the board.

The BBS software you see here asks for your first and last names individually; other boards allow you to enter your name in one line.

```
First  Name?  Rocky
Last  Name?  Raccoon
Searching  User  File  ...
```

The BBS software takes this information and checks it against a list of users who have permission to use the BCS•Mac BBS. Your first time on, the BBS has no idea who you are, so it'll respond as follows:

```
Calling  from  (City,State)?
```

Yet another demonstration of the friendliness of telecommunications: The BBS knows you're not a recognized, authorized user, but rather than zap you off the system, it collects all the information it needs to *make* you a recognized, authorized user.

Other BBS programs are a little savvier, recognizing that at 3 A.M. you sometimes can't spell your own name correctly. When you type in a name that such a BBS doesn't recognize it responds:

```
Rocky  Raccoon,  is  this  correct?
```

If you are a registered user of the BBS named Lil McGill (and not Rocky Raccoon), you can just type Lil McGill at this prompt, then continue with the logging on procedure.

About names: In the actor's union, no two people are allowed to have the same name, but that's not the case in the real world. If you make your first connection to a BBS and enter your name, and then the BBS asks for a password, now you know another user named Lil McGill is already on the board. You'll have to pretend your first name is Nancy (or anything but Lil) so the BBS can tell you and the other Lil McGill apart.

Second, don't use a name that is obviously phony. Many systems allow you to use handles—Doctor Midnight, The Hammer, and far worse—instead of the moniker your parents gave you, but on most systems that practice is either prohibited or discouraged. Usually the BBS will post a list of on-line rules for public reading.

Setting Up a New Account

Generally, to get an account on a BBS you have to give some info to two different entities. You have to tell the BBS what name you're going to use to log on, and what hardware you're using, so that any quirks in your terminal program can be dealt with. You also have to give some personal data to the sysops so they can make sure you're a decent, upstanding individual who won't cause any trouble.

Usually, the BBS requests the info it needs automatically. If you haven't done so already, soon after you offer your name you'll be asked where you're calling from.

Answering Questions about Your Computer

Next, the BBS probably asks for information about your terminal. Hundreds of machines exist, from Macintoshes to IBM PCs to pocket organizers that can operate as a terminal and log onto a BBS. Though all of these work just fine with almost all boards, many of them have small differences that have to be accounted for. The BBS probably asks you about a half dozen questions, detailed in the following sections.

Terminal Width and Height How big is your terminal window? The safe answer to give here is 80 characters wide and 24 lines of text high; that's the size of a standard (dumb) terminal, as defined a couple dozen years ago. When a BBS has to format some information for display (such as a menu or a list of files) it assumes an 80-by-24 window. Of course, on most Mac telecom programs, you can resize your terminal window to nearly any size, but it's usually not a good idea to go beyond 80 characters.

Pause between Terminal Pages Do you want the BBS to pause every 24 (or whatever the length of the terminal window is) lines? On standard terminals, you want this feature; when text scrolls off the top of the screen, it's gone for good. With the Mac, of course, you can always click on a scroll bar to have a second look at anything you've missed, so you probably want to avoid the pause, which saves you from having to press a key (usually Return) every 24 lines.

Uppercase and Lowercase Characters Years ago, some computers couldn't display lowercase characters. Answer yes and move on.

Terminal Emulation Ninety percent of the time you spend on a BBS, your terminal isn't doing much; it's just putting characters into the terminal window one line at a time. Some on-line services like to get fancier, though, and use inverse video, special graphics characters (which allow lines, boxes, and the like to be drawn), and color, and move the cursor all over the screen when editing files and messages. To make sure all these tricks work properly (since the BBS has to send specific codes to get this magic to work), the BBS needs to know what kind of terminal you're using.

Most Mac telecom programs give you three choices: VT100/ VT102, which is the most popular terminal standard; IBM-PC/ANSI, which takes advantage of color, simple sound, and some graphics characters; and TTY (TeleType), which has no enhanced features. Usually, you want to default to VT100/VT102, though you may want to choose IBM-PC/ANSI if you know you're working with a PC-based BBS. Make sure your telecom program has been configured for the terminal emulation you specified to the BBS. Choosing the wrong emulation probably won't have any dire consequences, but it can result in some weird-looking characters appearing in the place of special graphics symbols:

```
ƒƒƒƒƒƒƒƒƒƒƒƒƒƒƒƒƒƒƒƒƒƒƒƒƒƒƒƒƒƒƒƒƒƒƒƒƒƒƒƒƒƒƒƒƒƒƒƒƒƒƒƒƒƒƒƒƒƒƒƒƒƒƒƒƒƒƒƒƒƒƒƒƒ◊
≥               *  Thanks for calling Channel 1  *                    ≥
≥                       Call again soon!                             ≥
¿ƒƒƒƒƒƒƒƒƒƒƒƒƒƒƒƒƒƒƒƒƒƒƒƒƒƒƒƒƒƒƒƒƒƒƒƒƒƒƒƒƒƒƒƒƒƒƒƒƒƒƒƒƒƒƒƒƒƒƒƒƒƒƒƒƒƒƒƒƒƒƒŸ
```

Line Feeds Do you want the BBS software to send a line feed at the end of each line transmitted (to put the cursor on a new line)? If you answer no, putting the cursor on a new line and shifting up the previous line of characters will be the responsibility of your telecom program, and all text will be crammed into one line. In most cases, answer yes. If all text comes out double-spaced, then you can go back later on and change this option to no.

Nulls A null is a delay the BBS transmits after each line. In the early days of telecommunications, a BBS had to transmit a couple of nulls after every line, or else the first few characters of every line would get lost; the null characters would be the victims rather than real ASCII data. Nowadays, you don't have to give the subject a thought; set the number of nulls to 0 and forget about it. If you notice that the first one or two characters of every line are missing when you sign on, though, go back and change the number of nulls to whatever number of characters are missing on each line.

Everything Else Most boards stop right there, but sometimes you run across a system that also wants to know such things as what file-transfer protocol you want to use, what message area of the BBS you want to find yourself in after logging in, and anything else the system operators arranged for when they set up the board. Until you understand what all these concepts are, just accept whatever defaults the BBS mentions. You'll learn all about protocols, message areas, and the like later in this chapter.

The good news is that many BBSs save you the trouble of making all those selections, and just ask you what sort of hardware you're using:

```
<A>VT-100/102    <B>VIDTEX        <C>VT-52          <D>Mac WtKnight  <E>Mac ZTerm
<F>Mac Generic   <G>IBM, ANSI     <H>IBM, No ANSI  <I>ANSI BBS       <J>Tandy TRS-80
<K>Tandy CoCo    <L>Tandy Compat  <M>Atari Generc  <N>H19/H89/Z19   <O>Televid 925
<P>Commodore

Enter letter of your terminal, <CR> if not listed: E

Terminal Profile Set to:
ANSI codes Allowed
IBM Graphics Allowed

Upper/Lower Case
Line Feeds Needed
0 Nulls after each <CR>
Do you wish to modify this? N
```

Here, selecting *Mac ZTerm* automatically loads all the right settings for you. (Or, select *Mac WtKnight* if you're using White Knight, or *Mac Generic* if you're using any other software.)

Password: It's Not Just a Game Show Any More

The next step in setting up an account is choosing a password for yourself. A password is a magic word that you and only you know; it's the only way the BBS can verify whether that's really you trying to log on. Probably more than a dozen people can spell *LeVitus*, but the BBS knows that only the true Bob LeVitus will type **NOT@DVORAK** as his password.

You'll find a detailed discourse on password security in Chapter 10, but here are four important points to consider—we call them the four "nevers"—when selecting a password:

- **Never** use a password that anyone might guess. Don't use your name, your spouse's name, those of your kids, birthdays, or anything like that. If everyone knows you're a big fan of the *Star Wars* movies, don't choose Luke-Skywalker or Wookie or other word combinations that can be easily guessed.

- **Never** write down your password anywhere. No matter how private your office is, writing your password on a yellow sticky note and putting it on the side of your monitor is about as good an idea as spray-painting it on your door.

- **Never** share your password with anyone. It's not a good idea to let a friend log onto a BBS or commercial service with your name and password, but if you absolutely must, then change your password *immediately* after the pal's finished his or her business.

- **Never** use the same password on two different services. Almost all sysops are trustworthy, decent folk, but an evil sysop may try to log onto other services with users' names and passwords.

Common sense aside, you can pick just about anything for your password. Many systems impose a limit of eight characters, though, with no internal spaces:

```
Please Enter a 1-8 character Password to be used for future logons.   This
password may have any printable characters you wish.   Lower case is considered
different from upper case and imbedded blanks are legal.   REMEMBER THIS
PASSWORD.   You will need it to log on again.

Your password? stimpy
Re-enter New password to verify: stimpy
```

It's generally a good idea to keep your passwords all in lowercase; most BBS systems consider *stimpy* and *Stimpy* to be two different passwords. Trying to remember what letters you capitalized can lead to endless frustration.

Now that you've given the BBS all of your hardware particulars and chosen a password, you're halfway home. Most boards then immediately give you limited access to the board and present you with some info especially for new users:

```
You have read through message 0
Current last message is 6754
You are caller number 432938
You are authorized 30 mins this call


              *************************
              *    FOR  NEW  USERS    *
              *************************


Welcome to the BCS Mac Multiline TBBS!  If this is the first time that you've
called, please heed these words of wisdom:

You can't break anything!

The Bread Board System (TBBS) is the name of the software that runs this
```

Typically a BBS takes this opportunity to tell the first-time user about what sort of software and hardware the BBS is running on, about the people who've set up the board, and most important, about the rules you're expected to follow!

Validation

Most boards will grant you visitor-level access once you've done all of the above; this is a special access level that allows you to take a good look around the BBS and decide whether you'd like to stop by again later on. *Some* boards give you top-level access right away, but most limit your access somewhat while you're at visitor level. When you're a visitor, you can usually read messages but not send any replies or leave any new ones of your own, and you can browse through lists of files available for downloading, but not download any files. Before the sysops let you do nifty stuff like *that*, they'll want to know more about you. You have to fill out a validation survey.

Validation is a simple, fairly automatic procedure by which the system operators of the board check you over. When you press *V* to select *Validate me!* (or something similar) from one of the board's menus, you're presented with a simple questionnaire to fill out:

```
Welcome to The Boston Computer Society's Online User Validation

You've already given us your name : ROCKY RACCOON

  Street Address => 1313 Mockingbird Lane
           City => St. Canard
          State => ND
Zip/Postal Code => 91827
   Phone Number => (213) 555-1212
```

Why are the sysops asking for all this info? Generally, it's insurance; if you run amok causing lots of trouble, they want to know where to find you.

More often than not, the validation survey also gives you a couple of lines in which you can tell everyone about yourself and your computer system. They're not trying to pry; if you report technical problems in using the board, the sysops will know what your hardware setup is. Also, it's a way for other users to find people with similar likes, problems, and interests:

```
You have two lines to input this information.

line 1 => I've got a 4 meg Mac IIsi with a USRobotics Courier HST modem, and my
line 2 => telecom program is ZTerm.  I also dig Led Zeppelin and needlepoint.

Is the above correct? (Y/N)
y

Creating record for ROCKY RACCOON
```

On most public systems, that would be the end of the questionnaire. If the board requires a usage fee, payment info is requested at this point. On the BCS•Mac board, extra privileges are accorded to Boston Computer Society members, so the next step is to enter your BCS membership card number. On other systems, you can sometimes buy extra privileges by specifying the privileges you want and typing in a credit card number.

Warning: Avoid entering financial info such as credit card numbers on line if you can. You can usually trust a commercial on-line service or a smaller commercial board if it's been around for a few years, but hand over your MasterCard number to some fly-by-night local board, and you may find a couple grand worth of stereo components on next month's bill.

The final thing you might encounter in a validation is a legal disclaimer. Usually, they boil down to "Hey, look, we're just distributing info and software here...if you read a message saying Tabasco makes a great mouthwash, don't blame *us* if you try it and have to eat through a straw for the next few months!"

On a more serious note, if the board has any licensed software available for downloading (such as Apple System software), you may be asked to verify that you've read the statement defining what you can do with the software. Legalese is, unfortunately, becoming more popular these days.

You've done everything necessary to get full access to the system, and now it's in the hands of the system operators. Conferral of your powers isn't automatic, usually: some boards give you full access as soon as you complete the survey, but usually a sysop has to look through your replies and manually grant you access. Some sysops phone your house to verify that you didn't fib on the particulars, and a bizarre few require that you follow up the survey with an actual written letter, but normally after 24 hours you'll have complete access.

Logging On

Fortunately, you don't have to go through all of that every time you want to use a board. Once you've been validated by the sysops, the BBS welcomes you. Let's look at the logging-in sequence for a validated user:

```
First Name? Rocky
Last Name? Raccoon
Searching User File ...
Calling From ST. CANARD, ND
Enter Your Password: ********
```

This time the BBS knows you are a registered user and asks for your password. Notice that the BBS replaces your password with asterisks. This is to prevent malicious coworkers from looking over your shoulder and ripping off your password.

Don't worry if you enter the wrong password; most boards will give you three opportunities to get it right before they disconnect you. If you forget your password, log on as a new user again and send a message to the sysops explaining what happened. They'll probably ask you to verify your identity by reciting the info you provided in the validation survey.

Once the BBS recognizes you, you're in:

```
TBBS Welcomes ROCKY RACCOON
Calling From ST. CANARD, ND
Your last time on was 12/23/91 14:31
You have read through message 0
Current last message is 6744
You have called this system 1 times before
You are caller number 432932
```

These may seem like dull statistics, but they're quite important. Be sure to check this data every time you log on. If you've been out of town for the past month but these user statistics say you were on line yesterday, you know that someone else has been using your account. Change your password and notify the system operators immediately.

Next, you see this line:

```
You are authorized 60 mins this call
```

Almost all boards put limits on how much time you can spend on the BBS each day. It's logical; they want to give other users a chance to log on. The amount of time you're granted depends on how generous the sysops are and how much you've contributed to the system. If you're an infrequent, passive user, you'll probably have half an hour or less, but if you make some sort of contribution—taking an active part in the message bases, uploading interesting files, or maybe sending in some cash—you'll probably be rewarded with more time.

The next screen you see will look something like this:

```
Type P to Pause, S to Stop listing
```

```
Please support the companies that support BCS*Mac through donation of
products and technical support:

    eSoft, Inc. .............Producers of The Bread Board System (TBBS)
    GCC Technologies, Inc. ............................... Hard drives
    US Robotics, Inc. ........................................ Modems
    APS .................................... Hard drives & DAT software
    Hayes Microcomputer Products, Inc. ....................... Modems
    Prometheus Products, Inc. ................................ Modems
    Shiva Corporation ............... Net modems and Net serial modems
```

Call me overly sentimental, but I think a company nice enough to donate equipment to a nonprofit BBS is worthy of my support. Many companies make donations with the proviso that they get credit up front.

Now that you're past all the credits and whatnot, the board will alert you to the presence of any new mail that's been sent to you since your last visit:

```
Searching  Message  Base  ...

Msg # From              To              Subject           Board Name
__ _____  _____ _____ _____   _____       _____
6701  SYSOP             ROCKY RACCOON     YOU'RE VALIDATED  E-MAIL
6723  LIL MCGILL        ROCKY RACCOON     HOWDY, ROCKY!     BEGINNERS

These  2  message(s)  are  marked  for  retrieval

Read  Now(Y/N)?  N
```

This feature greatly simplifies things. There can be thousands of messages on a BBS at once; grouping all your incoming messages in one list when you sign on saves you a lot of time. Let's ignore these messages for now; you'll see them in the next section. If you had answered Y to that *Read Now (Y/N)?* question, you'd be reading both those messages and have the opportunity to type in your replies.

Usually, the board clues you in on any news its users should be aware of. Look here for information on problems and improvements to the board, days when the board will unexpectedly be unavailable, and community events and announcements:

```
BCS MACINTOSH Multiline BBS — Newswire                    Updated 1/08/92
 ─────────────────────────────────

  * TBBS 2.2 is here! Full-screen message editing, ZMODEM file transfers,
    and international netmail access are just a few of its new features.
    Many menus have changed; you may need to adjust macros.

  * (P)revious and (T)op may not work on some menus. We are working on a fix.
    (U)tilities will usually get you out.

  * No BCS*Mac Main Meeting this month because of the San Francisco Expo.
    Watch for the February Main Meeting with Apple's QuickTime development
    team.

  * Design Group meeting Thursday Jan. 9 Read Msg #516 in <I>nfo <M>eetings.

  * NBC's "Golden Girls" canceled...a nation mourns.
 ──────────────────────────────────────────────────────────────────────────


-Press Any Key-
```

The next thing you'll see should be the BBS's main menu:

```
BCS MACINTOSH Multiline BBS —  MAIN MENU
 ─────────────────────────


(I)nformation ........ BBS help; BCS meetings and general info
(P)ublic-Files ....... All callers can download these essentials

(M)essages .......... BCS Macintosh message bases
(F)iles ............. BCS Macintosh file libraries
(S)Premium Services .. Extended subscription features

(A)ctivists ......... BCS volunteer work area
(W)riters ........... Submit an article to The Active Window
(J)umpToGroups ....... Jump to BCS Main Menu (Access other groups)


(G)oodbye    (=)Utilities    (?)Help

Command:
```

Congratulations—you've joined the on-line community. But this is merely the beginning. In the following sections I'll guide you through the ins and outs of sending, receiving, and reading messages. In Chapter 6, you'll learn how to upload and download files.

Messaging

Here's something for you to try. Go to your local mall, theater, health club, anywhere you can find a large number of strangers milling about. Yell "The Boston Red Sox will not win a World Series within my lifetime" and see what happens. Unless you live in a rather odd neighborhood, the result will probably be people walking a bit faster and clutching their bags a little tighter as they pass by you. When you do this on a BBS or on-line service, though, those same strangers will actually engage you in intelligent conversation, debating the importance of relief pitching and the inanity of the abrupt firing of former manager Joe Morgan.

There's no comparable experience anywhere else; messaging is 90 percent of what makes BBSs so swell. The term *bulletin board service* connotes an area with public notices tacked up for all to read and post their own responses to.

Mail on on-line services is broken down into two main areas, depending on where in the system you post it. Most messages are *public*, which means that anyone can read them and post their responses to them. Because sometimes you don't want to air your dirty laundry to the whole world, most systems also allow you to send *private* messages to another specific BBS user. These private messages are usually called *E-Mail*—electronic mail. On a commercial on-line service, your E-Mail can be read only by you and the person you send it to. On a BBS your mail can also be read by the sysop, though we consider it somewhat rude for sysops to read private E-Mail not addressed to them. Areas for private and public messaging are usually kept under separate menus in the BBS. When you select **M** for *Messages* from the main menu, you see this screen:

```
BCS MACINTOSH Multiline BBS — MESSAGE BASE Menu
─────────────────────────────────
Roz Ault and Cathy Rudolph, Managing Sysops

(R)umor Manager ....... Read/send general Macintosh messages
(C)ombined ........... Select message areas for combined reading

(B)BS Help Desk ....... Questions about how to use the BBS answered here!
(E)cho Manager ....... National & international message base

(M)ailbox ........... Private messages

(P)revious   (T)op-Menu   (G)oodbye   (Z)ap-Logoff   (=)Utilities   (?)Help

Command: r
```

All BBSs set up their message areas a little differently, of course. Here on the BCS•Mac BBS, in addition to the public and private message areas, you can find the Help Desk, for new users who have questions about using this board. BCS•Mac also has the Echo Manager, where the board shares messages with other BBSs all across the country. The Rumor Manager is the BCS•Mac BBS's name for its public message area:

```
Command: r

BCS MACINTOSH Multiline BBS — RUMOR MANAGER Menu
─────────────────────────────────
Roz Ault and Cathy Rudolph, Managing Sysops

(1)Beginners Come First !   ... Moderated by Andy Ihnatko

(2)Hardware Messages        ... Moderated by David Walsh
(3)Software Messages        ... Moderated by Glenn Parker
(4)Modem Madness Messages   ... Moderated by Roy Eassa
(5)Buy/Sell & Swap          ... Moderated by Craig O'Donnell
(6)Jobs/Help Wanted         ... Moderated by Steve Semple
(7)Rumors/News Messages     ... Moderated by Ilene Hoffman & Cathy Rudolph
(8)After School             ... Moderated by Jeff Carson
(9)Health'n Fitness         ... Moderated by Gretchen MacDowall & Rodney Smith

(0)Legal User Subgroup      ... Moderated by Harley Hiestand
(A)HyperCard Subgroup       ... Moderated by Bob Soron
(B)MacTech Subgroup         ... Moderated by Glenn Rosen
(C)Music Subgroup           ... Moderated by Rodney Smith

(E)BMUG<->BCS (MACQA)       ... A transcontinental message echo
(F)System 7                 ... National Apple System 7 discussion

(P)revious   (T)op-Menu   (G)oodbye   (Z)ap-Logoff   (=)Utilities   (?)Help

Command: 1
```

At any one time, a BBS has hundreds, even *thousands* of messages available for reading. For a commercial service such as CompuServe, that number can go into the *tens* of thousands. To help you manage this mound of data, all BBSs divide their message base into areas of specific interest. When I go to read some messages, therefore, I can avoid the hundreds of messages on topics that don't concern me, such as politics, health, and education, and zoom right in on the area that maintains in-depth discussions on the most recent episode of "The Simpsons."

Leaving New Messages

Let's look at how to create a new message and post it to the BBS. Whenever you start using a new BBS, it's usually a good idea to leave a brief message saying "Howdy!" to everyone. It's also a good opportunity to ask some preliminary questions about what the most popular areas of the board are.

When should you leave new messages? Anytime you feel like it—if you have a pressing question, when you've learned a juicy new rumor or factoid you'd like to share with the world, when you're mad as heck and not going to take it any more. Take comfort that benevolent angels are always watching over you in the form of sysops. If you post a totally inappropriate message, the sysop will let you know. If you post a message in the wrong area of the BBS, the sysop will move it into the proper area *for* you. Nothing will break, so as they say in those sneaker commercials, Just Do It.

Since you're entering this arena as a beginner, I'll zip over to the Beginners section, which is moderated by Andy:

```
Command:  1

BCS MACINTOSH Multiline BBS — BEGINNERS Message Menu
──────────────────────────────────────

Moderated by Andy Ihnatko

(R)ead  ............  Read messages
(S)can  ............  Scan messages
(L)eave a Message ..  Add comments and ask questions
(K)ill a Message ...  Delete a message FROM/TO you

(P)revious    (T)op-Menu    (G)oodbye    (Z)ap-Logoff    (=)Utilities    (?)Help

Command:  L
```

That's something you'll run across a lot in the larger boards: The BCS•Mac BBS is so big and handles so much mail that no one sysop can manage it all. A team of assistant sysops (or subops) handle each area. Take note of the names you see in those positions on a BBS: These folks usually log onto the board at least once a day, and a message left to a subop is apt to be answered promptly.

You are now in the Beginners section. Think of it as entering a room in a hotel; technically you're in your own little world right now. Any message you leave here won't be read by someone who's in the Rumors/News section at the moment. Issue the command for leaving a new message:

```
Command: L
Who is the message to?
```

The first thing the BBS has to know is who you want to send a message to. That way, when whoever you're sending a message to logs onto the BBS, he or she can be alerted to the presence of the message you left.

```
Who is the message to? ALL
```

As you want everyone to read your message of greeting, type in **all**.

You could type *everyone*, or even *left-handed cellists* for all it matters (though *all* is the usual term); BBS users reading your message will understand that you're leaving this message for public consumption.
   Sysop may have special significance when you use it as an address, however. Most BBS software flags your message to the attention of either one of the lead system operators of the board or the person in charge of that specific message section.

All messages have a subject line. This is a short phrase describing the message's contents. As you'll see a little later on when you're reading messages, this subject line is another cue the BBS gives you to help you zero in (or avoid) messages of a specific interest:

```
What is the subject?
```

Select your subject line with care. If you're trying to sell your car and you post a message in the Classified message area with the subject *Black Sabbath Rules!* you're probably not going to find any buyers.

```
What is the subject? Howdy! New user here
```

Yet another example here of the forgiving spirit of modern computers. If you did in fact enter "Black Sabbath Rules!", here's your chance to make a correction.

```
To: ALL
Subj: Howdy! New user here
Is this correct(Y/N)? Y
```

Now you can start typing in the message itself:

```
Enter text of message.
<CR> by itself ends input.

01:
```

Unfortunately, this represents the state of word processing on a BBS. For Mac users, word processing means mousing a pointer around, clicking, cutting, copying, and pasting, using buttons and menus and having a jolly easy time editing and writing your letters and memos. Since almost all BBSs are text-based, you have no friendly icons to click on. Worse, because the connection between your Mac and the BBS is so slow, and full-page editing requires a lot of data to go back and forth between the two, most BBSs have you edit your text line by line. The *01:* tells you you're typing in the first line.

Now, type in the text of your message:

```
01: Howdy all!  This is my first time leaking on to the BCS•Mac BBS.  Looks
02: pretty nice so far.  I just got my modem last weekend (a DiscoModem 9624),
03: and this is my first time on-line.  Any hints or tips you people can give me
04: would be really appreciated.  Oh, and the Boston Red Sox will not win the
05: World Series within my lifetime.
```

> For the record, Andy's a Red Sox fan. Like most of his Massachusetts brethren he thinks the team is great, has all their albums, and so on. He created these examples, thus the repeated references to the Red Sox.
> Me? I'm a dyed-in-the-wool Mets fan.

On some systems the BBS automatically moves text to a new line for you and you need not add carriage returns at the end of each line.

When you've finished entering your message, just press Return on an empty line; this tells the BBS your message is complete:

```
06:

<L>ist, <V>iew, <E>dit, <R>cpt, <F>ile, <Q>uit, <S>ave, or <H>elp?
```

> If you want a blank line in your message, you'll have to type a single space in that line; it'll *look* blank to the reader, but the BBS will allow you to go on entering text.

Once you've pressed Return on that empty line, the BBS asks you what you want to do with the text.

For now, type **E** to select the Edit option so you can correct the typo in the first line: Change *leaking* to *logging*.

> If you're wondering about those other options: List displays your message with the line numbers; View displays it as others will see it when it's posted; File lets you send a Macintosh file—a word processing document, application, or whatever; Quit aborts the message without sending; Save sends the message; Help displays help text for messages.
>
> On many advanced boards, you have two additional options when posting a message. The BCS•Mac board allows you to make enclosures: You can include a file along with the message by pressing F before sending the message. The reader can download the enclosed file after reading the text of the message. It's a nifty feature; without it, the only way to send a sensitive spreadsheet file to your partner via the BBS would be to upload it to the general files area, where *anyone* could get at it!
>
> Another widespread messaging feature is requesting a receipt for that message (on the BCS•Mac BBS use the R option). As soon as the addressee reads your message, the BBS automatically sends you a private message notifying you that the message was received, along with the time and date.

Editing text in a BBS's line editor isn't as simple as using a commercial word processor, where you click your mouse on the misspelling and type in a replacement. Instead, you have to retype the whole line to make any corrections in it. Happily, you still have a search and replace option.

The pokiness of your modem mandates line editing. If you have a nice, fast modem (9600 bps or better) some BBSs allow you to use an advanced, screen-based editor in which you can jump from line to line with cursor keys and edit text willy-nilly. It's not as nice as even the most rudimentary Mac word processor, but it's a quantum leap ahead.

Once you select the Edit option, most BBS systems give you several editing functions:

```
<L>ist, <V>iew, <E>dit, <R>cpt, <F>ile, <Q>uit, <S>ave, or <H>elp? E

<C>ont, <I>ns, <T>ext Subst, <D>el/Repl Line or <H>elp?
```

Cont   Allows you to enter more lines after the last one you entered. If you pressed **C** here you could continue entering text at line 6.

Ins   Allows you to insert a line within your message. If you wanted to say you were using our book for reference, right after saying what kind of modem you're using, press **I**. When the BBS asks what line you want to insert new text after, enter **2**, and then you can insert as many new lines as you want.

Text Subst   Same as search and replace.

Del/Repl Line   Specify which line you want to work on, and the BBS allows you to retype that whole line, or leave it blank to delete that line.
    Let's fix the typo by pressing **T**:

```
<C>ont, <I>ns, <T>ext Subst, <D>el/Repl Line or <H>elp? T
String to edit? leaking
Replace with? logging
time leaking in
Replace here(Y/N)?
```

When you choose the Text Substitution option, the BBS asks you to verify that you want to change each occurrence of the word or phrase. Select **Y**.

```
Replace here(Y/N)? Y
<L>ist, <V>iew, <E>dit, <R>cpt, <F>ile, <Q>uit, <S>ave, or <H>elp?
```

Next, type **L** to select the List option, so you can see the message again and make sure that was the only mistake. Finally, you can send the message by typing **S**. The Save option saves the message on the BBS and makes it available for public view:

```
<L>ist, <V>iew, <A>gain, <E>dit, <R>cpt, <F>ile, <Q>uit, <S>ave, or <H>elp? S

Saving message to disk...
BCS MACINTOSH Multiline BBS — BEGINNERS Message Menu
_____

Moderated by Andy Ihnatko

(R)ead ............. Read messages
(S)can ............. Scan messages
(L)eave a Message .. Add comments and ask questions
(K)ill a Message ... Delete a message FROM/TO you

(P)revious    (T)op-Menu    (G)oodbye    (Z)ap-Logoff    (=)Utilities    (?)Help

Command:
```

> Not all boards use the same terminology to send a message, either. Some use a Save option, others use a Send option or a Post option. Whatever term is used, they all do the same thing.

You've successfully posted a public message. For detailed instructions on how to send messages on other sections of the BBS and how to send private messages that can be read only by you, the recipient, and the sysops, follow the same instructions. Primitive as it is, a BBS's user interface is at least consistent. You leave messages exactly the same way in all message areas. When you send private mail, however, you *must* address it to a specific person.

Selecting Messages to Read

Most of your quality on-line time will probably be spent *reading* messages, which is somewhat more complex than sending messages. The method for entering a message is the same no matter what section of the BBS you're visiting, but with thousands of messages on a typical BBS, a BBS offers a many ways to read messages.

The first step is familiar. You have to navigate through menus to get to a specific message section. Here's the menu you see in the Beginners section on the BCS•Mac BBS:

```
BCS MACINTOSH Multiline BBS — BEGINNERS Message Menu
────────────────────────
Moderated by Andy Ihnatko

(R)ead ............ Read messages
(S)can ............ Scan messages
(L)eave a Message .. Add comments and ask questions
(K)ill a Message ... Delete a message FROM/TO you

(P)revious   (T)op-Menu   (G)oodbye   (Z)ap-Logoff   (=)Utilities   (?)Help

Command:
```

> Many boards—including BCS•Mac—also have a Combined message area that allows you to access all new (since the last time you logged on) messages *everywhere* on the board. Use this area if the board is so infrequently used that only a small number of new messages are posted between logons, or for a script that grabs all new messages from every section on the BBS. Otherwise, stay away from the Combined area. It's a good way to waste a lot of time getting swamped with a lot of messages.

Reading messages is a straightforward, two-step process: You tell the BBS what sort of messages you want to read, then the BBS accesses them and you can read them.

> Reading private messages is simplest. Since the BBS assumes you'll be interested in all private messages addressed to you, you just go to the proper area and send whatever command lets you see your private mail.

For most of your day-to-day business, the "what sort of messages" options on a BBS usually boil down to either all new messages or only messages that interest you.

Reading All New Messages   A BBS keeps track of when you last logged on and what messages you read. Using this info, it can assemble all the new messages that have been left since the last time you had a look around. Start by pressing **R** to read messages. From the list of Read options, select **N** for new messages:

```
Command: r

<F>orward or <R>everse Multiple
<N>ew Messages
<M>arked Messages
<S>elective Retrieval
<I>ndividual Message(s)
<A>bort Retrieve

Which One? N
```

The BBS lets you read every message that's been left in the Beginner's section since you last logged on.

> Not all BBS programs are particularly clever when deciding what constitutes a new message. Some BBSs assume that *new* means "messages left after you last logged off the system," so if you were to log on, look around for private mail, then log off, on your next session none of the *public* messages left before that quick visit would appear under new messages. The smart BBSs track the most recent message you've read in each section, so checking your private mail every day won't affect your ability to read all new public messages once a week.

You can read all new messages on smaller, friendly BBS systems that you visit frequently. On a commercial service such as CompuServe, where hundreds of new messages per section per *day* is the norm, trying to read *everything* can take all your time and all your money. On most on-line services, you'll want to use the second method of reading messages.

Reading Only Messages That Interest You   Most systems allow you to scan a list of available message subjects and, from that list, choose to read only those that interest you.

Searching the message base on a set of criteria you specify, the BBS can summarize each message in one line:

```
Msg # From            To              Subject              Mark for later
—  _____  _____   _____  _____   _____   _____
7028   ELIOT AXELROD     VICTOR EHRLICH     MRS. HUFNAGEL'S HEAR Mark(Y/N/S)?
```

At your discretion, the BBS can tag individual messages you're interested in, so later on you can read all the tagged messages as a group. The BBS can find and summarize messages based on several criteria:

```
BCS*Mac Multiline BBS — BEGINNERS Message Menu
─────────────────────────────────

Moderated by Andy Ihnatko

(R)ead ............ Read messages
(S)can ............ Scan messages
(L)eave a Message .. Add comments and ask questions
(K)ill a Message ... Delete a message FROM/TO you

(P)revious   (T)op-Menu   (G)oodbye   (Z)ap-Logoff   (=)Utilities   (?)Help

Command: s

<F>orward  Scan
<R>everse  Scan
<N>ew  Message  Scan
<S>elective  Scan
<A>bort  Scan

Which One?
```

Forward and Reverse Scan summarize all messages left after or before a certain date, respectively. New Message Scan summarizes all messages left since your last visit. Abort Scan returns you to the Message menu.

Selective Scan is different from the rest—it can home in on messages sent to or from a specific person (handy for reviewing all the messages you've had a hand in, or for seeing if Cher has been on line recently). More usefully, it can find every message that contains a keyword or phrase in its Subject field.

Let's say you're interested in learning about color monitors. Set up a search to find all messages with the word *color* in their subject field, and tell the BBS to pause after each summarized message so you can tag it for further reading:

```
Which One? S

Select <F>rom, <T>o, or <S>ubject? S
Enter text to select by: color
Mark for Later Retrieval? Y
```

When asked for the type of scan, select **N** for New:

```
Select <F>orward, <R>everse or <N>ew? N
```

After a moment, the board shows you summaries:

Msg #	From	To	Subject	Mark for later
4115	ROBERT PLANT	ANDY MACKAY	COLOR MONITORS	Mark(Y/N/S)? Y
4126	JAMES PAGE	STEVE VAN ZANDT	POSTSCRIPT COLOR	Mark(Y/N/S)? N
4154	ANDY MACKAY	ROBERT PLANT	COLOR MONITORS	Mark(Y/N/S)? Y
4159	ROBERT PLANT	ANDY MACKAY	COLOR MONITORS	Mark(Y/N/S)? Y
4185	JOHN BONZO	J.P. JONES	CAT COLORINGS	Mark(Y/N/S)? N
4250	BRYAN FERRY	BRIAN ENO	EMAC 19" COLOR	Mark(Y/N/S)? Y
4443	NANCY WILSON	BRYAN FERRY	EMAC 19" COLOR	Mark(Y/N/S)? Y
4445	ANDY MACKAY	ROBERT PLANT	COLOR MONITORS	Mark(Y/N/S)? Y
7015	ANN WILSON	PHIL MANZANERA	THE COLOR OF MONEY	Mark(Y/N/S)? N

After each line, the BBS stops and asks if you want to see this message later on. As you can see, you can mark the messages that seem to be about color monitors and avoid having to read the rest. You'd use the same procedure no matter which selective retrieval method you used.

Other Ways to See Messages Once you've made your way down the list, the BBS zaps you back to the Message menu. To read only those messages you've marked, select Marked Messages from the Read menu:

```
BCS*Mac Multiline BBS — BEGINNERS Message Menu
─────────────────────────────────────────────

Moderated by Andy Ihnatko

(R)ead  ............  Read messages
(S)can  ............  Scan messages
(L)eave a Message ..  Add comments and ask questions
(K)ill a Message ...  Delete a message FROM/TO you

(P)revious   (T)op-Menu   (G)oodbye   (Z)ap-Logoff   (=)Utilities   (?)Help

Command: r

<F>orward or <R>everse Multiple
<N>ew Messages
<M>arked Messages
<S>elective Retrieval
<I>ndividual Message(s)
<A>bort Retrieve

Which One? M
```

Marking individual messages for later reading and reading all new messages en masse aren't the only ways to get the BBS to show you messages, of course. On the Read menu, you can also specify a single message to be read by number (this feature lets you get at the message without mucking through what came before and after it). You can read messages in forward or reverse chronological order, either to skip ahead to the most recent messages, or catch up with old messages.

Numbers are assigned to messages chronologically as they're posted. Unfortunately, some BBSs can only determine a message's age by its number. Only one message can come between message 1294 and 1296, but you can have a dozen messages that were posted at 8:23 A.M. on January 12. The more accurate numbering method doesn't help, however, when you're looking for a message posted a week ago last Wednesday.

The BCS•Mac BBS doesn't support one of the most common methods of selecting messages for reading. Many boards can present you with a list of all message subjects. If the BCS•Mac board had this feature, it'd probably show you a list like this:

```
Subjects in BEGINNERS:

Subject              Msgs   Mark all for later


CAT COLORINGS          3    Mark(Y/N/S)? N
COLOR MONITORS        12    Mark(Y/N/S)? Y
MY DISKS GOT HOSED!   26    Mark(Y/N/S)? Y
NEXT BCS*MAC MEETING   7    Mark(Y/N/S)? Y
SAD MAC ICON          12    Mark(Y/N/S)? Y
SCSI HARD DRIVES?      2    Mark(Y/N/S)? N
THE COLOR OF MONEY     1    Mark(Y/N/S)? N
```

Normally, a subject-listing function lists the subjects alphabetically, lets you know how many messages have that subject line, and lets you read all those messages as a group if you want. Reading by subject gives you a simple way of reading a wide variety of messages you're interested in.

Telecom nuts often talk about the *signal to noise ratio* of a BBS's message bases. In the world of audio, it's the ratio of good sound to useless background static. On a BBS, it refers to the ratio of good messages you're interested in to junk messages. A BBS with a high S/N ratio has a solid message base. A low S/N ratio means that for every interesting, useful message there are two messages on topics as scintillating as how to care for shag carpeting.

Reading Your Messages

After you've marked the messages you want to read, or instructed the BBS to show you only new messages, the BBS will show you those messages. But first the BBS usually asks you:

```
Pause after each msg(Y/N)?
```

Normally, the BBS pauses after each message to give you the option of replying to it, rereading it, jumping around to read other messages like it, and so on. If you answer **N** here, the BBS spews all the messages in one uninterrupted scroll. You can save on-line time (and therefore money) by commanding your telecom program to capture all incoming text to a file on disk, listing all the messages, then logging off. You can then read all the messages at your own pace, while off line.

For the most part, though, you'll want to read messages interactively, so type **Y** and the BBS presents you with your first message:

```
Msg#:   202 *BEGINNER*
07/22/92  12:17:33
From:  ABNER RAVENWOOD
  To: ALL
Subj: ANY SHELLAC COLLECTORS HERE?

Hello, everyone!  My name is Abner and my hobby is collecting antique jars
of shellac!  I have over 230 items in my collection, including a half-full
jar of shellac that was used to seal the finish on the deck of the Mayflower!
It came with a certificate of authenticity to prove it!  I paid $144,928 for
it!  Anyone else here collect shellac?

<*>Replies
<C>ubby, <D>el, <R>eply, <A>gain, <N>ext, or <S>top?
```

Assuming we had selected New Messages from the Read menu, this would be the oldest message you hadn't yet read. (If you had selected Marked Messages from the Read menu, this would be the first message you marked.)

The first line tells you the message number and in what area the message was left. Jot down the message number if you think you'll want to reread that message later. The second line gives you the time and date the message was posted. The third line tells you who left the message. The fourth line tells you who Abner left the message for: everyone. The fifth line is the subject Abner provided, describing what the message is about. After that, you can see the message text.

Finally, the two lines at the bottom list all the things you can tell the BBS to do next:

* **Replies**   Use this option to read replies to this message.

C **Cubby**   Use this option for individual messages of interest. It sends them to your cubbyhole—you can later choose to have the contents of your cubby electronically sent to your Mac as a text file.

D **Delete**   Use this option to delete the current message. You can delete only messages you sent or received.

R **Reply**   Use this option to reply to the current message.

A **Again**   Use this option to reread the current message (helpful if it's scrolled off your screen.)

N **Next**   Use this option to go to the next message.

S **Stop**   Use this option to stop reading messages.

F **Forward**   Use this option to take a message that's already been posted to the BBS and send a copy of it to another user. It's useful if someone sent you a list of light bulb jokes and you want to pass it on to a pal.

Relationships between Messages

If you were to break into the room housing the BBS, ignore all the hand-lettered signs promising swift revenge upon interlopers, and look at the files on the computer that runs the BBS, you'd see that each message is a distinct entity on the BBS's hard drive. You could single out one message for reading, but that's not how you generally read messages. The BBS program keeps track of two relationships between messages: Chronology and message threads.

First the BBS tracks the order in which the messages were created. As messages are saved, the BBS numbers and saves them on the BBS computer's hard drive. This keeps messages in a chronological order. On most boards, when you've read one message and ask to read the next one, the BBS looks for the next-higher-numbered message and puts it on your screen.

More powerful than chronologies are message threads. Let's say someone asks a question and two or three people write replies to that message. More folks read those responses and add their own replies. All of these messages make up a thread.

To help users follow a thread (make sense of the messages and their replies), the BBS always keeps track of related messages. If a day or two has elapsed between the posting of the original message and its first reply, you don't have to trudge through a couple dozen messages about shrubbery maintenance and the world's greatest bread recipe before finally getting to the reply.

Chronological Messages   Let's look at both chronologies and threading in action by picking up where I left off. On the next to last line, *
Replies tells you that at least one person has replied to the message. Nearly all BBSs give you some indication when replies have been posted. If you're not interested in shellac, you can move on to the next message, whether it's related or not, by pressing **N** to select the Next option. The next message is as follows:

```
Msg#:   208 *BEGINNER*
07/22/92 15:47:10
From: LEE VING
   To: ALL
Subj: WHERE CAN I FIND MACINTALK?

Hey, does anyone know where I can get a copy of MacinTalk? It's a
software-based speech synthesizer that Apple used to give out.   I
think it's free, but I can't seem to find it anywhere.   Any help
would be appreciated!

<*>Replies
<C>ubby, <D>el, <R>eply, <A>gain, <N>ext, or <S>top?
```

A free piece of software that gives a Mac a human voice? I'd like to
know more about *that*. Fortunately, there are some replies to this
message.

> You may have noticed that this message is number 208 and the
> previous message (from Abner) is number 202. That's not a mistake.
> The missing messages (numbers 203–207) were posted to other
> sections of the board; we're still in the Beginner section.

Message Threads   To follow this message thread, enter an asterisk
and you'll see the first reply to this message:

```
<C>ubby, <D>el, <R>eply, <A>gain, <N>ext, or <S>top? *
Msg#:   232 *BEGINNER*
07/22/92 17:09:52
From: DEAN WITTER
   To: LEE VING
Subj: REPLY TO MSG# 208 (WHERE CAN I FIND MACINTALK?)

You can find it right here on the BBS...it's the file MACINTLK.SIT in
the Music/Sound file area.

<-> <C>ubby, <D>el, <R>eply, <A>gain, <N>ext, or <S>top?
```

A couple of dozen messages (numbers 209–231) were posted
between the original message and this reply, but the BBS takes you
right to the reply. Also, note that the Subject field has been changed so
you can identify the parent—the original message this one is replying
to. If you want to reread the parent message, use a new command that's
been added to the line of commands: - (hyphen). Pressing hyphen right
now will tell the BBS to display Message 208.

Power User Flourishes   Since message 232 has no replies, press **N** to go to the next message in the thread:

```
Msg#:   241 *BEGINNER*
07/23/92  02:01:44
From: DIANE CHAMBERS
  To: LEE VING
Subj: REPLY TO MSG# 208 (WHERE CAN I FIND MACINTALK?)

> Hey, does anyone know where I can get a copy of MacinTalk? It's a
> software-based speech synthesizer that Apple used to give out.

Actually, you probably don't want to be using MacinTalk at all these days.
Apple officially gave it the kiss of death years ago (swearing off
making any new versions or even supporting any of the old versions) so if
there are any huge incompatibilities with System 7 you'll be truly stuck.
Though it's useful if you really, really like system crashes. :)

BTW, if you can stand to wait some more, Apple is working on this amazing
kick-*** speech code for an upcoming version of the System Software.  I
saw a demo of it a while ago...perfectly natural human voice (as opposed
to MacinTalk's drunken Swede dialect) PLUS it'll recognize _spoken_ commands.

<*>Replies
<-> <C>ubby, <D>el, <R>eply, <A>gain, <N>ext, or <S>top?
```

Let's take a look at all the power telecom user flourishes in Diane's reply: quoting, insider lingo, censorship, and italics.

Diane has quoted the important parts of Lee's message at the top of her reply, and started each line with an angle bracket (>) to distinguish them from the body of her reply. This is a friendly gesture. People who haven't been following the thread from the beginning will know what Lee was asking without having to read the original message, and if Lee waits two or three weeks before he logs on again, he won't have to ask Diane what he had asked in the first place. Putting an angle bracket in the leftmost column to demarcate a quote is the most popular convention. Some folks specify who wrote those lines by using their initials before the arrow, as in:

```
LV> Hey, does anyone..."
```

Insider telecom lingo is those words that do such a wonderful job of confusing new modem users. First, she's used a popular on-line acronym, BTW, which stands for "by the way." (You can find a long list of acronyms in Chapter 8.) After your first few weeks on line, the most popular and useful acronyms will start to roll off your keyboard naturally.

Diane has also incorporated a smiley (also known as an emoticon or an ASCII-gram) in the last line of her first paragraph. If you crick your neck to the left, the :) becomes a happy face. Here Diane is saying "I'm only kidding." You can find a guide to emoticons in Chapter 8. A vocal minority of BBS users think that emoticons, unlike acronyms, are the electronic equivalent of Smurfs and should be banned utterly.

In the second paragraph, Diane has substituted asterisks for the name of a small ungulate. If your vocabulary is questionable, it's a good idea to use asterisks. You never know when little kiddies will be reading your messages. For more common rules of BBS etiquette, see Chapter 8.

On-line text is limited to simple ASCII characters, so you can't use typographic enhancements such as boldfacing, italics, and so forth. By convention, though, when you want to italicize a word, surround it with _underline_ characters, as Diane has done with _spoken_. Boldface characters are represented by ALL UPPERCASE. THIS MAKES YOU SEEM LIKE YOU'RE SHOUTING (use it sparingly).

Tangled Threads   If you look at the bottom of Diane's message you can see that someone has replied to *her* message! Can you look at these replies and then continue reading replies to the parent message? That depends on the BBS program.

With *most* services, when you give the command to read the replies to a message, the BBS shows you *every* message that is a direct reply to that message. The same concept carries over when reading the replies. If you typed * after reading the reply, the BBS would show you all the replies to Diane's message, and then it would return to showing the replies to Lee Ving's original MacinTalk question.

A few BBS systems handle things differently, though. They show you all the replies, all the replies to the replies, all the replies to the replies to the replies, and so on.

Let's see this reply:

```
<-> <C>ubby, <D>el, <R>eply, <A>gain, <N>ext, or <S>top? *

Msg#:  258 *BEGINNER*
07/23/92  09:32:11
From: SAM MALONE
  To: DIANE CHAMBERS
Subj: REPLY TO MSG# 241  (WHERE CAN I FIND MACINTALK?)

Is that the "Casper" voice-recognition system I've heard so much about?
(and why do you think Apple chose "Casper" as a codename?  I thought those
old cartoons and comic books were long-forgotten...)

<-> <C>ubby, <D>el, <R>eply, <A>gain, <N>ext, or <S>top?
```

Notice that the Subject field identifies this as a reply to Diane's message (message 241) and not Lee's (message 208). And note that the focus has shifted from MacinTalk to Casper. Let's reply to this one.

Replying to Messages

When should you reply to a message? You should feel free to jump in and reply to any public message you want. Sure, that To: field says that this message is directed to Diane Chambers, but don't forget that all messages left in a public message area are posted for public consumption and comment. If you feel any ideas or questions bubbling to the surface after reading a message, go ahead and reply.

Occasionally, some self-restraint is an excellent idea. The first problem is one that *everyone* goes through when they start telecommunicating: You see all these messages, good conversation, great ideas, so you write a 100-line commentary on the trip to Yosemite you took last summer in response to a discussion on the impact of RISC technology. Always feel free to leave replies, but try to write short messages—not more than one screenful—and try to keep to the topic at hand.

The second problem is more serious. As you post public messages, *never forget that the person receiving the message is a human being*. A big software company once tested the use of electronic meetings; every other month, instead of all the department heads gathering in a room and talking face to face, they'd each stay in their offices and discuss their problems by typing into a terminal window shared by everyone. Without the visual reinforcement that they were talking to real human beings and not just a computer, the electronic meetings soon devolved into rude exchanges of insults.

Whenever you create a reply, the BBS gives you the opportunity to change the Subject string to something more appropriate, if necessary:

```
<-> <C>ubby, <D>el, <R>eply, <A>gain, <N>ext, or <S>top? r
Change the Subject(Y/N)?
```

Compare the content of Sam Malone's message to the Subject field, "Where can I find MacinTalk?" You can see that already the content has started to drift; he's not talking about where MacinTalk can be found, but about software speech synthesis in general. Every reply gets further off the subject until eventually that subject contains messages on how to properly seat and grout a bathroom tub enclosure. (That actually happened.)

People on line choose what messages to read based solely on the Subject, so it's important to pay attention and make sure your message relates to the stated subject. Folks who are paying $10 an hour to use a commercial on-line service get plenty ticked off when they spend a buck and a half to get a stack of messages on MacinTalk and find a series of chowder recipes instead. Whenever you're about to entirely abandon the topic at hand, be sure to change the Subject field to something more appropriate.

I have some info Sam Malone may find interesting—nothing whatsoever to do with speech synthesis—so I'll change the subject string:

```
Change the Subject(Y/N)? Y
Enter new subject: CASPER THE FRIENDLY GHOST
CASPER THE FRIENDLY GHOST
Is this correct?(Y/N)? Y

To: SAM MALONE
Subj: CASPER THE FRIENDLY GHOST
Use Full Screen Editor(Y/N)? N

Enter text of message.
<CR> by itself ends input.

01:
```

Advanced Message Editing   In the previous section you learned how to enter and edit messages. The technique for writing a reply to a message is no different from writing an original message, so here I'll show you some advanced message editing techniques.

First, I'll start by quoting the part of Sam's message that I want to reply to. I don't *have* to, but it's polite. I'll type it in manually:

```
01: > (and why do you think Apple chose "Casper" as a codename?  I thought
02: > those old cartoons and comic books were long-forgotten...)
```

You can enter a quote in two other ways: Using copy and paste or a text editor. The handiest way is to just type the > and then simply copy and paste the text of interest from the terminal window. Your telecom program can cut, copy, and paste any text in the terminal window or its scrollback buffer just as it would in a word processor. When you paste, the text is sent out the modem as though you had typed it in by hand.

But don't confuse this with cut and paste as it works in a word processor. In a word processor, you can click anywhere on the screen and paste in text wherever you fancy. In a telecom program, you can paste only to the bottommost line in the terminal window (unless your BBS supports full-screen editing); normally, when you use the Paste command, a Mac telecom program automatically pastes text in at the bottom of the terminal window, no matter where the cursor is.

Furthermore, you are limited to no more than 80 characters per line. With the > and the space that comes after it, a quoted line can exceed 80 characters, so you may have to copy and paste a little bit at a time. You can then continue typing in message text as usual.

If you write lots of messages and replies during a session, consider running a text editor alongside your telecom program. If you use MicroPhone II, you've got it made—it includes a built-in text editor called MicroEditor. Otherwise, rather than a full-featured program such as MacWrite or Microsoft Word, use one of the many freeware and shareware text editors available for downloading. They're generally faster, run in far less memory (a big plus when you consider that it has to run alongside your telecom program), and best of all they're either free or nearly free. Andy's favorite is a shareware editor called ConTEXT II. It's simple, it's powerful, and it costs only $15. I like McSink or miniWRITER, two other nifty shareware editors.

Whichever text editor you use, launch it either right before or right after you launch your telecom program so it's always at the ready. The only preparation you have to do is to make sure the text editor is using a monospaced font such as Monaco or Courier. Because messages appear on the BBS in monospaced fonts, when you use fonts where characters have varying widths (such as Helvetica, Times, and Geneva), text doesn't appear with the same formatting as when posted to the board.

Using a Text Editor   Let's look at how to enter text with a text editor. To quote those two lines of text, I select the lines in my terminal window, select Copy, select my ConTEXT II window, and select Paste. The text shown in Figure 5–1 appears on my screen.

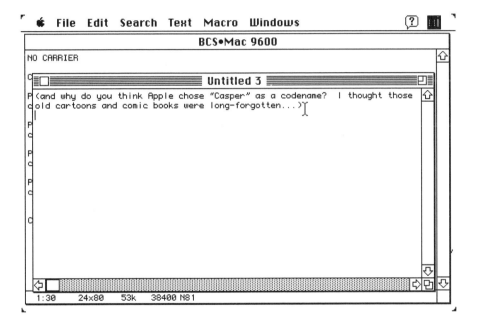

Figure 5–1: First step of message editing with an external text editor

Now you can edit and enter text just as in any word processor. You can add the comment symbols by clicking at the head of each line and typing a >.

You can also use a handy free utility to make those comments for you. Quoter is a desk accessory (Figure 5–2) that takes whatever text you've copied into the Clipboard and automatically adds comment symbols. In addition, Quoter reformats the text so that each line doesn't exceed the maximum allowed by the BBS.

Figure 5–2: The Quoter DA

To use Quoter, copy the text from the terminal window and click on Quoter's OK button. When you paste into your text editor, the quoted text will be perfectly formatted. Quoter isn't the only program that can do this for you, and some freeware editors have this feature built in, but ConTEXT and Quoter together make an excellent solution.

Look for Quoter, miniWRITER, McSink, and ConTEXT II on your favorite BBS or on-line service. They're worth downloading!

Now you can compose your text as you would in any word processor. Don't forget that even though you're in a word processor, your telecom program is still in the background and you're *still* connected to the on-line service. If you spend too much time working on the message, the BBS may log you out automatically. Since nothing's being typed into the telecom window, the BBS may interpret this inactivity as a user who's fallen asleep or given up, and will kick you off the system to make room for a more productive user. Every five minutes or so, it's a good idea to go back to your telecom program and tap the spacebar so the BBS knows you're still alive. Or, log off, compose your message, then log back on.

The last step you have to perform is to reformat your reply so that no line exceeds the maximum set by the BBS (usually 80 characters). Most freeware and shareware text editors can do this for you automatically; you can find that feature behind a menu called something like word wrap. In ConTEXT, you select Adjust Carriage Returns (Figure 5–3) and specify how many characters should be on every line.

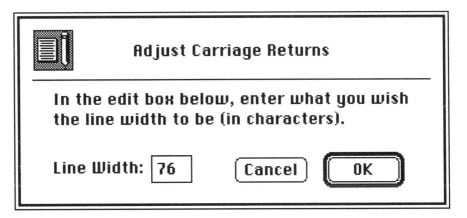

Figure 5–3: Reformatting your text so that no line exceeds 76 characters

I've specified 76 characters to allow a 4 character safety margin. Some boards include the line numbers (01:, 02:, and so forth) in the characters per line count. Keeping your line length on the conservative side can head off potential problems. If you have a utility like Quoter, you might want to use it to add the quotes as a last step; often, the text editor's line-length transmogrifier can mess up the line formatting of the quoted text. Finally, remember that when you press Return in a blank line, the BBS assumes you're done entering text. If you want a blank line in your message to separate paragraphs, make sure to add a space or two on blank lines before pressing Return.

My final message looks like Figure 5–4:

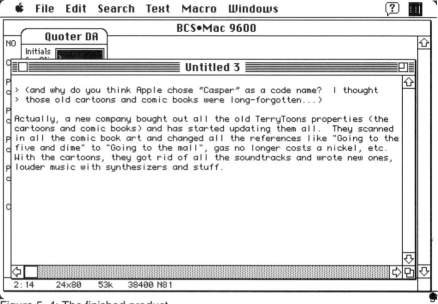

Figure 5–4: The finished product

All that's left is to select the text, issue the Copy command, and then paste it into your telecom program. Some BBS programs allow you to upload a text file as a message, but I think that's too much work.

If the BBS seems to freeze or skip characters when you paste your message in, you'll have to slow down your telecom when you paste text into the terminal window (Figure 5–5). BBS programs expect text to be entered manually, not pasted in and sent at 2400 bps.

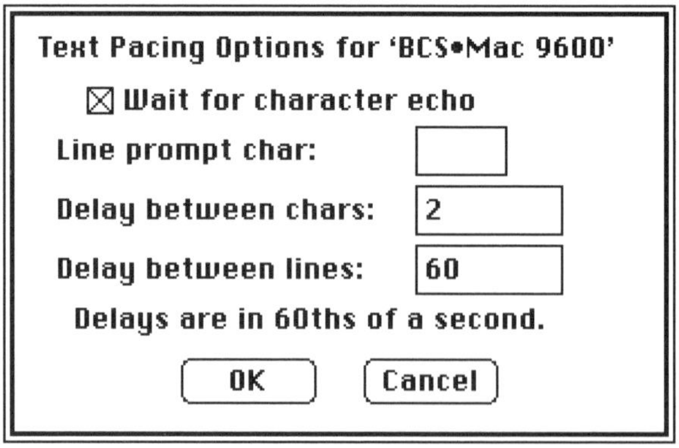

Figure 5–5: Changing how the telecom program transmits text

Normally, a telecom program lets you adjust text pasting three ways. First, it can slow things down by waiting a few fractions of a second between transmitting each line or each character. A faster solution (though not foolproof) is to have the program wait for a certain character to be transmitted by the BBS before sending the next line. This way, your telecom program won't send another line until the BBS sends, for example, a colon—on the BCS•Mac BBS a colon signifies that it's ready for another line.

The surefire method, which results in slow pasting, is to wait for the BBS to echo a character back before proceeding to the next character. A message that might take half a second to paste without any slowdowns can take twenty times as much time to transmit when the telecom program has to wait for confirmation on each character.

The first few times you paste messages in, you may want to view the message, if the View option is available. The View option displays the message as other users will see it and allows you to make sure everything went both hunky and dory. For instance, if a View command displays the message like this

```
Actually, a new company bought out all the old TerryToons properties (the cartoons
and comic books) and have started updating them all.  They scanned in all the comic
book art and changed all the references like "Going to the
```

you'll know that you set the line lengths too long.

The last step is to tell the BBS you're done entering text the way you normally do, by pressing the Return key on an empty line:

```
To: SAM MALONE
Subj: CASPER THE FRIENDLY GHOST
Use Full Screen Editor(Y/N)? N

Enter text of message.
<CR> by itself ends input.

01: > (and why do you think Apple chose "Casper" as a code name?  I thought
02: > those old cartoons and comic books were long-forgotten...)
03:
04: Actually, a new company bought out all the old TerryToons properties (the
05: cartoons and comic books) and has started updating them all.  They scanned
06: in all the comic book art and changed all the references like "Going to the
07: five and dime" to "Going to the mall", gas no longer costs a nickel, etc.
08: With the cartoons, they got rid of all the soundtracks and wrote new ones,
09: louder music with synthesizers and stuff.
10:

<L>ist, <V>iew, <A>gain, <E>dit, <R>cpt, <F>ile, <Q>uit, <S>ave, or <H>elp? S

Saving message to disk...

<*>Replies
<C>ubby, <F>wd, <D>el, <R>eply, <A>gain, <N>ext, or <S>top?
```

The BBS saves your reply, where it instantly becomes available for everyone else to read. Once it's been saved, the BBS reverts to its message-reading mode and you can continue reading messages. The BBS keeps serving up messages for you until either you've read them all or you tell it you're ready to stop (by issuing the Stop command).

Deleting Your Messages

It's usually a friendly gesture to delete all of your private mail (using the Del option) after you've read it, to free up space on the BBS's hard drive. But you ought to leave your public messages alone, so other BBS users can read them. When you delete your public messages, you run the risk of breaking a message thread; people who try to follow all the related replies to a question may find that the link between one half of the thread and another has been severed with the deletion of a critical message. You might want to delete one of your public messages if you jumped in to answer someone's question, saved that reply, then found that three other users had already answered the question in exactly the same way you did.

Parting Shots

There you have the basics of sending, receiving, and reading messages. It's easy once you get the hang of it, so go on, try it. I'll wait…

In the next chapter, you'll learn how to download tons of free and almost free software.

6

Downloading Files

Acquiring lots of free and almost free software.

There's a wealth of interesting and useful files in the on-line universe, just waiting for you to come along and download them. In the following sections I'll tell you what to look for and how to download the files you find.

Freeware and Shareware Programs

Whenever I run into problems with my Mac, I don't send away for a commercial set of utilities. I log onto a BBS or on-line service and have a shareware or freeware utility transmitted to me. It arrives on my hard drive in minutes, not days. And because it's available on the BBS the instant the programmer transmits it, I'm sure to get the latest, greatest version.

All across America, thousands of computer nuts like you and me are writing their own software, from simple disk utilities to full-blown word processors and spreadsheet programs that would cost hundreds of dollars if sold commercially. Instead of marketing their software traditionally, some programmers upload it to major on-line services and BBSs, where anyone can get a copy free or for a low shareware fee. *Freeware* is software you can use without paying a red cent (except for the normal cost of the phone call to your BBS or hourly connect charges on a commercial online-service). *Shareware* is software you can use on the honor system. Try it out, put it through its paces, and if after a month you still find it useful, you are honor-bound to send the programmer a modest registration fee (usually ranging from $5 to $20). Some philanthropic programmers even have you send your check to their favorite charities or donate a pint of blood to your local Red Cross chapter.

The quality of shareware and freeware software can range from barely useful (hacked out in a couple hours and not fully tested or debugged by the author) to slick and professional. I've already devoted plenty of space to praising the shareware telecom program ZTerm. As another example, I'll plug BiPlane, a monstrously great full-featured shareware spreadsheet program.

Shareware and freeware software is available in all categories: business, music, art, educational, entertainment, scientific, utility, telecom, and so on. And because distributing a shareware program is as simple as uploading it to a BBS, many programs exist in the shareware/freeware arena—especially cool little one-function utilities—that aren't available in commercial, over-the-counter software.

One of my favorite one-function utilities is Michael Whittingham's Screen Flipper ($10 registration fee). If you have a color monitor, you know what a hassle it is to change color settings. If you want to change from black-and-white to 256 colors, you ordinarily must use the Monitors control panel. It's much easier with Screen Flipper—hold down a modifier key (the Command, Option, Control, or Shift key, or any combination of the four) and click anywhere on screen. A pop-up menu appears that allows you to change color settings immediately (Figure 6–1); no time-consuming control panel to deal with.

Figure 6–1: Screen Flipper's color settings menu

Templates and Sample Files

Don't go to all the trouble of putting together an Excel spreadsheet for selecting a home mortgage. If you look on line, you're likely to find a spreadsheet that *another* potential homeowner created and left on the BBS for everyone's benefit.

Many software publishers also distribute sample documents on on-line services. UserLand Frontier, a commercial package for writing scripts to automate Macintosh activities, comes with dozens of sample scripts on disk, but you can find hundreds more on CompuServe and other on-line services. Sometimes the publishers also post files detailing additional hints and techniques for using their software that never made it into the program's manuals.

Information Files

Want to know what features to look for when buying a car stereo system? What radio frequencies the Massachusetts state police use when they patrol the highways? A definitive list of every light-bulb joke ever written? Many boards have text files offering information on lots of different subjects.

Bug Fixes and Updaters for Commercial Software

Every now and then, you'll find the word processor you just bought for $300 was shipped with a serious bug. Normally, you'd have to call the software publisher, send your original program disks and $10, and wait a week or so for a corrected version. The on-line alternative is a *bug-fix* (often called a *patcher*) program. Many big-hearted publishers write a special program that, when run, yanks out the flawed bits of their application and replaces them with new, corrected code, effectively eliminating the bug. The bug fixes are then uploaded to BBSs and commercial on-line services, where anyone can download them and fix their software for free.

Even bigger-hearted software publishers distribute updater programs that, like the bug fix, add extra code to an old version of their software to upgrade it with new features.

Demo Software

Wouldn't it be great if you could try out that $300 word processor before you actually plunk down your hard-earned dough? Some publishers create a special demo version that anyone can get from their local BBS for free. It has all the features of the real version, with certain key operations removed. A demo word processor can't save or print files, or prints files with the banner DEMO! in the margins, for instance.

Sending Files

You can contribute to the on-line treasure trove by sending your own files. You can post a magazine article you wrote about PostScript printers that no one wanted to publish. Other users may find it useful, and a powerful magazine editor might read it and offer you a lucrative monthly column. On a more practical side, if you find yourself in a long-distance business relationship with someone hundreds of miles away, rather than using Federal Express, why not just send that spreadsheet file electronically?

Uploading works exactly the same way as downloading, only in reverse. If you can download a file, you'll get the hang of uploading a file in seconds.

How to Download Files

If Webster's was hipper, it'd define *download* as "To have a file transmitted from a BBS or on-line service to your own home computer."

Downloading a file involves four steps:

- Find a file on the BBS you want to download.

- Tell the BBS you want to download it and how you want it to be transmitted.

- Tell the telecom program on your Mac to start receiving the file.

- Do something else until your Mac beeps to let you know the file has been received.

The transmitted file appears on your hard drive just like any file you copied off a floppy.

Where to Find Files to Download

To find a cool file you want to download, look in the Files area of a BBS:

```
BCS MACINTOSH Multiline BBS —  MAIN MENU
───────────────────────────


(I)nformation  .......  BBS help; BCS meetings and general info
(P)ublic-Files  .......  All callers can download these essentials

(M)essages  ..........  BCS Macintosh message bases
(F)iles  .............  BCS Macintosh file libraries
(S)Premium Services  ..  Extended subscription features

(A)ctivists  .........  BCS volunteer work area
(W)riters  ...........  Submit an article to The Active Window
(J)umpToGroups  .......  Jump to BCS Main Menu (Access other groups)


(G)oodbye    (=)Utilities    (?)Help

Command: f

BCS*Mac Multiline BBS — FILES MENU
───────────────────────────

Becki Sherman & TJ Creamer, Managing Sysops

(B)est of the Board  .......  Files that every Mac User should have!

(F)iles Area  ............  BCS Macintosh Files Download Areas
(U)ploads/New Files  .......  Upload/Download new files (untested area)

(A)pple Software  .........  Apple Computer, Inc., Macintosh Systems & Tools
(M)DN Files  .............  Macintosh Distribution Network Files

(P)revious    (T)op-Menu    (G)oodbye    (Z)ap-Logoff    (=)Utilities    (?)Help

Command:
```

Like the message area, the files area has several categories. All the utilities are in their own area, as are communications programs, games, and so on. As with message sections, these categories let you find what you're interested in without having to scroll through endless lists of irrelevant (to you) files:

```
Command:  f

BCS*Mac Multiline BBS — FILES AREA Menu
──────────────────────────
Becki Sherman & TJ Creamer,  Managing Sysops
 (A)rtwork/Graphics              ... Moderated by Carl Swanson
 (B)usiness                      ... Moderated by Ray Cochrane
 (D)A/FKey/INIT/CDev/Extension   ... Moderated by Glenn Berntson
 (E)ducation                     ... Moderated by Cathy Rudolph
 (F)onts                         ... Moderated by Jonathan Duke
 (H)yperCard                     ... Moderated by Nick Lauriat
 (K)Communications               ... Moderated by Mike Newman
 (L)ibrary/Information Files      ... Moderated by Craig Finley
 (M)usic & Sounds & Related       ... Moderated by Rodney Smith
 (Q)uickTime/MultiMedia           ... Moderated by Ian Maclennan
 (S)ystem 7 Programs              ... Moderated by Farokh Lam
 (U)pdaters/Demos - Commercial    ... Moderated by Juan Montoya
 (V)irus Protection Software      ... Moderated by Andy Weiner
 (X)Utilities                     ... Moderated by Yacine Ait Sahalia
 (0)Legal User Group              ... Moderated by Harley Hiestand
 (1)MacTech                       ... Moderated by Glenn Rosen
 (2)Games                         ... Moderated by David Pinkowitz
 (C)ombined Download              ... Merged area download

(P)revious    (T)op-Menu    (G)oodbye    (Z)ap-Logoff    (=)Utilities    (?)Help
Command:
```

In theory, all the files in these sections have been inspected by one of the sysops and deemed suitable for public consumption—they run without causing any damage, they're free of viruses and other nastiness, and they're not commercial programs.

Untested Files

It takes a while for the sysops to inspect a new file and put it in its proper file area. It can be anywhere from a day, on a well-staffed system, to a week for systems run by a single, part-time sysop. Sometimes you know that the exact solution to all your problems is on the BBS, but it won't be out of quarantine for days.

That's why most boards have a special New Files or Untested section for the most recently posted files. When someone sends a file to the BBS, it goes to this section and is immediately available for downloading. The only caveat is that the sysop has *not* inspected any of these files, so you may spend an hour downloading something and find out it doesn't work. It's not a serious risk, though, and all the latest, hottest files are usually found in the Untested section. But if you download a huge file from there and it just doesn't run at all on your Mac, you shouldn't get cross at the sysop.

Commercial on-line services don't have this feature. If you want to download a file from CompuServe or America Online, you have to wait for the sysop to clear it.

Let's browse through a list of untested files on the BCS•MAC BBS. To get to the Untested section (called Uploads/New Files), start from the main File menu:

```
BCS*Mac Multiline BBS — FILES MENU
─────────────────────────────

Becki Sherman & TJ Creamer, Managing Sysops

(B)est of the Board ....... Files that every Mac User should have!

(F)iles Area  ............ BCS Macintosh Files Download Areas
(U)ploads/New Files ....... Upload/Download new files (untested area)

(A)pple Software ......... Apple Computer, Inc., Macintosh Systems & Tools
(M)DN Files .............. Macintosh Distribution Network Files

(P)revious  (T)op-Menu  (G)oodbye  (Z)ap-Logoff  (=)Utilities  (?)Help

Command:  u
```

Type **U** to go to the Uploads/New Files section:

```
BCS*Mac Multiline BBS — NEW FILE UPLOADS
─────────────────────────────

Moderated by Becki Sherman

NOTICE : Files uploaded within the past 7 days may NOT have been checked
yet by our sysops for suitability of use or for lack of viruses.

(D)ownload/List .... View List of Files & Select for Download
(U)pload .......... Upload a File
(C)ut/Kill ........ Kill a File
(M)ove ............ Move a File to This Area
(V)iew directory ... Examine TBBS file (includes who uploaded each)
(!)Download ....... Download from Unprotected Directory

(P)revious  (T)op-Menu  (G)oodbye  (Z)ap-Logoff  (=)Utilities  (?)Help

Command: d

Type P to Pause, S to Stop listing
```

Type **D** to view a list of the latest files that were sent to the BBS:

```
                   *** Newly Uploaded Files! ***
                      USE AT YOUR OWN RISK!


   ****************************************************************
   * Most of the files on this board are Stuffed (.sit) or Compacted  *
   * (.cpt). You will need the applications UNSTUFFIT (for .sit) and   *
   * EXTRACTOR (for .cpt and many .sit files). Download them from the  *
   * Public Files Area, accessible from the Top Menu.                  *
   *                                                                   *
   *    You can stop this list at any time by pressing the 'S' key.    *
   *                                                                   *
   * Hint:   You can save time typing by using COPY and PASTE to enter *
   *           the name(s) of the file(s) you want to download.        *
   ****************************************************************

CONTXTII.SIT    66954   Ver. 1.01 of CONText II, great text editor    (07/10/92)
RAGE.SEA       129408   Shoot holes in your screen    (07/09/92)
PROGMKEY1.42     2048   Turns pwr key on kybd to progrmrs switch    (07/09/92)
TIDBITS167      36123   Mac news for 7/5/92 Word 5 info text form   (07/09/92)
MEMINIT.SIT     26240   &7 v2.0.2 Quietly shows foreground mem usage   (07/09/92)
EFFN203.TXT     30000   ElecFrntFndn newsletter 1/7/92 #2.03 text     (07/09/92)
CACHE040        43136   Turns on/off Cache for 68040 machines    (07/08/92)
PEEK-A-BOO     198016   A Hypercard game that teaches mousing skills   (07/08/92)
COMPCHART        3712   Compares compression utilities-very handy    (07/08/92)
IN.CONTROL     271232   demo of new outlining app, this one works    (07/08/92)
BEAM23.CPT     407424   BeamWars 2.3 - color Tron-like game - Mac II   (07/08/92)
FANFARE          6272   MIDI file: Fanfare for the Common Man    (07/08/92)
HCINTERNET     322176   Internet Guide and Tour (HC Stack)    (07/06/92)
DIPSTATION     506624   DIP Station Manual (MSWord)    (07/05/92)

<D>ownload, <P>rotocol, <E>xamine, <N>ew, <L>ist, or <H>elp
Selection or <CR> to exit:
```

The leftmost column has the names of the files (as they appear on the BBS's hard drive), the middle column shows the size of each file in bytes (for example, CONTXTII.SIT is roughly 66K), and the last column contains a short description and the date the file was sent to the board.

Because I'm so enthusiastic about CONText II (see "Replying to Messages" in Chapter 5), I'll download it now. Before giving the BBS the command to transmit the file, you have to specify *how* the file should be sent. You do this by telling the BBS what *file-transfer protocol* you want to use.

File-Transfer Protocols

All methods of sending a file from one place to another work in essentially the same way. The sending computer (here, the BBS) takes the file and breaks it down into small chunks for easy manageability. The BBS then sends one chunk of data across the phone line at a time to your Mac. Your telecom program receives each chunk, again one at a time, and puts all those pieces back together, reconstructing it as a file on your hard drive.

Ever heard the story about the guys who took a friend's car apart and put it back together in the bedroom of his fourth-floor apartment? Same situation. You can't drive an entire Volkswagen up three flights of stairs, but you can get it up there by reducing the car into smaller, easier-to-manage chunks.

A file-transfer protocol performs another important function: error checking. Phone lines aren't flawless. If a lot of static disrupts the line when you're reading messages, every now and then an *a* might get switched to a *$* or some other character. When every number in a file making up a computer program on your Mac represents an instruction the Mac must follow, even *one* incorrect digit can lead to disaster.

To prevent such disasters, almost all file-transfer protocols have a built-in error checking scheme. After each chunk of data is transmitted, the BBS essentially sends some codes to your telecom program that ask whether that bit of data was received without error. If an error was detected, that chunk of data will be sent again (and again, if necessary), until it's transmitted correctly.

Although dozens of file-transfer protocols exist, here are the protocols you're most likely to deal with, starting with the worst, slowest protocols and ending with the best, fastest ones:

- **ASCII** Not a protocol, but most BBSs include it in their list of protocols anyway. Use ASCII *only* to transmit a text file.

- **Kermit**   One of the first protocols, and one of the slowest. Use Kermit for file transfer only to talk to a university computer that hasn't been updated for use with more efficient protocols; few BBSs or on-line services support it. (Contrary to what I said in the first edition of *Dr. Macintosh*, it *is* named after the famous frog.)

- **XMODEM**   The first protocol to become popular after Kermit. Nearly every computer everywhere supports it, and its simplicity can be an advantage. Sometimes, when phone-line conditions are bad, a more complex protocol won't work. XMODEM is slow, but it almost always works; reserve it as a backup. It's sometimes referred to as XMODEM (Checksum) to differentiate it from the next two versions.

- **XMODEM CRC**   CRC stands for cyclical redundancy checking, a method of error checking that's more effective than XMODEM (Checksum). XMODEM CRC and XMODEM Checksum are sometimes segregated on a BBS, but in most Mac telecom software they're part of the same XMODEM protocol.

- **XMODEM 1K**   A simple but significant enhancement to XMODEM that speeds things up. The size of the data packets it sends are 1 kilobyte, instead of 128 bytes for XMODEM (Checksum), so it spends one-eighth as much time asking your Mac "Hey, did that packet arrive OK?".

- **YMODEM**   Not much faster than XMODEM 1K, but has extra features. Unlike XMODEM, a file downloaded with YMODEM retains the file name and date of creation. (With XMODEM, you have to name the file, and the date you *downloaded* the file becomes the file's creation date.) Also, YMODEM can do batch file transmission: You can specify a list of files to be downloaded, and YMODEM sends each one in turn.

Caveat: Often a BBS mistakenly lists its XMODEM 1K protocol as YMODEM. If your attempt at a YMODEM download fails, try setting your telecom program to XMODEM 1K.

- **YMODEM-G** YMODEM without error checking. If you connect to the BBS with MNP or V.42 error-checking, YMODEM-G is *great*; otherwise, it's a disaster, as any errors that creep in during transmission are *not* fixed later on.

- **ZMODEM** ZMODEM is the fastest of all the popular protocols, and it adds one or two cool new features. If you're using an error-checking modem, it automatically turns off its own error checking to boost efficiency. Unlike other protocols, if you lose a connection (say your dog pulls the phone wire out of the outlet) ZMODEM picks up where it left off. When you log on and once again try to download that same file, the ZMODEM protocol can detect that you already have most of it and transmits only the remaining few minutes' worth.

Those are the protocols you're likely to have to deal with at some point, but there are a bunch of notable also-rans, which are popular on other machines and may become more commonly available in Macintosh telecom software sometime.

- **BiModem** Allows you to send and receive files simultaneously. At the same time, it lets you specify more files you'd like to download and exchange typed messages with someone at the BBS end at the same time.

- **HyperProtocol** Performs its own data compression on the file as it's transmitted, which can result in higher efficiency—like having V.42bis as part of your communications program, with many of the same advantages and limitations.

- **B, QuickB, and B+**   Protocols peculiar to CompuServe that are supported by some Mac telecom programs.

- **WXMODEM**   A faster, version of XMODEM.

Of the bunch, you're most likely to encounter B, and QuickB in Macintosh telecom software. Unfortunately, they're only useful when downloading files from CompuServe.

Let's see what protocols are available on the BCS•Mac board:

```
<D>ownload, <P>rotocol, <E>xamine, <N>ew, <L>ist, or <H>elp
Selection or <CR> to exit: p
Select from the following transfer protocols:

T - TYPE file to your screen
C - ASCII with DC2/DC4 Capture
A - ASCII only, no Control Codes
X - XMODEM
O - XMODEM -1k
Y - YMODEM (Batch)
G - YMODEM-g (Batch)
S - SEAlink
K - KERMIT
W - SuperKERMIT (Sliding Windows)
Z - ZMODEM-90(Tm)

Choose one (Q to Quit):
```

Always use ZMODEM if both the BBS and your telecom program support it; it's by far the fastest protocol in wide use today. If the board didn't support ZMODEM, my next choice would be YMODEM (YMODEM-G if my modem told me that V.42 was enabled when it established a connection to the BBS), then XMODEM-1K, then XMODEM. (When XMODEM doesn't work, it's time to give up and go to bed.)

```
Choose one (Q to Quit): Z

<D>ownload, <P>rotocol, <E>xamine, <N>ew, <L>ist, or <H>elp
Selection or <CR> to exit:
```

Transmitting Files

Now that you've chosen a protocol—ZMODEM—you're finally ready to command the BBS to send you that CONText II file. Enter **D** for Download:

```
Selection or <CR> to exit: d

File Name? CONTXTII.SIT
```

Make sure you enter the file name *exactly* as it appears in the file listing. If you don't, the BBS tells you there is no such file and you have to give the Download command once again.

The BBS reminds you how big the file is and gives you a very rough estimate of how long it'll take to transmit it:

```
File Name: CONTXTII.SIT
File Size: 66954 Bytes
 Protocol: ZMODEM-90(Tm)
Est. Time: 1 min, 32 secs at 9600 bps

Awaiting Start Signal
(Ctrl-X to abort)

rz
*
```

As a rule of thumb, at 2400 bps it takes one minute to transmit 20K of data; at 9600 bps, roughly 60K per minute. But these are only estimates; as in MPG stickers on new cars, your mileage will vary (and probably won't be nearly as good).

Another thing to consider: If you're using a commercial on-line service, try not to download large files. CompuServe users who downloaded Apple's entire System 7.0 upgrade when it came out wound up spending about $130 in connect charges for the download, versus $99 to walk into a computer store and buy the upgrade on disk, complete with manuals.

Finally, file transfers are affected by the number of users currently logged onto the system. For best results, save big downloads for the wee hours of the morning—say 3 A.M.

What happens next depends on the selected protocol. Generally, once the BBS has told you it's ready to start sending data (Awaiting Start Signal or Initiate Download Now or something like that), it's time for you to give your Mac's telecom program the command to start downloading a file, using the proper protocol as shown in Figure 6–2.

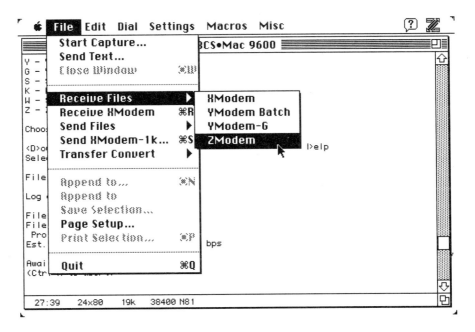

Figure 6–2: Selecting a download protocol in ZTerm

The BBS and your Mac chatter at each other for a moment, to make sure they're both using the same protocol and that everything's in order for the transfer. After a second or two, your telecom program puts a dialog box like the one in Figure 6–3 on the screen and starts receiving actual data.

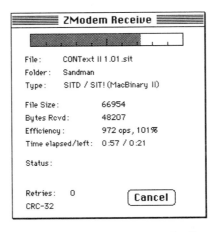

Figure 6–3: Dialog to keep you posted on the status of a file transfer

When you use ZMODEM to download a file, you don't have to explicitly tell your telecom program to begin receiving data. The BBS sends your telecom program a special code (the *rz ** after *Awaiting Start Signal*) that tells it to start receiving a file using the ZMODEM protocol. This isn't a standard feature of the other protocols, but some telecom software can sense when a BBS is sending data with YMODEM or XMODEM and automatically start receiving data.

All telecom programs display some sort of progress monitor, to keep you informed on how well the file transfer is coming along; everything you want to know is neatly presented here. At the top of Figure 6–3, the progress bar tells you that the download is almost three-quarters done.

Next, the progress indicator tells you about the file you're down-loading: its name, the folder on your hard disk where the file is being sent, and what kind of file it is. *SITD/SIT!* are the file's Creator and Type (standard file attributes given to all Macintosh files). These codes tell you the file was created with StuffIt Deluxe and it's a StuffIt document. (You can learn more about this in the following section, "MacBinary.")

Then you see the file size and bytes received—a quantitative corollary to the graphic progress bar at the top of the screen.

After that, the dialog box lists the efficiency (see "Throughput" later in this chapter).

Like many telecom programs, ZTerm estimates how much more time before the download is finished.

Finally, Status and Retries are windows on the technical progress of the transfer. As problems and important events occur, ZTerm posts status reports. When ZTerm is trying to begin the transfer, it tells you so. When blocks of data were received incorrectly, it tells you which block got garbled and that it's going to be sent again. When the transfer is over and ZTerm is tying up some loose ends, it reports that, too. And a constant count of the number of re-sent blocks of data is kept under Retries.

If the number of retries starts to mount up, you can tell that the download might be unsuccessful.

Use the Cancel button to tell ZTerm to give up on the download and return you to the terminal window.

When the download is received, the BBS returns you to the line of commands:

```
<D>ownload,  <P>rotocol,  <E>xamine,  <N>ew,  <L>ist,  or  <H>elp
Selection or <CR> to exit:
```

MacBinary Now let's back up and look at the file name in Figure 6–3 again. Where did *CONText II 1.01.sit* come from (we typed *CONTXTII.SIT* to start the download), and how did the BBS record the Creator and Type information? This info comes from MacBinary, a protocol incorporated into all Macintosh telecom programs. MacBinary takes all of a Macintosh file's Finder info (its full name, Type and Creator, creation and modification dates, and distinctive icon) and blends it into the file when uploading it to another computer. Similarly, whenever a Mac telecom program receives a file and detects that it's been encoded with MacBinary, it takes all that Finder info out of the file and uses it to recreate the Macintosh file exactly as it originally appeared. The upshot of this is that a Macintosh file always retains its original name, icon, and the like when it's transmitted from one Mac to another, even if it has passed through several non-Macintosh BBSs in between.

> More accurately, MacBinary solves a rather unique (and sticky) problem that arises when you transmit a Mac file to a non-Macintosh computer. Most computers store individual files (whether they're programs, documents, or whatever) in one continuous stream of data. Macintosh files are much more complex.
>
> Rather than putting all that data in one place, the Mac stores every file in two *forks*: a resource fork and a data fork. When a Mac file is transmitted to a DOS machine, MacBinary folds both forks together along with the Finder info into one easy-for-non-Macs-to-deal-with pile. When a Macintosh telecom program downloads the file, the MacBinary code in the program automatically senses that the file has been encoded and splits it back into its native, two-fork format.

MacBinary is found in all Mac software. All you have to do when you install your telecom program is make sure that MacBinary has not been inadvertently turned off.

Throughput If you've connected to the BBS at 9600 bps, that's the physical speed of the raw data zooming across the phone lines, but is good use being made of those 9600 bits per second? The speed of communications is insignificant; what you really want to know is what kind of *throughput* you're getting. Of those 9600 bits transmitted every second, what percentage is actual data from the file you're down-loading?

Normally, throughput is given in characters per second, or cps. When your communications setup is working at 100 percent efficiency, its throughput in cps is one-tenth the operating speed of your modem. For a 9600 bps modem, 100 percent efficiency is 960 cps; at 2400 bps, 240 cps.

All file-transfer protocols come with a certain overhead, in terms of extra error-checking data that's transmitted along with the actual file, and the pauses that occur as the two computers try to verify that data was sent correctly. Normally, the best you can do with ZMODEM is 98 percent efficiency. XMODEM, at the bottom of the heap, usually tops out at around 74 percent.

Noisy phone lines are also a leading culprit. All that static means the same block of data may have to be retransmitted several times to ensure that it's been received properly. Performance plummets when you use a multiline service in which more than one user is being served at once. With the big, commercial services—at peak hours, they can have hundreds of users active at any given moment—you might find that you're getting no better than *30 percent* efficiency in a file transfer! Think about it: Seventy cents out of every dollar you spent while downloading that file is *wasted*.

In Figure 6–3 you can see that efficiency is 101 percent! To boost performance, you use hardware error checking and data compression. Here's where the extra dough you spent for V.42bis pays off. With hardware error checking only, the file transfer protocol can concentrate on sending data through the modems, and efficiency soars. Better yet, with modems that can compress and decompress data as they transmit and receive it, you can get efficiencies *greater* than 100 percent! Andy claims his record throughput is 1740 cps at 9600 bps—it's as if he had a 17,400 bps modem!

File Archives

With the download complete, there's now a new file on your hard drive, *CONText II 1.01.sit*. If you used a protocol like ZMODEM or QuickB where receiving the file is begun for you automatically, the file can be found in a file that you've designated as the *Receive Folder*, the destination for automatically downloaded files. Otherwise, when the file transfer is complete, your telecom program will ask where the file should go.

So that's it, then? Now you can just double-click on this *CONText II 1.01.sit* and run that great text editor I told you about? If you try it your Mac will probably give you that infuriating "Application not found" error message. No, that little *.sit* at the end of the filename tips you off that this file isn't actually "CONText" at all; it's an *archived copy* of CONText and its related files, and more processing has to be done to the file to transmogrify it into an application you can actually open and run.

Archiving files solves two big problems with downloading files. First, very few of the programs you'd want to download exist as just one, single file. Usually there's the program itself, and a file containing documentation, and often there's a *Read Me First* file, a file containing registration info. In some cases there will be sample documents, too. Rather than download five separate files, it'd be great if all those little files could be combined into one big one, one file that includes the program and all its necessary supplemental files. This is exactly one-half of what an archiving program does.

The second half is more unique. A standard lament of anyone that uses a BBS is, "Isn't there a way to get these files to download faster?" And a standard lament of a sysop is "Isn't there any way my BBS can store more files in the same amount of disk space?" An archiver suits both interests by *compressing* files. Basically, the program looks for patterns and regularities in the file, which can be expressed in a different fashion more efficiently. A file that may once have taken up 100K of space on the sysop's hard drive now only takes up 75K, and when there's 25% less information to be downloaded, the file can be transmitted in 75% of the time it'd normally take.

The final upshot is this: an archiving program can take the four files comprising *CONText II* that take up 230K and turn it into one file (an *archive*) that only takes up 130K. The only bad side effect of all this is, of course, that the Mac can no longer recognize this file as an application. The file must be un-archived back into its original, full-size components before they can be used.

In the Mac world, there are only two popular archiving programs. You can tell which program is used by the *.xxx* extension at the end of the archive's filename. *.sit* means the commercial program StuffIt Deluxe or the shareware program StuffIt Classic, both published by Aladdin Systems, was used. The suffix *.cpt* means the archive was created with Compact Pro (formerly known as Compactor), a shareware achiver written by Bill Goodman. Both archive formats are equally popular.

Because both formats are so widely used, and both of the programs' creators would very much like you to use *their* standard, there are free programs available that will extract files from both archive formats. Though StuffIt Deluxe is a commercial program, it's also available in a stripped-down shareware version, StuffIt Classic, and an even further stripped-down version, UnStuffIt Deluxe, which only extracts files (it doesn't compress) and is freeware. Compact Pro is shareware to begin with, but similar to StuffIt, there's a freeware extract-only version. Not to be outdone, though, Aladdin Software, creators of StuffIt, has written a dandy free utility, *StuffIt Expander*. It's an agreeably small utility (quick and cheap to download) which will extract files from both StuffIt and Compact Pro files.

Decompressing Files

StuffIt Expander is your best bet, because it can decompress files compressed with all of the StuffIt variants as well as files compressed with Compact Pro.

A brief note on terminology: *Extracting, decompressing, expanding, de-archiving,* and *un-archiving* all mean the same thing—to restore files from an archive to their original state.

Un-archiving a file with StuffIt Expander is trivially simple. If you're running System 7, you can un-archive a file merely by dragging it on top of Expander's icon. If you're using System 6.0.x (or don't feel like using System 7's drag-and-drop feature), just double-click on Expander. It was designed to be a bare-bones program, so its menu bar has only one menu, File, with only two items in it: Expand... and Quit. Select Expand, select the .sit or .cpt file from a standard scrolling list, and the program goes to work right away (Figure 6–4).

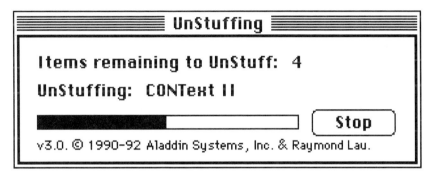

Figure 6–4: StuffIt Expander's status indicator

The extracted files will appear in the same folder as the original archive, and if the archive contains more than one file a new folder will be created to hold them all.

The simplicity of Expander makes it great for the beginner, but after a few weeks you may want to either download the more functional StuffIt Classic or Compact Pro or purchase the commercial StuffIt Deluxe. These give you much greater control over the extraction process (Figure 6–5).

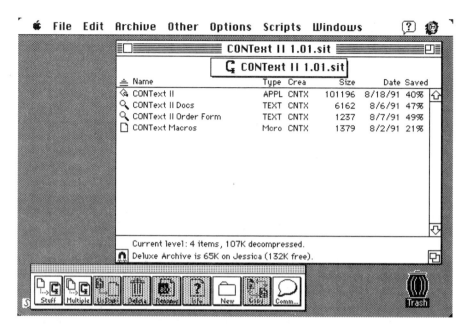

Figure 6–5: The CONText archive, opened with StuffIt Deluxe

When you open the archive with StuffIt Deluxe, you're presented with a list of the archive's contents and you can manipulate each file individually, extracting only those you want and storing them wherever you please. Items with a magnifying glass next to them can also be viewed from within StuffIt by double-clicking the magnifying glass icon.

In addition to .sit and .cpt, there are three other extensions you may run across from time to time:

- **.sea** This denotes a self-extracting archive, a special sort of archive where the code for extracting all its files is built into the file itself. Just double-click .sea files and they magically decompress themselves.

- **.hqx** This is a file that's still in MacBinary format (one big pile of data instead of the Mac-like two forks). You rarely see this sort of file, and when you do, it's usually on Unix systems. To turn it into a Macintosh file, the file must be *decoded* (restored to its native two-pile format) using either a freeware program called *BinHex*, or more commonly the "Decode MacBinary" functions of StuffIt or Compactor Pro.

- **.ZIP** This isn't a Macintosh standard at all, but the most popular archiving format found in the IBM world. Files in .ZIP format can be extracted either with StuffIt Deluxe (which prides itself on being able to deal with many different formats) or a shareware program called *MacZip*.

Another advantage of the shareware and commercial archiving programs (as opposed to the freeware ones) is that they allow you to create archives of your own, which is essential when you want to upload a file. Almost all online services insist that you archive (compress) a file before uploading it. Again, it saves space and allows more files to be on the BBS at once, and it saves time and frustration for those who download the file.

Creating Your Own Archives

Creating a new archive is straightforward; all it involves is creating an archive file and telling the archiving program what file or files to put in it. The program will compress and combine all those specified files into one neat bundle (Figure 6–6).

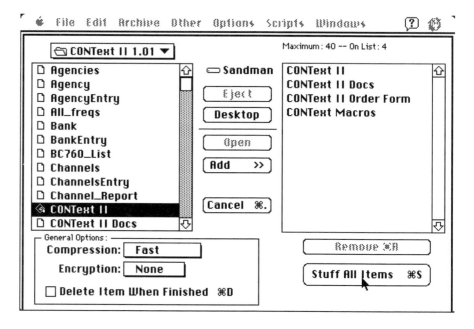

Figure 6–6: Creating a new archive with StuffIt Deluxe

Most archiving programs give you the option of *encrypting* your archive—scrambling the data so that it can only be unscrambled with a special password. Only those people you've given the password to will be able to decompress the files.

Uploading

If you understand how to download a file, uploading (sending a file from your Mac to the BBS) will seem like familiar ground. You should feel free to upload just about any file you think other BBS users will benefit from having, within certain limits. Commercial software is, of course, forbidden. Also, you should always make sure the file doesn't go against any of the set policies of the BBS. Some systems, for example, prohibit the uploading of complex color graphics, as they take up too much space. Others insist that the files you upload be germane to the focus of the BBS. Finally, make sure you've archived the file, in the format adopted as the standard by the BBS (either .cpt or .sit); almost all BBS use one format exclusively, to keep things simple.

Finally, make sure the BBS doesn't already have the file. Space on a BBS is limited and is best not wasted on duplicate copies of the same software. Even though most sysops screen newly uploaded files for duplicates, do the sysop a favor and check before you upload. You can search for a duplicate file the same way we searched for an existing file when we wanted to download. Use the BBSs file-search capability and look for files with keynames likely to match the file you're about to upload.

If you're satisfied that all the rules of good taste and etiquette have been satisfied, you're ready to upload the file. Issue the Upload command by typing a **U**:

```
BCS MACINTOSH Multiline BBS — NEW FILE UPLOADS


_____

Moderated by Becki Sherman

NOTICE : Files uploaded within the past 7 days may NOT have been checked
yet by our sysops for suitability of use or for lack of viruses.

(D)ownload/List .... View List of Files & Select for Download
(U)pload .......... Upload a File
(C)ut/Kill ........ Kill a File
(M)ove ............ Move a File to This Area
(V)iew directory ... Examine TBBS file (includes who uploaded each)
(!)Download ....... Download from Unprotected Directory
(*)Upload ......... Upload to Unprotected Directory

(P)revious   (T)op-Menu   (G)oodbye   (Z)ap-Logoff   (=)Utilities   (?)Help

Command: U
```

The first step is usually to give the file a name as it should appear on the BBS. As most BBSs are based on IBM PCs, this usually means giving it a name in the format FILENAME.TYP—a maximum of eight letters followed by a period and three letters which describe the format of the file (usually .sit or .cpt). We're going to be uploading CONText II 1.01 (I know, I know, they already have it; but this is just a book so there's no harm done).

```
Enter 1-12 char full file name: CONTXTII.SIT
```

Because the name took so many characters, I didn't bother mentioning the version number. I don't really have to, as I can add a description line of info to the listing. This is the information that users will base their downloading decision on, so make it worthwhile. Try to mention what kind of file it is, the exact version number, and a brief blurb on why it's worthy of downloading:

```
Description:
      1–5—10–15–20–25–30–35–40–!
01: ConText II 1.01 -Nifty text-editing program
02: features multiple documents open, complete
03: font support, and text-bashing features.
04:
```

On most systems, you can write multiple-line descriptions, but some allow you only one 40-character line.

You'll generally be asked for a list of keywords next. This will help folks using the BBS's database of files find CONText II if it's exactly the file they're looking for, so choose wisely.

```
Keywords for CONTXTII.SIT: TEXT EDITOR WORD PROCESSOR CONTEXT STRIP
```

Good choices for keywords are the program's basic name, the sort of program it is, and one or two key features. For instance, at the end I've included STRIP, for folks who are looking for a program that can strip IBM-type characters from text files.

The next-to-last step is to select a file-transfer protocol, just as you had to when downloading. I typed **Z** to choose ZMODEM:

```
Select from the following transfer protocols:

T - TYPE file to your screen
C - ASCII with DC2/DC4 Capture
A - ASCII only, no Control Codes
X - XMODEM
O - XMODEM -1k
Y - YMODEM (Batch)
G - YMODEM-g (Batch)
S - SEAlink
K - KERMIT
W - SuperKERMIT (Sliding Windows)
Z - ZMODEM-90(Tm)

Choose one (Q to Quit): Z


File Name:  CONTXTII.SIT
  Protocol:  ZMODEM-90(Tm)

Ready to receive
(Ctrl-X to abort)
```

Now that the BBS has all the info it needs to accept a new file, it goes into receive mode. All that's left for you to do is select the Send a File (or Upload) command from your communications program, with the file transfer protocol you've selected. After the file's been sent, the BBS returns you to its command line.

Remember that all the files you upload are tagged with your name; something to give one pause before uploading Microsoft Word for public consumption.

Other Stuff

In Chapter 5 and this chapter we've covered the real biggies of BBS operations. You *must* know about how to log on and set up an account. You *must* know how to send and receive files and messages. That's what you spend most of your time doing on a BBS; that's where the fun is. Of course, there are infinite variations in the BBS structure, and each sysop will try to add extra features or activities to make things more enjoyable for the users. Here's a brief list of some of the added attractions found on many BBSs.

On-line Conferencing

One of the biggest advantages of using a multiline BBS is the fact that its line won't be busy when you call as often as if it were a single line BBS. But there's another cool feature—on-line conferencing—that allows people on the system to talk interactively with each other. You enter a special conference room or chat area, where everything you type can be immediately read by everyone else in that room. You join a conference merely by entering that area of the BBS, much as you enter a file or messaging area. A typical conferencing session looks something like this:

```
> Andy Ihnatko -> Really?  Why do you think so?
> Lee Loyota -> Well, look at what he had to contend with.  Shemp may not...
have been the most talented Stooge, but he had the highest expectations...
going in.
> Mike Sullivan -> He wasn't half the Stooge Curly was.  Case closed.
> Andy Ihnatko -> Really.  Next you'll be praising Joe Besser to the high...
heavens!
>>> ENTERING CONFERENCE: MAURA WEGENER
> Mike Sullivan -> Hi, Maura
> Lee Loyota -> Howdy there, Maura. Andy, who's Joe Besser?
> Maura Wegener -> Hey there.  What are we talking about?
```

An on-line conference can go on for hours, begun by one group of people then maintained as old people leave and new users join. On local boards, a conference is generally done for fun, but many commercial services schedule conferences as national meetings for user groups and lectures. For instance, important BCS•Mac meetings are often simulcast over commercial on-line services as conferences; all during the meeting in Cambridge, Massachusetts, an attendee types in everything that's going on and a rough transcript of what's being said. All over the country, other folks can follow the meeting and even jump in and ask questions.

There's a topic related to conferencing: the concept of paging. Because BBSs are so highly interactive, it's possible to send someone else on the system a quick, instantaneous one-line message. For instance, in the conferencing area of the BCS•Mac BBS, I can get a list of everyone who's on the BBS right now:

```
Line    User
 —      ————
  1     Andy Ihnatko
  2     Linda Borzono
  3     Steve Sweeney
  4     Diane Loyola
  7     Bob Hoffman
```

And while I'm in the conferencing area, I can send them a quick one-line message by typing a command (in this case, **/s,2,** to send a message to Linda who's on line 2):

```
/s,2 Hey, Linda, how's your project coming along?
```

Unless Linda's in the middle of sending or receiving a file, that message will immediately appear right on her screen. Paging someone is good if you have a fairly urgent need to speak with them—to break an imminent date or something. But remember that a page can be a minor annoyance for the receiver—it cuts right in the middle of whatever they're doing and can be quite disruptive. So don't just page someone to tweak his or her nose a bit…that ain't nice. Usually, you'd page someone just to ask if they could join you in a conferencing area to talk something over.

Parting Shots

There you have it. It's hard to believe it's that easy to download tons of free and useful software, but it is! And you now know all you need to know to dive right in and download some.

The next chapter will introduce you to the heavy hitters of the on-line world, commercial services such as CompuServe and America Online. These services are mega-BBSs, with tens of thousands of messages and files for your reading and downloading pleasure.

7

All About On-line Services

The concept of the on-line service—what's at the
other end of your modem...

For the most part, on-line services and BBSs operate in similar ways,
with similar functions and procedures, and identical logon procedures
(except for those local exceptions to every standard concept).

Messaging is largely the same whether you're using a small local
BBS for free or a large, national commercial on-line service for $12.50
an hour.

In this chapter, I'm going to talk about all the entities that can
answer your modem when it calls.

> There's no *big* difference between a bulletin board service (BBS) and
> an on-line service. For the most part you can use the terms inter-
> changeably. By convention, though, *on-line service* usually refers to a
> large commercial system that's used by people all over the country.
> On-line services generally bill your credit card for the time you spend
> logged on.
>
>   *BBS*, on the other hand, brings to mind a smaller, local board run
> by volunteers that you can log onto for free and whose membership
> consists mostly of people for whom the BBS is a local phone call.
>
>   *On-line service* is the more generic of the two terms.

Types of On-line Services

You're probably wondering, "What kinds of services can I call? What
can I do once I get there? What'll it cost me?" The answers are, in order,
oodles, oodles, and anywhere from zilch to oodles.

Not only are a lot of on-line services available, but they fall in many
categories. You don't need a license from the government or permission from the phone company to run a BBS, so services can run the
gamut from a single college student turning the Mac in his dorm into
a BBS on weekends, to a huge, multinational conglomerate with tons
(literally) of hardware running a similarly huge, multinational commercial on-line service. Usually, services fall into one of these four
categories: public bulletin boards, commercial on-line services,
superboards, and corporate BBSs.

Public Bulletin Boards

What garage bands are to music, public BBSs are to telecommunications. A public BBS is usually a small, local BBS run by people who love
telecommunications. Sometimes these people are an organized Macintosh user group (such as the Boston Computer Society Macintosh User
Group or the Berkeley Macintosh User Group, both of which have
excellent boards). More often, it's one slightly crazed but big-hearted

individual who pays for a computer, a modem, an extra phone line, and countless other expenses out of his or her own pocket simply because he or she wants to create a forum that other telecom nuts (and non-nuts) will want to visit.

Advantages of Public BBSs   Public BBSs are usually free! You can use most public BBSs without any fees whatsoever (except for the cost of the phone call, naturally); those that do charge money usually ask a modest ($10 or $20) sign-up fee. Typically, you have a daily time limit of a half an hour to an hour, but if you become an involved user of the board (contributing to the message and file bases, helping the sysop with your time and money on occasion), the sysop gives you more time. The local nature of a public BBS also means it's easier to find information specific to your region. Finding out which local theaters serve real buttered popcorn is next to impossible on a national on-line service, but that info is only one message away on your local board. Finally (and this is generally an advantage) a public BBS tends to take on the personality of the person running it. A good example is *The Graphics Factory* in Boston. Its sysop lends two things to the formation of the board: a keen interest in desktop publishing (DTP) and an "anything goes" attitude toward messages. Thus, it's one of the best sources of info for DTP and a great place to spend an evening reading messages. (Appendix E contains a short list of BBS phone numbers including the Graphics Factory's.)

Disadvantages of Public BBSs   Since a public BBS is generally being run on a shoestring budget, most of them can support only one user at a time. If the board is a popular one (like The Graphics Factory) the line might be busy for a solid hour before you can get through (even if your modem is autodialing the number over and over again).

Second, public boards can sometimes vanish overnight. A college student can go home for the summer along with his or her BBS, a sysop can go away on vacation for a couple of weeks and shut his or her BBS down for the duration. Worst of all, the sheer cost of maintaining the board may become so prohibitive that the sysop shuts it down for good.

Commercial On-Line Services

Commercial on-line services such as CompuServe and America Online are everything public BBSs aren't.

Advantages of Commercial Services Commercial on-line services are generally national in scope; instead of your messages and questions being read by hundreds of users who live nearby, they're read by *thousands* of users living all across the country, maybe even the *world*. This also means that the array of message topics gets a lot more diffuse than is generally found on local boards. Almost every commercial service has a section for folks who are into making wine and/or home-brewing beer, for instance; I've yet to see a single public BBS that caters to those users.

Furthermore, many software publishers offer technical support through commercial services. You can log on, leave two questions for Aldus about your problems with PageMaker, and pick up the three messages Adobe sent you on how to get color output from Illustrator.

You rarely get a busy signal with a commercial service, as they can generally support hundreds if not thousands of people simultaneously.

In addition, a commercial service is generally reliable. Part of your usage fee goes to paying hundreds of people to constantly monitor the system and keep it running.

Finally, even though commercial on-line services are national, even worldwide in nature, accessing one almost always involves a local phone call. Whereas with a public BBS you must dial the number of the BBS directly, with commercial services you dial the number of a local computer that does nothing but establish a link across a huge nationwide telephone/computer network to the service's central computer. For most major services, no matter where you are there's a local access number nearby; if a BBS isn't right in your neighborhood, it may be an expensive toll call.

Disadvantages of Commercial Services First, they aren't free. Whenever you're using a commercial service, *time is money*. The clock is running. Typically you're charged an hourly fee for using the system ($5 to $50, depending on the particular on-line service), and sometimes a monthly fee besides. So users of commercial services have to remember this: *Like sand in the hourglass, so are the dollars in your checking account.* If you're concerned about cost, though, many commercial services offer flat-fee services. For a modest monthly fee (usually $10 to $20), you can have unlimited access to a small subset of the on-line service's...er...services.

Superboards

A superboard is a large public BBS with many features that's being run as a commercial concern. It's a happy medium between small public BBSs and huge commercial on-line services. Most superboards started out as common, public BBSs that grew. One year it was an IBM PC and a single modem, then as more people started to use it they added a second machine, more modems, more phone lines, and better BBS software, until it became a roomful of personal computers supporting a hundred people logged on simultaneously.

The Channel 1 BBS in Massachusetts is such a monster. Look at some of the specialty areas of this board:

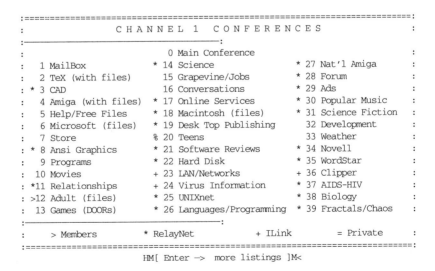

```
:==============================================================================:
:                 C H A N N E L   1    C O N F E R E N C E S                   :
:------------------------------------------:                                   :
:                              0 Main Conference                               :
:     1 MailBox           * 14 Science            * 27 Nat'l Amiga             :
:     2 TeX (with files)    15 Grapevine/Jobs     * 28 Forum                   :
:   * 3 CAD                 16 Conversations      * 29 Ads                     :
:     4 Amiga (with files) * 17 Online Services   * 30 Popular Music           :
:     5 Help/Free Files   * 18 Macintosh (files)  * 31 Science Fiction         :
:     6 Microsoft (files) * 19 Desk Top Publishing  32 Development             :
:     7 Store             % 20 Teens                33 Weather                 :
:   * 8 Ansi Graphics     * 21 Software Reviews   * 34 Novell                  :
:     9 Programs          * 22 Hard Disk          * 35 WordStar                :
:    10 Movies            + 23 LAN/Networks       + 36 Clipper                 :
:   *11 Relationships     + 24 Virus Information  * 37 AIDS-HIV                :
:   >12 Adult (files)     * 25 UNIXnet            * 38 Biology                 :
:    13 Games (DOORs)     * 26 Languages/Programming * 39 Fractals/Chaos       :
:------------------------------------------:                                   :
:     > Members         * RelayNet         + ILink        = Private            :
:==============================================================================:
                  HM[ Enter -> more listings ]M<

Help, NS, N=Stop, (Enter)=More?
```

This is only the first of five pages of listings. It has thousands of files available for downloading, supports users of many different computers, and subscribes to most every electronic journal available. As you might guess, a great service like this isn't free. Although nonpaying users can indeed log in, they have no access to file downloading, on-line texts, a lot of messaging, and other valuable features. But a superboard generally isn't nearly as expensive as a large commercial board. Typically, you pay a yearly usage fee that grants you a set number of hours of access per day, with a set number of file downloads per month.

Superboards are often excellent choices for people who want something more than a simple public board, but aren't ready to spring for the expense of a commercial on-line service.

Corporate BBSs

Many manufacturers of computer hardware and software maintain their own BBSs for the benefit of registered users of their products. Use of the BBS is free (though for most of us, it's a long-distance phone call), but usually the board's sysops will validate you only if you can provide the serial number of a product you purchased.

These corporate support BBS's are great resources. Since the board belongs to the company, it can make anything and everything available for downloading. Bug fixes, program updaters, sample files, documents full of tips and techniques, information on upcoming releases, and more are all available. Best of all, such a BBS gives you a chance to leave concise questions that, chances are, will be answered quickly and more completely than if you simply talked to a technical support person on the phone.

Choosing a BBS

You'll doubtless run into all four types of services. The first service to try should be a public BBS—no question about it. As with any new activity, learning telecommunications involves quite a few nights of trying out stuff you've learned from this book and picked up on the street, and you're better off doing that for free than paying $12.50 an hour. After a few weeks or months, when you understand what telecommunications is about, you *might* consider getting yourself an account on a major on-line service, too. If you can afford it, a commercial service is great in that it's both wide and deep. A public BBS usually has a sizable user base that's knowledgeable in one or two areas; on a national service, you can ask a question about movie making and the guy who worked the cameras filming *Batman Returns* (hi, Rob!) might answer you. You don't get that with a local public BBS (unless, perhaps, your local BBS is in southern California).

Superboards aren't widespread, but generally they're a good value if the annual fee is reasonable. They provide an inexpensive way to get lots of files and other valuable information. Corporate BBSs are great if you have a question about a commercial product, but you have to pay long-distance rates.

Finally, you don't have to choose one type of BBS, or even limit yourself to one BBS. Andy and I have accounts on about thirty different on-line services of all types.

Special Features

Once you've found a BBS or on-line service to log onto, check to see if it offers any special features that make it more useful or easier to use, such as networking, a graphical user interface, Premium Services packages, games, or on-line shopping. None of these is essential to your telecommunications experience, but one or more may be of interest to you.

Networking

One of the drawbacks of a local BBS is that it's a *local* BBS; you can send mail only to other users on the BBS, so generally you can send mail only to people within your rough geographical area. If you're in Boston and you want to send a message to someone in Berkeley, California, one of you has to make a long-distance phone call to the local public BBS that the other person uses. You can avoid long-distance charges and converse bicoastally if you both use local boards that are part of a nationwide network.

Networked Boards What if you could link the thousands of local BBSs between Boston and Berkeley bucket-brigade style, from BBS to BBS all the way across the country? That's precisely how a network of BBSs works. If your local BBS in Boston is part of a network, to send a transcontinental message all you have to do is go to a special Netmail messaging area, write your message, and specify which BBS in the network it should be delivered to and which user it's for. At night, usually sometime between three and six in the morning, the BBS transmits all its netmail to a larger BBS nearby. That BBS checks the address of your message and sends it to *another* BBS that's closer to the target—and so on, until it reaches your friend's BBS in Berkeley.

> Parents take note: To see this concept in action, get out your video-tape of *101 Dalmatians*. (As parents, I know you're required to own tapes of all major Disney releases.) The twilight bark, used by the dogs of England to spread the word of the puppies' kidnapping, works in almost the same fashion as a BBS network.

The actual address varies depending on the network. By far the most widely supported network for public bulletin boards is a system called FidoNet. A FidoNet address might look something like this: *1:101/640* (the FidoNet address for The Graphics Factory). The *1* means North America, the *101* is the computer that handles messages in that area of the Northeast, and the *640* is The Graphics Factory. You don't have to memorize anything; most BBSs on a network have an on-line database of network addresses. To find The Graphics Factory's address you need only do a search based on the name of the BBS, the sysop, or the rough geographical area.

Echoed Message Forums You can get involved with national messaging without bothering with network addresses if your local BBS has an echoed message forum. These are message bases (just like the ones you used in Chapter 5) that are shared across the network by all subscribing boards. You can't send private mail, but when you read a message in that forum, you're reading messages from users all across the country; likewise, when you send a new message or write a reply, it's seen by everyone across the country.

Point Software   How about setting things up so messages can be sent *directly to your Macintosh*? This is a great concept. With *point software*— a special program that handles network communications activities— your Macintosh can become a *part of the network*, just like one of those BBSs. After your point software has been properly configured, your Mac automatically calls its local *boss node* (a local BBS on the net) at a preset time every morning, and it receives all the messages that've been sent to you—both those that've been sent from faraway BBSs *and* those left for you on your local BBS!

It's called *point software* because your Mac becomes a *point* on the network. To set it up you have to contact the sysop of the local BBS you want to get your mail from (your boss node), and have him or her issue you a point number. This number distinguishes your Mac from all others calling in with point software. On The Graphics Factory, Andy's point number is 8 (which means he was the eighth person to ask for one). Therefore, if anyone anywhere in the world sends a message on FidoNet to 1:101/640.8, it'll be delivered directly to his Macintosh a few days after it's sent.

A great point program is available as shareware—*MacWoof*. It does everything a point program is supposed to do, and if you're still using it a month after you get it, it's only $25. Andy uses MacWoof every day—he says it's great!

BBS's with Graphical User Interfaces

The user interfaces on most BBSs are text-based, and that's what we Mac owners have been trying to avoid ever since we saw the first 128K Mac.

Some services, however, try to make BBSs as easy to use as Macs. The user runs special software that can accept commands from the BBS: Draw an icon here, put a window there, stick some text in that other place. These graphic-interface systems tend to work more slowly than a text-only interface, but the result can be an on-line service that takes minutes to learn instead of hours.

Some commercial on-line services offer such software as an option (CompuServe); others (AppleLink, Prodigy, and America Online) require special user-interface software to access the service.

> Requiring special software is a real disadvantage of those services. When you have a text-based interface, you can access the service with almost any computer. On cross-country trips, Andy claims he could log on and get his CompuServe mail with an electronic pocket organizer equipped with a portable modem. If he wanted to keep in touch with America Online, he'd have no choice but to lug a Macintosh with him from coast to coast.
>
> I, on the other hand, always lug a portable Macintosh with me when I travel. It *is* a PowerBook, so I'm not sure I'd call it *lugging*. I can write an entire product review or column, create screen shots, compress the file, then modem it off to my editor. Plus, I can play Spectre. Let's see Andy do *that* with his pocket organizer!

You learn about these commercial services and their special software later in this chapter, so instead I'll show you TeleFinder, a special graphical BBS program. It's commercial software, from Spider Island Software (see Appendix D) consisting of a BBS and special client software. A TeleFinder BBS can work in one of two ways: If you log on with a telecom program like ZTerm, it presents you with a familiar text-only interface. If you log on with TeleFinder's special client software, though, you see a thoroughly Mac-like interface, like the one shown in Figure 7–1.

In Figure 7–1, the windows you see open are areas of the BBS I've opened up (Conferences is a list of message conferences available for reading; the other two windows are lists of files I can download). The row of icons on the far right represents the volumes on my hard drive, the row next to that represents areas of the BBS I can access. Everything works more or less as it would in the Finder. If I want to download the game Asteroids, for instance, instead of entering various downloading and protocol commands I drag its icon to one of my hard drives. If I want to start reading messages in the TeleFinder News conference, I double-click on the document icon that represents it.

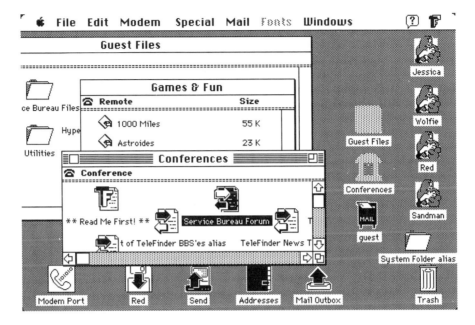

Figure 7–1: TeleFinder's Mac-like interface

You do need special TeleFinder client software to use the graphical user interface but—and this is a nifty touch—whenever you use generic software to log onto a TeleFinder BBS, it asks if you want to download a copy of the TeleFinder software!

Are the graphical interfaces worth the trouble of having to use special software and the expense of the extra time that's wasted as the special software communicates with the BBS program? Ease of use is essential in welcoming new telecom users into the fold. After six months of using the graphical user interface, however, many users decide to switch to a text-only interface for the speed advantage.

Premium Services Packages

Say you run a popular public BBS. You want to add some of the new features you see on other boards—FidoNet mail, on-line magazines, and such advanced messaging features as file enclosures and receipts—but you can't afford it. You want to keep your BBS free for everyone, so instituting a membership fee is out of the question.

The answer is BBS Premium Services. The idea is simple: If you want to use most of the common BBS features (public and private messaging, uploading and downloading files, reading news bulletins), it doesn't cost you a cent. But if you want to use a feature that costs the sysop money (such as network mail or advanced message handling) you have to subscribe to a Premium Services package. It's usually another $20 to $30 a year, but it allows the expensive services to be subsidized only by those who use them.

Games

Many systems have on-line games of many varieties that you can while away many hours playing. It can be fun, but never forget that a commercial on-line service charges you by the hour whether you're there on business or pleasure!

Usually the sort of games available are limited by the text-only interface of most on-line services, but there's loads of fun to be had nontheless. There are many Dungeon games, where you're in a maze with several other users currently on the system, smiting orcs and collecting treasure. There are stock-market simulations, racing games, text adventures, just about anything that can be covered in ASCII characters. Many UNIX systems even have a version of the game Tetris, where the tumbling tiles are drawn with asterisks!

For the most part, you're limited to ASCII, but some systems provide graphical front-ends to their on-line games. GEnie has a system available for downloading that allows you to dogfight other users in full graphic splendor in real-time while connected to their service. But as cool as on-line games are, I think that the games available on commercial on-line services are best avoided. Even at $5 an hour, the most modest game can eclipse the list price of much better and more graphically interesting games available from your local software store.

On-Line Shopping

This is one of those features with which an on-line service will try to snag folks who don't normally use computers. Many commercial and public systems have fully stocked on-line stores. You can browse through electronic catalogs of merchandise (housewares, home electronics, books, records, movies, clothes, even airline tickets and stocks and bonds, if you're so inclined), call up a list of prices, and actually order real merchandise. You enter a credit-card number, and the merchandise is shipped to your home address.

It certainly is handy. I can relate a personal experience where I realized, quite late, that it was suddenly my parents' anniversary, and with one phone call to an on-line service, located a boxed set of jazz CDs that were delivered to my doorstep the next day. However, on-line shopping is somewhat like those phones you can rent in an airplane: You use it because you *can*, not because you need to. It's neat to never leave your chair or pick up a catalog and magically have something arrive within a day or two, but to be perfectly honest, you can often do just as well shopping by phone or in person. Here's a word of advice: Don't buy something on-line unless you know exactly what it is you're getting (that is, you've already seen it for real somewhere else) and have a good enough sense of prices to know you're getting a good deal.

Specialized Commercial Services

There's only one thing as painful as paying for a commercial on-line service: deciding which one you're going to subscribe to.

Over a dozen commercial services exist, but only a few major, popular commercial services are of general interest to all Macintosh users: America Online, CompuServe, and GEnie, plus the Internet (which isn't really a commercial service). You'll learn about all four of those in some detail in the section called "The Big Four" toward the end of the chapter.

The rest, for one reason or another, are probably not your best choice for a general on-line service. Some cater to a specific interest, others are weak in certain areas. All have some value.

Accu/Weather

As the name implies, Accu/Weather is an electronic information service that provides up-to-the-moment weather forecasts for any part of the country you're interested in. You can pull down all that meteorological data either in text format or as color radar maps, weather pattern maps, or charts and graphs of temperature, humidity, and barometric pressure.

If the name sounds familiar, it's because Accu/Weather is one of the private companies that supplies weather data to some television and radio stations for their newscasts.

AppleLink

Apple set up this moderately nice on-line service so that people who develop products for Apple computers could have a formal way to talk with Apple and each other. If you're an Apple developer, AppleLink is useful. It's one of the easiest mediums for asking Apple direct questions and getting direct answers. It's a solid source for learning from your peers how to make and market Macintosh products. Best of all, all Apple software and official Apple information (technical notes, spec sheets, and the like) are available on line. All of this is on a service with one of the niftiest graphical user interfaces on any on-line service. You can't use AppleLink without Apple's custom software, though.

If you work with Macs on a professional basis and can get your boss to pay for an AppleLink account, then go for it. If it's your own money, go elsewhere. The fact is, AppleLink is expensive and many of its features are duplicated on other on-line services.

Byte Information Exchange

The Byte Information Exchange (BIX) is a rather funky haven for wireheads and propellerheads (hardware hackers and software hackers) of all varieties. If you want to know everything there is to know about simple knot theory and ways to model it on a computer, BIX is the place to go.

Pricing (combining an annual fee with a modest hourly rate) is competitive with other services. If you're a technoid and the preceding paragraph brought a maniacal grin to your face, BIX is worth checking out. If you read the first sentence and then anxiously skipped ahead to this paragraph, you're obviously too weak of spirit to handle BIX. You're better off leaving it alone.

Dow Jones News/Retrieval

Dow Jones News/Retrieval is a specialized service tailored for business users. News/Retrieval is a pretty nice combination of on-line services and Mac software that, if their brochure is to be believed, allows you to make a great deal of money very fast. Not only does News/Retrieval give you news, financial data, and facts and figures on most segments of the business world, but it also provides you with Macintosh software for organizing and interpreting it all.

My idea of financial high-rolling is signing up for credit cards to get the free gifts, but Dow Jones News/Retrieval still got me excited about investing.

Lexis/Nexis and Dialog

Lexis and Nexis (owned by Mead Data Central) and Dialog (owned by Dialog Information Services) are for people who need to research information, research it exhaustively, and research it *fast*. Lexis is for legal research, and Nexis and Dialog are for news information. These databases contain the full text of thousands of publications, which you can search electronically with almost any criteria you specify. If you wanted to know, say, whether David Letterman ever appeared in a show with Mary Tyler Moore, you could do a search on LETTERMAN and MOORE, and within a minute Nexis (or Dialog) would produce a magazine article about Dave in which it's mentioned that he worked on a short-lived variety show of hers called "Mary."

What power. But they're all very expensive services; you're charged for the search itself, as well as for individual articles retrieved. Still, for some folks it's money well spent; several people I've described this service to have instantly said they'd have gladly paid twice those high charges for such a service while preparing their doctoral theses.

MCI Mail

MCI Mail is a mail service—that's it. If a big corporation wants to set up an EMail system for its executives, it buys them all MCI Mail accounts. If you're not one of the industrial bourgeoisie, however, your money's better spent on CompuServe or another *real* on-line service. The only reason to use it is because someone you need to communicate with electronically makes you join.

> That's the only reason I maintain an account. I only use it to communicate with people I can't reach via CompuServe, America Online, or AppleLink.

One benefit is that you can send paper via MCI Mail. For a slight additional charge, you can have a message—created and uploaded from your Mac—delivered in hard copy, via U.S. mail, overnight courier, or fax.

OAG Electronic Edition

OAG (Official Airline Guide) is an incredibly neat service for frequent travelers. It maintains current listings of plane schedules, airfares, seat availability, and hotel availability so that you can (theoretically) save a good piece of change the next time you travel. You can search based on any criteria; for instance, try to find a United flight to Chicago sometime between Friday and Sunday leaving in the morning. A list comes right back, complete with flight numbers, departures, arrivals, and seat availability; if you see a fare you like, you can book the seat yourself and pay at the airport. And the morning your plane leaves, OAG can tell you whether the plane's on time or has been delayed.

Once Andy did a search based on "Get me to San Francisco as cheaply as you can, I don't care what airline or what time I leave," and he wound up saving $130 off the lowest Boston-San Francisco price he could find elsewhere.

OAG is also available as a surcharged service through CompuServe. Check it out by typing **GO OAG** at any prompt.

Prodigy

(Sigh). Okay, I'll say it: Prodigy stinks. Avoid Prodigy unless you have kids.

Frankly, that's consistent with the majority of the on-line community's opinion about Prodigy (sometimes called Plodigy because it's so darn slow). Here's the original concept: Put together an online service where instead of charging by the hour, users are charged a flat monthly fee. You can stay on-line for three weeks or three minutes and you pay the same amount. Fill it with lots of useful services: an online encyclopedia, games, and current news, sports, and weather information. Put in lots of on-line stores so folks can do their shopping by placing orders with their modem, and even provide access to stock quotes, financial information, and banking by modem.

Pretty good so far. But how to make it profitable? First, put graphical ads at the bottom of every screen of information. You're reading an encyclopedia article about Lincoln, say, while some guy at the bottom of the screen is trying to sell you flowers. Annoying, but acceptable. Here's another idea: Every time a user buys something, make a note of the item so Prodigy can sell the person's name, address, demographics, and buying profile to people in the direct mail industry! (What do you expect? Prodigy is owned jointly by IBM and Sears.)

On top of all that, it has no areas to download files. It has message areas, but get this: There are limits to how many messages you can send (exceed a set limit and you have to pay a surcharge). Worst of all, messages can be censored before they're posted. When I started seeing messages critical of Prodigy being deleted, I closed my account.

So why subscribe to Prodigy? It might be acceptable as a toy for the kids. There's lots of electronic graphics and games to keep them enthralled, and with the flat fee, they won't run up huge bills. But never, ever think of Prodigy as a *real* on-line service.

ZiffNet/Mac

ZiffNet/Mac (formerly ZMAC) is an electronic service created and maintained by the creative folks at *MacUser* and *MacWEEK* magazines, and it is totally dedicated to the Mac. It offers lots of great brains to pick with just about any question, always some hot files to download, and every now and then, useful software that's available nowhere else.

Setting up a complete on-line service all by yourself is a daunting (not to mention expensive) proposition, so ZiffNet/Mac rents space from CompuServe. And even though ZiffNet/Mac walks, looks, and quacks like a part of CompuServe (and you get charged the same rates as on CompuServe), it calls itself an independent entity. (That's why it gets its own section.) Like CompuServe's Macintosh forums (which we'll get to in a minute), ZiffNet/Mac has a variety of discussion forums and file libraries. Most of the editors and writers check in at least occasionally, which makes ZiffNet/Mac a good place to leave a message if you need an authoritative answer and you need it now.

Think of it like this: When you sign up for ZiffNet/Mac, you get a CompuServe membership for free.

> In the interest of fair play, Andy and I are obligated to include the following conflict of interest disclaimer: ZiffNet/Mac is part of the same company (Ziff-Davis) that sends us both a check each month for our column in *MacUser*. In addition, we are both close personal friends with the folks who run ZiffNet/Mac (Andy's even a sysop).
> We still recommend it highly.

The Big Four

All of the commercial services described so far (with the exception of ZiffNet/Mac) have something in common: They're focused services with a narrow audience. With those on-line services, it's easy to decide why or why not to subscribe. An AppleLink account comes in handy if you want to make a living writing Mac software, for instance. And Prodigy is a good deal for your kids; for a modest monthly fee, they can cavort in a graphical system that contains loads of useful information.

America Online, CompuServe, GEnie, and the Internet are different; you can't justify the cost by saying "I need this so I'll get an account." Why pay for your on-line experience when you can use public BBSs for free? What does an account with a major on-line service give you?

The benefits of the big four boil down to two things: more people and more stuff (messages, files, and things to see and do). When you send a message on a public BBS, you're sending it to an audience of a few hundred people who live in your general geographical area. When you send a message on a commercial on-line service, *thousands* of people from all walks of life all over the planet can read it. It's a subtle concept, one you won't understand fully until you leave a message asking, say, how a special effect in the summer's highest-grossing film was done, and out of the blue you get a reply from one of the people who *worked* on that film.

Whereas most BBSs have maybe 80Mb of space for files (if that), a commercial service has literally *gigabytes* of files available for downloading. This means, in part, if you need a specific type of utility for your Mac and you can't find it on a commercial service, then chances are it's not available as shareware or freeware, and you have to buy a commercial product.

Most commercial services make databases of raw information available to their users. Many services make agreements with major magazines to make articles available to their users for downloading. Most services have electronic newspapers, encyclopedias, movie reviews, weather forecasts, stock quotations, and all kinds of other electronic information available for your perusal—all the information you could ever need, available from a single source.

Almost everyone can find *something* of interest in a commercial service. You have to experience it firsthand to appreciate the concept, so here's what I suggest: Set aside some money for the purpose of exploring commercial services; say $100. That's generally enough for ten to fifteen hours of connect time. Consider that money gone and spent, and over a month, spend a few hours on each commercial service that interests you. If, after you've spent every penny of that budget, you still want to explore one service above all others, then you know you're ready for a commercial service. Otherwise, you can probably go on using public BBSs and be satisfied that you're not missing anything. But if you want to sample the *complete* on-line experience, it's important to try out commercial services.

In each of the next four sections, you'll learn about America Online, CompuServe, GEnie, and the Internet. Andy and I will give you a good overview to help you decide whether to try them out.

America Online

Of the several attempts to create a graphically oriented on-line service that's not merely easy to use, but actually *fun*, America Online is known as the one that succeeded.

AOL (as its users call it) is a graphical tour de force. Because you use a custom communications program supplied by the service (for free!) instead of a generic telecom program, America Online has a completely graphical user interface. From the buttons and windows that are endemic to Macintosh software to the use of pictures and sound, America Online has an inviting look and feel. In addition to the software, though, there is an attitude endemic to the system that AOL should be made as accessible as possible. When you log on (by clicking one button and supplying your password), for instance, instead of being presented with a menu of commands, you'll see the screen shown in Figure 7–2.

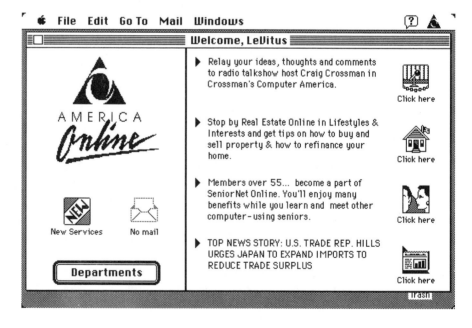

Figure 7–2: America Online's welcome screen

This is a great idea. Right after a cheerful "Welcome!" and "You have mail!" (if you do) comes out of your speaker, America Online gives you a "cover page" to the entire service, calling out items of interest (or areas they're trying to plug), each with an icon you can click on.

Just about the only time you need to use the keyboard during an America Online session is when you type in messages. Everything else—navigating from area to area, reading messages, downloading files—is done by selecting onscreen items with the mouse. Clicking on the Departments button yields a dialog containing AOL's major areas of interest, shown in Figure 7–3.

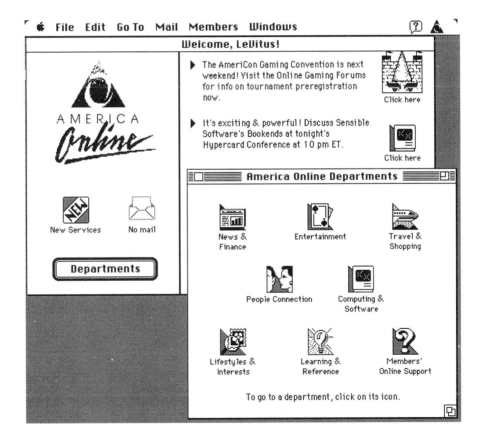

Figure 7–3: AOL departments

Notice that whenever you go somewhere in America Online, the place you just left remains in a window in the background; this lets you go back and pick up your private mail easily instead of having to backtrack. Clicking on one of the department icons in Figure 7–3 will take us to one of AOL's special interest groups. For example, if you click on the Computing and Software icon, you'll see the screen shown in Figure 7–4.

Even though you've now gone from a general to a more specific menu, AOL still reserves the right-hand portion of most windows for buttons that can instantly take you to other areas of the service. This is another nice touch that enhances the browsability of America Online. Double-clicking one of these folders in the Computing and Software window (such as Communications & Networks, the selected folder in Figure 7–4) will bring you to that particular sub-forum.

As you can guess, messaging and filing are greatly simplified with this system. Downloading a file from a forum is as simple as two clicks. You bring up a file list, as shown in Figure 7–5, select the file you want, and click on the Download File button.

America Online's custom software handles everything. It selects its own protocol, synchronizes the data flow, and handles all error checking automatically. Literally one mouse click delivers a file to your Mac.

Selecting and reading messages is also easy. As with most other elements of the service, message reading doesn't involve much more than selecting items from a list, as in Figure 7–6.

File Edit Go To Mail Windows
Computing & Software
Computing Forums:
Tonight in The Forums
Check for Active Rooms
Beginners
Business
Communications & Networks
DeskTop Publishing
Development
Education
Games & Entertainment
Graphic Arts & CAD
Hardware
HyperCard
Music & Sound
Operating Systems
Utilities/Desk Accessories
User Groups
MW
Macworld Online
Software Libraries
Industry Connection
News & Reference
Conference Center
System 7 Resource Center

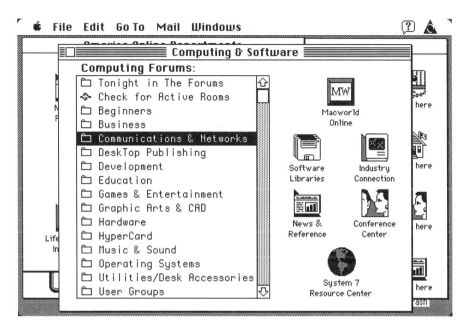

Figure 7–4: Inside the Computing & Software Forum

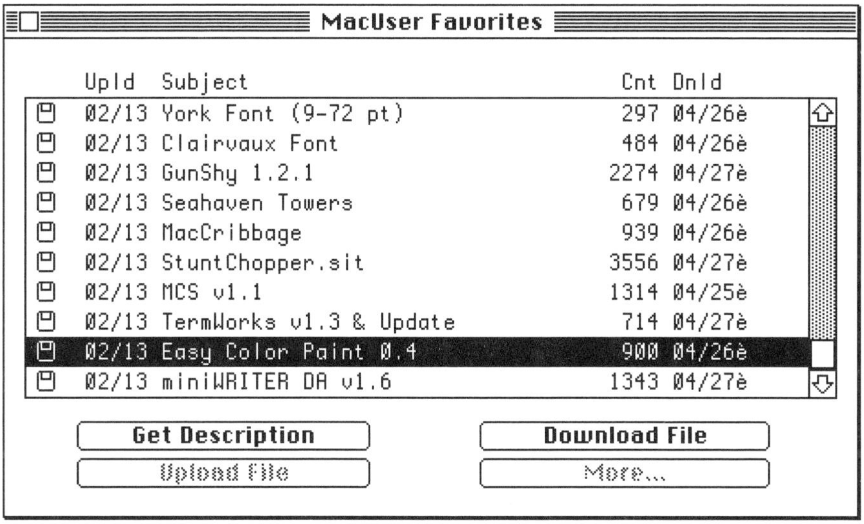

MacUser Favorites
Upld Subject Cnt Dnld
02/13 York Font (9-72 pt) 297 04/26è
02/13 Clairvaux Font 484 04/26è
02/13 GunShy 1.2.1 2274 04/27è
02/13 Seahaven Towers 679 04/26è
02/13 MacCribbage 939 04/26è
02/13 StuntChopper.sit 3556 04/27è
02/13 MCS v1.1 1314 04/25è
02/13 TermWorks v1.3 & Update 714 04/27è
02/13 Easy Color Paint 0.4 900 04/26è
02/13 miniWRITER DA v1.6 1343 04/27è
Get Description
Download File
Upload File
More...

Figure 7–5: Downloading made easy

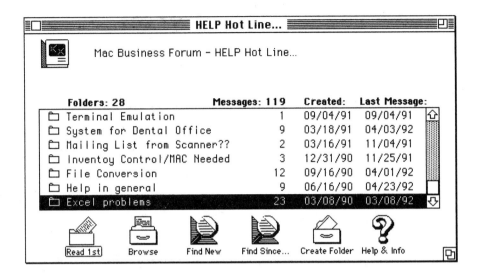

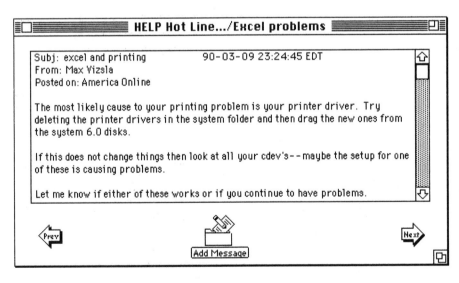

Figure 7–6: Message browsing and reading

But although it's a clean, straightforward way to read messages, you get a minimal set of message-selection options: you can select all new messages, or messages posted *since* a specific date. It'd be nice if AOL allowed you to do searches based on subject, or to look for messages posted by a specific user, or on a specific day.

Once you've selected a message to read, your message-reading options are likewise sparse. You can read the previous message or the next message, or you can send a reply. What if you want to see the message this one was in reply to? Or read a bunch of *individual* messages?

My biggest complaint with America Online is that, unlike CompuServe or most BBSs, it has no threads. The only way to read an answer (assuming there is one) to a question is to read all the messages posted in that folder. On CompuServe or most BBSs, you can read all replies to the question—a thread.

Also, America Online uses nonstandard terminology in organizing its messages. On standard BBSs, you send messages, read messages by subject, and follow a thread. On AOL, you add messages and open folders of messages. It's not a major point, but an America Online user might get a bit confused when he or she jumps from AOL to another on-line service.

On the plus side: One of the areas in which America Online shines is in its Industry Connection forums, which are set up and controlled by software and hardware companies. Because you need AOL's special software to use the service, and as yet it's available only for Macintosh and IBM PC computers (and clones), many companies like to use America Online for support. Figure 7–7 shows the Claris Support Center, for example. It's easier for their customers than text-based on-line services such as CompuServe and GEnie.

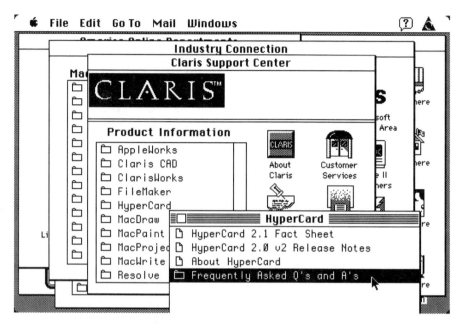

Figure 7–7: The Claris forum

Because the America Online forums aren't segregated into file and message areas as rigidly as forums on other services, companies can set up a support forum that has messages, documents, and downloadable files in the same area.

Now for the gripes. First, America Online has the same disadvantages as any service that has to be accessed with custom software. It can at times be slower that a text-based service; you *must* be using either a Mac or a PC to use the software (no logging on with your pocket organizer!); and it's impossible to soup up performance and maximize your time by writing your own scripts in a telecom program. Second, the message and file selection is significantly smaller than CompuServe's.

America Online is a fine choice for most telecom users who want a service that has a broad base of features and that is very easy to use.

AOL is an enjoyable on-line service, and I urge you to make it the first commercial service you try. It couldn't be easier to use, there's no charge to join, the software is free, and connect time is reasonable (about $6 an hour to connect evenings and weekends; somewhat more on weekdays).

Since prices are in a constant state of flux (hardware seems to get less expensive over time; software and connect charges seem to increase regularly), I've tried to give you a sense of relative cost, rather than absolute prices.

Connecting to America Online in the evenings currently costs about half as much as connecting to CompuServe. Since the services compete with each other, this could easily change by the time you read this.

CompuServe

In terms of size and scope, CompuServe is the world's largest commercial on-line service. It's also probably the oldest; CompuServe, among other services, got started back when telecommunicating was a hobby for dedicated enthusiasts, the computer equivalent of CB radio. Since then it has thrived on the premise that bigger is better.

First, CompuServe (shortened to CIS, for CompuServe Information Service, or CI$ after you get your first bill) has the largest user base. It's noteworthy that a sizable portion of the user base is made up of people who don't particularly like computers and are using CompuServe for its services. More than any other on-line service, on CompuServe you can communicate with the widest range of people. As you might expect, CompuServe hosts so many forums that it can support obscure and specialized interests as well as popular topics.

Second, CompuServe has more information than any other on-line service. Many other on-line services let you access OAG or Dow Jones News/Retrieval through their menus, but none of them come close to the number of independent databases CompuServe can access for you. You can have CompuServe search through Federal census data, trademark and patent applications, the complete text of hundreds of newspapers, magazines, and scientific, legal, and medical journals from the past decade, regional and national demographics, phone books for the entire country, *Books in Print*, the Associated Press wire, *Who's Who*, and more. If a piece of information is available electronically, it's likely that CompuServe can find it for you—though it may cost you an arm, a leg, and a kidney.

So why might you want to use Dialog, Lexis, or Nexis? First, their databases are even bigger than most of the databases on CompuServe.
Second, because information retrieval is all they do, their searching
technology is more powerful and flexible.

On the downside, Dialog, Lexis, or Nexis are complicated and hard to
use, and cost more than CompuServe's surcharged databases. In my
opinion, most people searching for most things will find them faster and
cheaper on CompuServe.

Third, CompuServe has the greatest range of services. Many services provide some way to send mail to another commercial service
(usually through the Internet), but CIS gives you a vast range of options
in directing a message. If you want to do *all* your correspondence
electronically, for instance, you can create a message and have
CompuServe print it out, stick it in an envelope, and physically *mail* it
to an address for you. CIS even has Congressgrams, where you can
write letters to any member of Congress. And though some services
can fax an electronic message to a phone number you provide, only
CompuServe (as far as I know) can arrange for the message to be
translated into another language before faxing it.

So what's the downside of all this? Imagine someone telling you
that California's a pretty cool place to visit. All you have to figure out
is what to do once you get there. Like California, CompuServe is *big*.
You can find your way to the Macintosh and industry-support forums
pretty easily, but as a new CompuServe user, you may get the impres-
sion that you *know* there's something else great going on somewhere,
but you have *no idea* where it is. Even with *The CompuServe Almanac*, an
essential, inch-thick book sold by CIS that simply lists the various areas
of the service, it can take months before you even begin thinking that
you know of all the services available to you and are seeing everything
of interest.

Which brings up another minor gripe: Thousands of messages get
posted to the service every week. If you leave a message on a local BBS,
you can go back there two months from now and it'll probably still be
there. On CompuServe, old messages are removed to make way for
new messages and the entire message base of a forum can roll over (if
your message disappears this way, it's said to have *scrolled off the board*)
in less than a week. Reading every message that comes along in a forum
is trivial in a BBS and merely challenging on most commercial services,
but nearly impossible on CompuServe.

Fortunately, you can use ZiffNet/Mac, the Mac-specific service created and maintained by the folks at *MacUser*. Because it's designed as a self-contained part of CompuServe, ZiffNet/Mac acts as a microcosm for all the Mac activity on CompuServe. Any hot Mac files posted in a CompuServe Mac forum wind up in ZiffNet/Mac's files area, and its smaller message base usually reflects the same issues and answers you can find in the several Mac forums in CompuServe proper.

Having plugged ZiffNet/Mac shamelessly, I should point out that CompuServe itself has an amazing set of Macintosh forums, known collectively as MAUG—the Micronetworked Apple User's Group. I've been a citizen of MAUG for about five years, and as nice as ZiffNet/Mac is, I find myself spending as much time visiting the MAUG forums, partly because of MAUG's more extensive message bases and partly because of its huge libraries, which are considerably better stocked than those of ZiffNet/Mac.

To access CompuServe's Macintosh forums, simply type **GO MACINTOSH** at any CompuServe prompt, then type the appropriate forum's number to see its main menu:

```
Enter choice   !go macintosh

Macintosh/Apple                MACINTOSH

 1 Applications Forum
 2 Communications Forum
 3 Community Clubhouse Forum
 4 Developers Forum
 5 Entertainment Forum
 6 Hypertext Forum
 7 New Users and Help Forum
 8 Systems Forum
 9 File Finder
10 Mac Vendor Forums
11 Apple News Clips
12 Zmac: MacUser/MacWEEK On-line
13 Macintosh System 7 Forum

Enter choice !1
```

In this example, I typed **1**, so the next menu I'd see would be the main menu for the Macintosh Applications forum.

MAUG and ZiffNet/Mac have a wealth of messages and files; I urge you to explore both as soon as you can.

Folks have only two serious gripes about CompuServe. First, it's expensive. CompuServe's hourly connect charges are usually about double what America Online's and GEnie's are (at this writing), and the plethora of information tends to make you linger on the service as long as possible.

Second, CIS is not nearly as easy to use as a graphically oriented service like America Online. The interface is 100 percent text-based, and even by that standard CompuServe's interface takes some getting used to. Whereas software designed for small BBS systems has been constantly improved over the years, CompuServe's software hasn't had a major overhaul for years.

Some diehard telecom junkies claim that this is an advantage: By leaving a lot of the old-style elements of the on-line experience intact, CIS has left in a lot of resources for power users to exploit. Most users conduct their business through CompuServe's standard menus, but power users can enter commands all at once. For instance, searching for and downloading a specific file usually means moving through a bunch of menus, wasting time. A CompuServe power user can just enter

```
BRO  KEY:SOLITAIRE  LIB:ALL
```

at any CompuServe prompt to find a specific solitaire game, then type

```
DOWN  SEAHAVEN.SIT  PROTO:YMODEM
```

to download it. With these CompuServe commands, writing scripts for automating messaging and file transfers is a minor breeze.

CompuServe sells two pieces of optional software that can mitigate ease-of-use and cost complaints. CompuServe Information Manager (CIM) puts a complete graphical user interface on CompuServe, enhancing ease of use by a factor of a zillion, and CompuServe Navigator cuts your CompuServe bill by letting you do most of your messaging and filing tasks while you're off line and the clock isn't running.

Information Manager doesn't make CompuServe like America Online, however. America Online was designed from the ground up as a graphical service. Information Manager is a graphical interface to a standard text-based service. Although CIM doesn't have some of the graphical niceties of AOL (such as icons for related areas next to a list of computing forums, as shown in Figure 7–4), CIM gives you almost all the features and functions available to you in the text interface. Check out CIM's interface when you're reading a message, as shown in Figure 7–8.

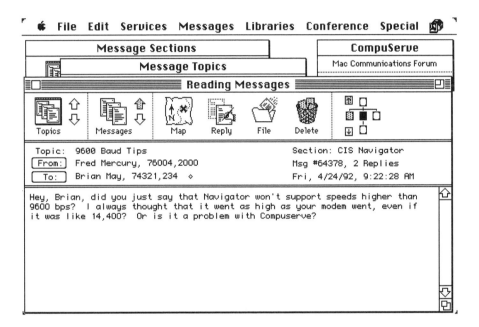

Figure 7–8: Reading messages in CompuServe Information Manager

Instead of AOL's Next, Prev, and Add Message buttons (see the bottom of Figure 7–6), Information Manager gives you tools for making your way through the message thread. That's an advantage of CIM over AOL. CompuServe is the only major commercial service that does support message threading, allowing you to read all messages and their replies in sequential order.

CompuServe Navigator can reduce your CompuServe bills by reducing the amount of time you spend on line. As you use an on-line service, you notice that your modem is idle much of the time you spend connected to the system. No data is exchanged between your Mac and the service because you spend so much time thinking about which message sections you'd like to visit, what messages to read, what you want to write in reply, what files to download, and so on. Navigator saves you money by allowing you to define exactly what messages and files you want to get from CompuServe and what messages you want to send, off line, while you're not connected to CompuServe and running up your bill.

Typically, the first step in a Navigator session is to tell Navigator to go to various CompuServe forums and summarize all the new messages it can find in specific message areas. When Navigator finishes this and logs off, it presents you with a list of messages and files. Figure 7–9 shows a summary of new messages left in CompuServe's Consumer Electronics forum.

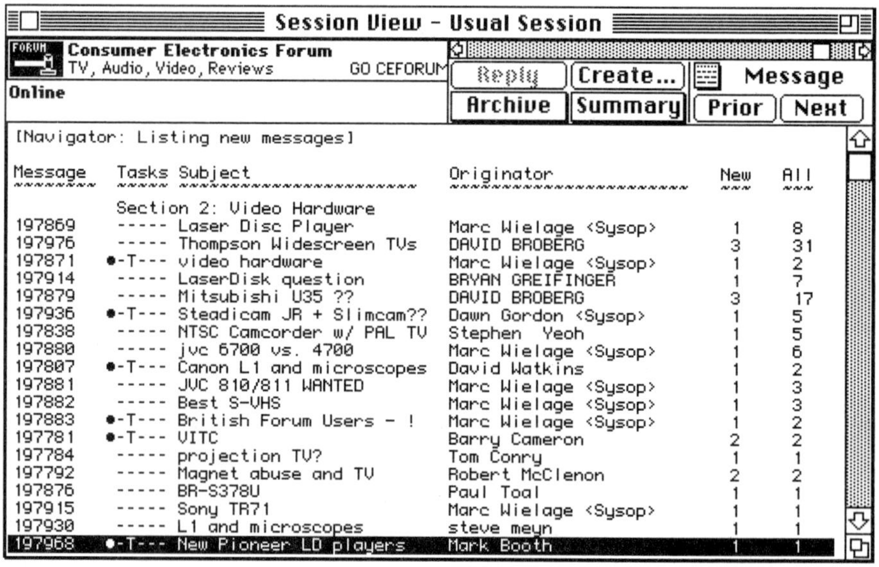

Figure 7–9: A summary of new messages presented by Navigator

For each of these summaries, you choose a message thread to read by double-clicking on its name in the list. Navigator can then fetch every message specified, log off, and display the messages as shown in Figure 7–10.

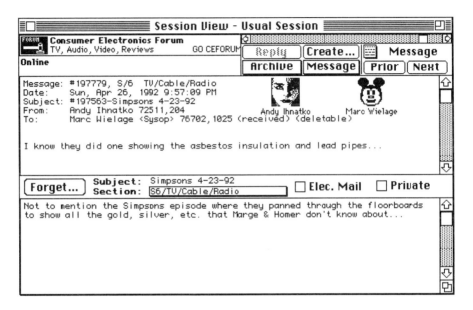

Figure 7–10: A message Navigator has retrieved

Here Andy has decided to reply to the message by clicking on the Reply button and typing in the lower part of the window. The reply is posted the next time he runs a Navigator session.

> Another Navigator bonus: The icons in the upper right of Figure 7–10 are Face Files—whimsical self-portraits that you can design and then upload to add a personal touch for other Navigator users reading your messages.

Navigator is not as polished as some other Macintosh software, but it can easily pay for itself the first month you use it. With Navigator, you'll typically spend 20 to 50 percent less time on line, and therefore your CompuServe bill is 20 to 50 percent lower.

CompuServe is a great service for just about everyone. The only stumbling block is its relatively high hourly connect rate, which may place it above the reach of many beginning telecom users. If your chief interest in an on-line service is information and noncomputer-related interest groups, you might want to start off with GEnie or America Online, both of which are less expensive. But sooner or later, you should give CompuServe a try. I think you'll come to agree that even though it's more expensive, it's worth it.

GEnie

GEnie, the on-line service owned and operated by General Electric, has always had a reputation not as a great service itself, but as a great, miniature alternative to CompuServe. It's text-based, but without the rich command structure of CompuServe. It's national in scope, but not nearly as big. It has many connections to other databases, but... you get the idea. Probably its best feature is that its hourly connect rates are about half as much as CompuServe's.

GEnie is an interesting service, but it can't match the scope of CompuServe or the ease of use of America Online. Also, its hobbled messaging features are a serious drawback. Its only real advantage is its thrift. GEnie delivers a handsome array of features at an attractive price. Even so, America Online, which is far easier to use, is priced about the same.

Try as we might, Andy and I couldn't find a compelling reason for using GEnie. Check it out if you like, but we feel confident that most of you will prefer America Online or CompuServe.

> My editor asked, "If you couldn't find a compelling reason to use GEnie, why do you have an account?" The answer is the same as it was a few pages back when I explained why I keep an MCI Mail account. I only use GEnie to communicate with people I can't reach via CompuServe, America Online, or AppleLink.

The Internet

Of all the on-line entities, the Internet is the most difficult to explain. Like the other services, the Internet allows you to exchange public and private messages, and download fun and interesting files. Unlike the other services, the Internet is not one computer somewhere in America that users log into; furthermore, using the Internet is free.

What our country's highway system is to transportation, the Internet is to data. The Internet is nothing more than a *huge* worldwide network that seemingly connects every large computer in the world to every other large computer. At this writing, it doubles in size every six months.

By *large computer* I'm generally talking about a minicomputer (or better) owned by a university, a large corporation, or the government and set up for the use of many people within one organization. If you're a student or a scientist, involved with the government, or work for a large company, it's likely that the computer system you use every day is part of the Internet, and you can take advantage of all the services the net has to offer for free. If you're not, you have to find a local company that rents computer time to the general public.

With the increasing popularity of the Internet, many local companies advertise themselves as Internet hosts for a nominal fee. Almost every geographical area has at least one computer set up as a public-access UNIX system—a computer running the UNIX operating system, which is a part of the Internet. Your modem dials a public-access computer nearby (to save on toll charges), and through it you're connected to the Internet. Since use of the Internet is always free, the only charges involved are for the use of computer time. This is almost always reasonable; the public-access UNIX system Andy uses charges a dollar an hour, and some systems allow Internet access for free.

The huge number of systems connected has several nifty ramifications. First, a phenomenally large private message system has sprung up. Just about every large computer in the world has its own mail system so its users can exchange messages with each other. If a computer is patched into the Internet, however, users can supply an Internet address for the message's destination. This means that any computer system can send private mail to any other computer system on the planet. This includes almost all major on-line services, too.

CompuServe, America Online, MCI Mail, and AppleLink are all part of the Internet, so whether you have an account on one of those services or not, you can send messages to those commercial services for free merely by directing the messages to that service's Internet address.

> For instance, a CompuServe address becomes an Internet address when you add the suffix @CompuServe.com. To send me a message through the Internet, which I'd get when I next logged onto CompuServe, you'd address it to 76004.2076@CompuServe.com. Notice that the comma in my CompuServe address has been changed to a period—76004,2076 vs. 76004.2076—as the Internet can't use commas in addresses.

Most services strive to put such a gateway into their service because it means that anyone on their service can send a message to anyone else on any other service.

Here's something else you can do on the Internet: The rough equivalent of a public message system is Internet *newsgroups*. These newsgroups started off as simple information files on various topics that one system would electronically transmit to other systems on the net, but they've gotten much more sophisticated. In terms of what you can do with them, newsgroups are now nearly identical to the message bases found on traditional on-line services.

Each newsgroup covers a different topic, and there are thousands of them. On commercial services in general, interest groups can have a narrow focus. That means you can find an impressive range of topics on CompuServe, but on the Internet, you'll find an even greater range of topics. One newsgroup, alt.fan.dan-quayle, is devoted to followers of our vice-president (and the verbal gaffes thereof); alt.folklore.urban is for swapping infamous stories that *everyone* knows happened to a friend of theirs. You can find newsgroups dedicated to just about every specialized branch of the sciences. And, of course, the Internet has several newsgroups for Mac users, comp.sys.mac.

So many newsgroups exist that not all systems can subscribe to them all. At regular intervals, new messages posted to a newsgroup are transmitted to Internet sites that subscribe to that newsgroup.

Downloading files from the Internet is more complicated than an on-line service, since the Internet is a network of thousands of computers, you can download files from *thousands* of places. Many computer systems on the Internet have set themselves up as anonymous FTP (*File Transfer Protocol*) sites. This means that Internet users, logged into their host computers, can open a connection to a faraway system even though they don't have an account there, look at what files are on the system, and download them. Two such anonymous FTP sites are

- **sumex-aim.stanford.edu**   A computer at Stanford University with a wealth of Macintosh files of all kinds

- **ftp.apple.com**   An area Apple Computer has set up for Internet users to download system software, technical notes, and other official and unofficial goodies.

When you use the Internet, you're using any one of thousands of computers. No two have precisely the same procedures for reading mail, browsing through newsgroups, and downloading files; each system has programs you run to do basic operations.

Two popular and easy to use programs are found on most UNIX systems, though: Elm and NN. Elm is a great UNIX mail program for reading, composing, and replying to private messages sent to you via the Internet. If you're logged onto Internet and you type **elm**, it neatly organizes all your messages into a text-based tour de force, as shown in Figure 7–11.

The program is called Elm with a capital E; the command to invoke it is elm with a lowercase e.

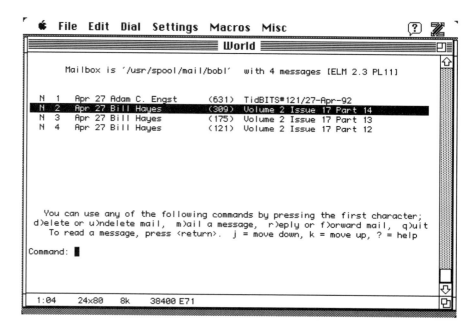

Figure 7–11: Reading Internet mail with the Elm mail reader

Elm is one of the slickest mail readers found on any on-line BBS or commercial service. Without any custom software running on the Mac, Elm organizes all your new messages into a list you can navigate with the cursor keys on your keyboard. Hit the spacebar, and the highlighted message is displayed. When you decide to create new messages or create replies, you use the system's full-featured word processor, not a text-editor. The word processor can vary from system to system, but most often it's a program called eMACS, a complete word processor with a spelling checker.

After I've read all my mail, I can scroll back through the list and mark which messages I'd like to delete, which messages I'd like Elm to save as text files that I can download later, and which messages I'd like to leave in the mailbox.

NN (NewNews) is a newsgroup reader that's as slick and easy to use as Elm. You type **nn** and then the name of the newsgroup you want to read, and after a little percolation NN pops up, as shown in Figure 7–12.

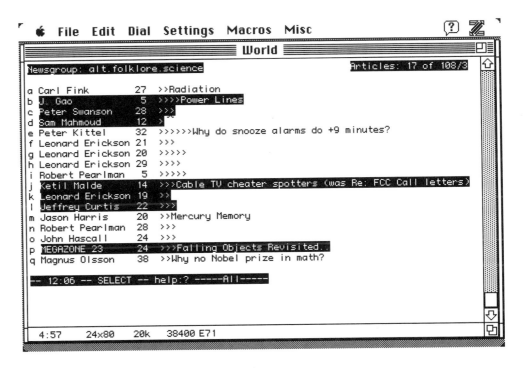

Figure 7–12: The NN newsgroup reader

The program is called NN with capital Ns; the command to invoke it is
nn with lowercase ns.

In Figure 7–12, I'm looking at items posted in the alt.folklore.science
newsgroup. Each highlighted line is a posting I've marked for reading
by hitting the letter in the leftmost column. After NN has given me a
listing of all the new postings, it displays the messages.

All bulletin boards and commercial services should handle public
and private mail this way. With only a text-based interface, Elm and
NN offer a powerful way of accessing huge amounts of data.

No services should handle file transfers like they're handled on the
Internet, though. It's a nonintuitive procedure, and you just have to
learn it. Here's how I get a file from Apple's FTP site. I start by entering
the command for my local public-access UNIX system (called The
World) to connect to Apple's FTP site: I use a program called "ftp" (for
File Transfer Protocol) which both establishes the link between your
host system and the FTP site and handles the file transfers.

```
world% ftp ftp.apple.com
```

The system outputs technical data to tell me it connected successfully.
Now I have to log onto the FTP site, as I would with any on-line service:

```
Connected to bric-a-brac.apple.com.
220 bric-a-brac.apple.com FTP server (IG Version 5.91 (from BU, from UUNET
5.51)
 Fri Nov 8 17:06:51 PST 1991) ready.
Name (ftp.apple.com:bobl):
```

I don't have an account on that system, but again it allows anonymous
FTP. To gain entry I can enter *anonymous* as my user name and type in
my user ID as my password:

```
Name (ftp.apple.com:bobl): anonymous
331 Guest login ok, send ident as password.
Password:
230 Guest login ok, access restrictions apply.
Remote system type is UNIX.
Using binary mode to transfer files.
ftp>
```

Now I've successfully connected to Apple's computer a few thousand miles away. I'm still at home, my Mac's talking to The World, and
I've established a link over the Internet to another computer.

To get a directory of the files available here, I use the UNIX
command **ls**:

```
ftp> ls
200 PORT command successful.
150 Opening ASCII mode data connection for /bin/ls.
total 339
drwxr-x—  3 ftp        6            512 Apr 13 21:38 .NextTrash
-rw-r—    1 ftp        6            296 Apr 23 17:03 .dir.wmd
-rw-r—    1 ftp        6           1095 Apr 13 19:40 132.203.58.244
-rw-r—    1 ftp        6           9856 Apr 22 18:07 GPIB
-rw-r—    1 ftp        6         119108 Apr 20 22:24 GPIB.CompactPro
drwxr-xr-x 5 sac       archivis   1024 Apr 20 22:06 alug
drwxr-xr-x 3 30233     6           512 Mar 19 22:37 apple
d—x—x—x   2 root      6           512 Jan 17  1991 bin
drwxrwx—x 3 fair      110         512 Apr 21 01:56 boot
drwxr-xr-x 2 blob      archivis    512 Apr 25  1991 cdrom
dr-xr-xr-x 2 root      6           512 May 15  1991 dev
drwxr-xr-x 9 mjohnson  archivis    512 Feb 19 03:17 dts
drwxr-xr-x 2 blob      archivis    512 Apr  6  1991 echt90
d—x—x—x   2 root      6           512 Jan 17  1991 etc
drwxr-xr-x 2 root      root       4096 Jul 25  1990 lost+found
-rw-r—r—  1 root      archivis  88393 Mar 20 09:37 ls-1R
-rw-r—r—  1 root      archivis  88394 Mar 20 09:38 ls-ltR
drwxrwxr-x 31 ftp      archivis   1024 Apr 27 17:57 pub
lrwxrwxrwx 1 root      archivis      3 Mar  5  1991 public -> pub
d—x—x—x   2 root      6           512 May 17  1991 shlib
drwxr-x—  2 ftp        6           512 Apr 21 02:45 xferit
226 Transfer complete.
ftp>
```

A UNIX-style file directory listing results. I want the file named ls-
lR transmitted from Apple to my place on The World, so I use the FTP
get command :

```
ftp> get ls-1R
200 PORT command successful.
150 Opening BINARY mode data connection for ls-1R (88393 bytes).
226 Transfer complete.
88393 bytes received in 3.8 seconds (23 Kbytes/s)
ftp>
```

The file is now on The World in the storage space allocated to me. I'm
done with FTP now, so I close the connection and quit:

```
ftp> bye
221 CUL8R.
world%
```

When I get a listing of what's in my area on The World, I find that
the ls-lR file is there:

```
world% ls -l
total 113
drwx——  2 bobl         1024 Apr 27 01:40 Mail
drwx——  9 bobl          512 Mar 20 03:00 News
-rw——   1 bobl          285 Feb  2 23:45 README
-rw——   1 bobl         1091 Feb  4 02:25 README.FIRST
-rw——   1 bobl         2282 Feb  4 23:22 Viewing PS file
-rw——   1 bobl         1522 Jan 26 18:00 bobsoron
-rw——   1 bobl        88393 Apr 28 12:08 ls-lR
-rw——   1 bobl            0 Oct 18  1991 stuff
-rw——   1 bobl        15805 Feb  4 02:17 | sz
world%
```

Finally, I have to have the file transmitted from The World to my Mac. The UNIX sz command transmits a file to you with the ZMODEM protocol:

```
world% sz ls-lR
sz: 1 file requested:
ls-lR

Sending in Batch Mode
*
### Receive (Z) ls-lR: 88393 bytes, 3:47 elapsed, 388 cps, 161%
world>
```

That's it. It's a long, complicated procedure involving a lot of arcane, nonintuitive commands. To use the Internet effectively, you have to amass some technical knowledge. At least CompuServe presents you with a menu of options. When you log onto your Internet host, however, all you get is a prompt. Still, you need only memorize two commands: **nn** and **elm**.

The Internet is not for beginners. Once you've had some experience with BBSs and major on-line services, however, an Internet account can be a wonderful component in your telecom bag of tricks.

Finding an Internet site to use regularly is the hard part if you don't have one waiting for you when you go to work in the morning. The best way to find an outfit in your general area that can sell you time on the Internet, as usual, is to use the experience of your fellow telecom users. Log onto any popular public BBS and leave a message somewhere asking if there are any Internet sites nearby you can dial into. Also, look in the board's files area for a national listing of public access UNIX systems. Keep looking; it's well worth the effort.

Parting Shots

You don't have to choose just one on-line service; you get the most out of telecommunications by getting accounts on a wide variety of free and commercial services because each has its own strength.

For example, Andy has accounts on dozens of systems. Typically, his daily telecom session begins with a trip to the BCS•Mac BBS, to stay up to date with local events and BCS•Mac business and immerse in the restorative waters of the Mac community for an hour. Then it's off to CompuServe (using Navigator, naturally) to check in on ZiffNet/Mac and see what's up on the national (and heavily used) forums on comic books and animation. After he's run up an uncomfortably large bill there, it's on to The Graphics Factory BBS, to prop up his feet and indulge in all the great discussions and arguments on subjects as deep as they are idiotic. Finally, at around 3 A.M. he lands in his Internet service, where he picks up most of his national mail. He also subscribes to a lot of electronic journals over the Internet, and after he's read all that, he spends the rest of the night wandering through newsgroups until he passes out.

My telecommunicating day is slightly different. Every morning, first thing, I run Navigator to check my E-mail and choose some messages to read on CompuServe, then I check my mail on America Online and AppleLink. A couple of times a week, I check my mail on GEnie and MCI. In the evenings, when its rates are lower, I log back onto America Online and peruse messages.

Between several different on-line entities, all our telecommunications needs are met. You're probably not as fanatical as we are (yet), but you could easily maintain a once-a-week schedule.

Here's how you'll probably evolve. You'll start by getting an account on a public BBS. After a couple of weeks, you'll probably start frequenting several boards. Soon, as your confidence soars and you know what you're doing, you'll subscribe to a commercial on-line service. America Online makes a dandy first choice for anyone; it's relatively cheap, it's easy to use, and it's a wonderland for Mac owners. You may sample GEnie a bit, but it won't be long before you long for the big time, CompuServe. Eventually—this is fate and you can't escape it—you'll come to the conclusion that although CompuServe is more expensive than the others, it's worth it. If the bug has bitten you badly, you'll probably start experimenting with the Internet.

The important thing is not to rush yourself. Sample each on-line service as you begin to learn more about telecommunications, and be sure to stick around on each one long enough to savor its unique essence.

8

The Strange and Peculiar Customs of the Natives

Or, when in Rome…

Ask anyone: The first thing you ought to do before traveling is to get to know about the people of that region. In England, you'll learn they dunk their French fries in vinegar; in France, Jerry Lewis is a much-loved star.

> One of the factoids I've collected on line: Jerry Lewis's popularity in France may be a misconception. Supposedly, for years they'd been using the same French actor to dub Jerry's dialogue; when they started using another actor, Lewis's popularity nose-dived.

The telecommunications community isn't as foreign as England or France, but it can seem like another planet if you're unaware of the strange and peculiar customs of the natives. The on-line tourist does well to observe its unwritten rules of behavior and arcane language. You could waste hundreds of hours learning these secrets on your own. Fortunately for you, those hours have already been wasted by Andy and me. We promise to teach you everything you ever wanted to know about on-line etiquette.

Mr. Modem Manners On-line Etiquette

You always telecommunicate from the sanctuary of your own desk, so it's unlikely that you'll be beaten up or even physically accosted should you do the wrong thing on line. This shouldn't prevent you, however, from trying to be as pleasant an on-line patron as possible. The following sections explain the major things to keep in mind, but they all boil down to two things: Follow whatever rules the sysop sets, and never do anything that might ruin someone else's good time. Following basic on-line etiquette is essential and will maintain your sterling reputation wherever you telecommunicate.

Honor Thy Sysop

Always be kind to your on-line host, the sysop. After all, the sysop keeps a bulletin board running at peak efficiency 24 hours a day. If you make the sysop's job as easy as possible, your reward is continued access to a great board.

If you want to keep in a sysop's good graces, *don't be a pig*. If every day you log on, spend an hour doing nothing but downloading, then log off, it's like going to a party, raiding the buffet table until there's nothing you like left, then leaving without saying good-bye. How rude. Though some sysops don't care how much you participate in their boards, *try* to make a positive contribution to the BBS. Participate in the message areas, and *upload interesting files*.

Note that this most important caveat applies only to BBSs; if you log onto a commercial on-line service, you're welcome to raid the buffet table to your heart's content. After all, you're paying for it.

By the way, a person who logs on and reads messages, but never contributes to discussions, is known as a *lurker*. Avoid being a lurker on a BBS; being a lurker on a commercial service is perfectly acceptable behavior.

Don't be intimidated if you're a neophyte, you think you'd have little to add to an on-line discussion, or you don't have any public domain or shareware files to contribute. Subjects of all kinds are discussed on line. You may have nothing to say when someone asks about proper initialization strings for Trailblazer modems, but when the talk turns to making bread by hand versus using breadmaking machines, the difference between white and dark chocolate, or why the original "Star Trek" was canceled, you may have a wealth of knowledge to share. *Participate.*

Don't laugh… all of these topics were recently big, raging discussions on local bulletin boards. The bread controversy came to such a head that an impromptu bake-off was put together at the sysop's house later in the month, with all users invited.

(The handmade bread won—no contest.)

You don't have to be a big-time programmer to have unique programs and files to upload. If you're a member of a commercial on-line service, keep an eye out for new files that people using a local free BBS might like. Look for information files of general interest that can be publicly distributed. On a regular basis, files you couldn't find elsewhere appear on on-line services, compiled by ordinary people just like you. A producer for "Late Night With David Letterman" uploads a regular list of reruns that will appear on cable the following month; a fan of "The Simpsons" maintains a definitive listing of all the episodes, detailing everything from what Bart wrote on the blackboard at the opening to the gag credits hidden in the closing.

You can upload other information, too. Any BBS has a dozen different shareware text editors, but how many have complete plans for building a computer desk? You created that file for your own use and now it's just sitting on your hard drive. Go on, upload it! It's bound to be useful to *someone*.

If you're unsure whether your text or word processor files, Hyper-Card stacks, spreadsheets, and the like, are of general interest, send a message to the sysop and ask. Sysops go ape over the prospect of being the first to have a hot, new file.

You can even make a more traditional contribution: cash and fabulous prizes. Running a BBS costs money. The sysop has to foot the bill for an extra phone line, equipment, maintenance, and so on; money is almost universally appreciated. Or donate some hardware! When you finally spring for a spiffy new V.32bis modem for yourself, why not lend your old 2400 bps modem to your favorite board? Modems that run 24 hours a day tend to melt, and a backup system is always appreciated.

Better than any of that, though, is your time. If a sysop has put together a great BBS without getting paid for anything, offer to help run the system! A popular BBS means lots of users, lots of messages, and lots of files, all of which have to be managed on a timely basis. By becoming an assistant sysop, helping out as needed and taking over while the main sysop goes on vacation or stays in bed with the flu, you can not only build up plenty of good karma, but you can gain a lot of valuable experience that can't be acquired elsewhere.

Deputize Yourself

While on line, always be on the alert for any problems on the BBS. Many sysops have jobs, and so aren't watching their babies all the time. If you had a hard time establishing a connection, if line noise uncharacteristically rained into your session, if you were suddenly disconnected, or if it seemed like you were teleported out of normal BBS user mode into a sysop mode, be sure to send a message to the sysop explaining the problem.

Report line noise problems directly to the phone company, too. The phone company tends to prioritize line maintenance by how many customers complain. A BBS in the Boston area had incredible line noise problems, to which the phone company responded not at all. But when the sysops sent mail to all the other local BBSs, advising them to call the phone company and report they were having trouble getting through to that BBS's phone number, the repairperson came out and fixed the problem within the week. And after only 350 complaints had been logged!

Message Manners

DON'T USE ALL CAPS. PEOPLE THINK YOU'RE SHOUTING WHEN YOU TYPE IN ALL CAPS.

Try to write tight. Don't go on and on and on, rambling with absolutely no point or rhyme or reason. When you drone on endlessly, people tend to ignore the point you're trying to get across.

Most BBS programs impose some reasonable limit to message length; that limit has a reason. Try to keep your messages to one screen in length (about 24 lines); at most, limit your logorrhea to two messages one after the other. If you have something important to say that takes more than a couple of screenfuls, upload it as a text file into the files area, and send a quick message referring people to the file.

You may love the idea of a sign-off—a cute little tagline at the end of your messages that becomes your trademark—but keep it within reason. One line with your name is fine, and a second line with a witty saying ("Truth is stranger than fiction because fiction has to make sense") is OK, but when you append a 12-line list of banned books to read, you're pushing things.

Please, get into the habit of changing the subject headings of your messages when you write replies that go off on a tangent. It's an understandable faux pas; you've become so wrapped up in this fascinating discussion of Byzantine pottery you've forgotten that the subject heading, originating from a month ago, still reads *Installing a frammus on '68 Ford Fairlane.* Many folks decide what messages to read solely by scanning the message subjects. You may think it's fun to read back and try to figure out how you got from cars to pottery, but other on-line patrons probably won't think so.

Avoid using harsh language; insert asterisks when appropriate. You never know when you'll encounter an on-line denizen offended by language that's too **** strong.

And no mudslinging. Personal attacks belong in private E-mail (if anywhere); not only do you avoid embarrassing your target by allowing strangers to read your comments, but you also avoid embarrassing yourself. All the public attacks I've witnessed had worse repercussions for the slinger than the slingee.

> By the way, this holds true even if you're talking behind someone's back. It's not nice, and keep in mind that the sysop can always read *everything*. He or she may pass along your message to an interested party.
>
> Another by the way: Be careful what you say even if you're sure the target will never read your message. On CompuServe, Andy was talking about TV theme songs and called the theme for a certain afternoon cartoon show "incredibly wimpy." Little did he know that the person who *wrote* that tune was a frequent CompuServe user.

For goodness' sake, rein in your impulse to *flame* on and on about a subject. In telecom parlance, *to flame* is to spit endless venom at a subject, without the least concession to logic or reason.

> To be honest, when a *flame war*—multiple individuals publicly flaming against each other—is in full swing, it can be quite an entertaining thing to watch.

Almost as bad as the flamers are the folks who enjoy reading their own messages. I realize that as a telecom nut newly fallen from the tree, you want to reply to every message you see, but please restrain yourself. Write a message or send a reply only if you have something to *say*, if you have a question or think you can further the conversation. Don't reply just to get your name in there.

Finally, try to maintain the integrity of the message base. On most boards, you can delete any public message you've sent or received, but don't exercise this awesome power unless you have a good reason (like the guy flamed you). Deleting public messages disrupts the natural flow of that message thread and makes it more difficult for other folks to follow along. Private E-mail, on the other hand, is for your eyes only, so it's considered good form to delete private mail after you read it. It helps free up space for more mail.

File Finesse

Before uploading a file to the BBS, check to make sure the BBS doesn't already have it somewhere. Storage space is always at a premium on a BBS, and the sysop doesn't want to waste space on duplicate files. Almost all BBSs offer you an easy way to search their libraries for a specific file. Use it!

Needless to say, don't upload commercial software. Most of you are smart enough not to upload, say, Microsoft Word to a BBS or on-line service. To be safe, always check anything you intend to upload for the phrase Public Domain or Shareware or Freely Distributable—anything to suggest the author says it's OK to give away copies. Many spreadsheet files, HyperCard stacks, and desktop publishing templates are sold as commercial products, and uploading them is not de rigueur.

Similarly, use caution when you reproduce copyrighted material electronically. I love my startup screen of the Batman logo, my beep sound from *Total Recall*, all those QuickTime movies of scenes from *Terminator II*—but even though none of these are commercial software products, they're all copyrighted material. Scanning the logo from a page on a comic book, digitizing the sound from the movie, and hooking up the VCR to a capture board to make the movie are all copyright infringements, and many BBSs are wary of such material. If you're in doubt, be sure to confer with the sysop before you upload any material that you even suspect may be copyrighted.

Never, ever upload files that you *know* harbor viruses. Everything you do on a BBS is being logged and printed. If you unknowingly pass on a virus to the BBS, then you'll earn nothing worse than the sympathy of your peers, but if you knowingly infect another system, expect a visit from local or national law enforcement authorities.

Finally, don't upload any materials that the sysop deems inappropriate—smut, for instance. Most sysops male and female would rather you kept that 24-bit PICT file of the playmate of the month (or worse) to yourself. Again, check with your sysop before proceeding.

Obey Time Limits

Stick to whatever time limits the sysop has imposed. Most BBS programs kick you off when you exceed your allotted time, but allow you back on if you call right back. Please let the next person have a turn. Every now and then you might have a legitimate need for more time, but in those cases the sysop will gladly arrange for a temporary boost in your daily allowance.

Be Real

How would you react to someone who introduced himself or herself to you as Doctor Blood, Scuzzy1, or Mr. Cool? You'd probably think he or she was a bozo. That's why you should probably use your real name on a BBS, and not use a *handle*. Granted, anonymity is desirable on some boards, but most BBSs discourage the habit and demand the use of real names. Since 1988, all the people I know who'd started logging in under handles switched to their real names soon thereafter.

The exception is America Online, where each account can support five separate screen names. A lot of people use their real name most of the time, and log on using a handle when they want to hang around in chat rooms with names like "M looking for wild F," or "Teenage sex talk."

Don't Try This at Home

Here are some things not to do. First, *don't* try to break the system. People who try to break into a BBS and wreak havoc are not much loved. If you find yourself in what appears to be the operating system of the computer running the BBS, switch off the modem and log back on.

Don't *ever* try to log on with someone else's user name and password without their knowledge.

Don't abuse the ability to page someone on the system. Think of what a page does on a BBS: It interrupts the user of your choice, disturbing him or her from the trancelike state accompanying quality telecommunications. In general, don't page someone unless you have an immediate need to talk (that last-minute file he or she just sent you got destroyed, for instance). If you page someone just to chat, don't be offended if he or she says no. Some people regard paging as an invasion of their privacy. The exception to this rule is America Online, where Instant Messages (IMs) are easily ignored. But even on AOL, be polite. If you send an Instant Message to someone and they refuse the invitation to chat (or don't reply, which usually means the same thing), don't send five more IMs, each worded more strongly than the last. If "live" interaction is what you're after, try AOL's chat rooms or CompuServe's CB simulator. People hanging out in those two places *want* to chat.

Paging the sysop on a BBS can be even worse. This causes an audible alarm to go off in the BBS computer, which (depending on the time) causes the sysop to bolt out of bed and check the system. Think of any pager as a 911 system. No one minds when you use it properly, but when you use it for kicks sysops get mad at you (at best).

Finally, don't end your BBS session merely by switching off your modem. Quit properly, by logging off in a civilized manner. Some antique BBS programs crash when you just switch off your modem, and they stay off line until the sysop wakes up and fixes it.

Dial Ahead

I've saved the scariest piece of etiquette for last, because this one potentially involves dealing directly with real people. Whenever someone gives you the number of a local BBS to try, be *sure* to pick up the phone and dial it yourself at a reasonable hour of the day. All too often, the number belongs to a person, not a BBS. Answering the phone at 3 A.M. to hear a modem shrieking in your ear is not the niftiest way to begin (or end) the day.

Remember, the things you've read so far in this chapter are guidelines; each sysop establishes a slightly different set of rules of behavior for his or her board. But all of these rules of behavior are reasonable and if you play by them you'll always be welcome on line.

A Guide to Acronyms

One of the symptoms of the telecommunications disease is that, subconsciously, you're always looking for a way to eke a little higher efficiency out of your telecom setup.

A more efficient method of message processing is to use placeholders, or acronyms, for some common phrases. For example, typing **BTW** instead of **by the way**, compresses that phrase *70 percent!* On a V.32bis V.42bis modem, use of that one acronym yields an effective throughput of over 100,000 bps! How can you afford *not* to use acronyms?

> Some of what we're calling acronyms (like CU for "see you"), are not acronyms—they're more like abbreviated homonyms. We refer to them collectively as acronyms to keep things simple.

Acronyms are in wide use all over the English-speaking world. Here are the most common ones you'll find on line:

ADN	Any day now
AFAIK	As far as I know
AOL	America Online (commercial on-line service)
BBS	Bulletin board system
BFD	Big *** deal
BIX	Byte Information Exchange (commercial on-line service)
BTW	By the way
CIS	CompuServe Information Service (commercial on-line service)
CI$	CompuServe Information $ervice (commercial on-line service)

CU	See you
CUL8R	See you later
DIIK	Darned if I know
ESAD	Eat Spam and die
FAQ	Frequently asked question. Many systems (especially Internet newsgroups) maintain an FAQ list, and refer new users to it.
FITB	Fill in the blank
FOAD	*** off and die
FOAF	Friend of a friend
FUBAR	***ed up beyond all recognition
FWIW	For what it's worth
FYA	For your amusement
FYC	*** You, Charlie! (sometimes C is followed by another sequence, like FYCITB—*** you, Charlie…I'm the boss!)
FYI	For your information
<g>	Grin. You tack this on to show you're only kidding, usually after you've made a joke at someone else's expense. Use more than one or capitalize for emphasis. Example: "Well, _sure_ you can afford it; after all, you've sold your soul to the Establishment! <G>" See also <gd&r> and <vbg>.
GA	Go ahead. In an on-line chat, GA signals that I'm done talking and now it's your turn.

<gd&r>	Grinning, ducking & running. A more intense version of <g>; you're running away to avoid the things that your target is surely going to throw at you.
GIGO	Garbage in, garbage out
GIWIST	Gee, I wish I'd said that
HHOK	Ha ha only kidding
HHOS	Ha ha only serious
IAE	In any event
IBM	Ishoulda boughta Macintosh
IC	I see
ILOL	I laughed out loud
IMHO	In My Humble Opinion. Use IMHO to get yourself off the hook if you say something factual that later turns out to be completely wrong . Example: "IMHO, it was space aliens led by Elvis that fired at Kennedy from the grassy knoll."
IMNSHO	In my not-so-humble opinion
IMO	In my opinion
IOW	In other words
KISS	Keep it simple, stupid
L8R	Later
LOL	Laughing out loud
LSTYD	Life stinks then you die
NBFD	No big *** deal

O&O	Over and out
OIC	Oh, I see
OTOH	On the other hand
PITA	Pain in the ***
POV	Point of view
ROFL	Rolling on the floor laughing (also ROTFL and rof,l)
RSN	Real soon now. When referring to the release date of a piece of software, RSN means never.
RTFM	Read the *** manual. Used as a response to an absurdly simple question.
RTM	Read the manual
SNAFU	Situation normal, all ***ed up
TANJ	There ain't no justice
TANSTAAFL	There ain't no such thing as a free lunch
TIA	Thanks in advance
TLA	Three-letter acronym
TNX	Thanks
TNXE6	Thanks a million (E6 = 10^6)
TPTB	The powers that be
TTBOMK	To the best of my knowledge
TTFN	Ta ta for now
TTUL	Talk to you later

<vbg>	Very big grin
WTF	What the ***
WYSIWYG	What you see is what you get

Emoticons (AKA Smilies, ASCII-grams)

I'm putting this section in only because I want this book to be as complete as possible.

The emoticon is a cute little symbol, made from regular ASCII keyboard characters, that you can see by cocking your head all the way to the left. Emoticons are also called Smilies and ASCII-grams.

Use them if you want. Emoticons remind me of dotting your i's with happy faces. On the other hand, they can sometimes say more than a thousand words.

Most emoticons consist of three stages, assembled from left to right:

:	Ocular Construct
-	Nasal Construct
)	Oral Construct

The stages are assembled like this:

:-)	I'm happy

This is the oldest known emoticon.

Pathology on other species is similar. Using a *B* for the ocular construct yields

B-)	Cool guy with shades on

There are some variants to the classic three-stage pathology. The more limited two-stage emoticon provides a 33 percent increase in throughput:

:)   Micro happy

More baroque entries feature more stages:

+-<|:-)   The Pope

*<|:-)   Santa Claus

The first class of emoticon depicts human or humanoid faces. Normally they're used to comment on the mental, emotional, or physical state of the sender or receiver.

:-)   Happy

:-D   Very happy or big mouth/blabbermouth

:-i   Half-smile

:-]   Dopey grin

:-(Sad

:-C   Truly bummed out

:-P   Sticking your tongue out

;-)   Wink

:-o   Shocked!

:-?   Pipe smoker

:-\   Uncommitted

:-x   My lips are sealed

:-*   Ate a sour pickle

:-|	No reaction
:-)#	Has beard
:-{	Has moustache
:-{#	Has beard and moustache
(:-)	Is bald
:-9	Licking his chops
:-′	Spitting
:-′|	Runny nose
:-)′	Drooler
B-,	Bruce Willis (smirking dude with glasses)
:-@	Screaming
::-)	Eyeglass wearer (four eyes, get it?)
O-)	Scuba diver (or cyclops)
(-:	Left-handed
{(:-)	Wearing a toupée
}(:-(	Losing toupée in wind
*:o)	Person is a bozo
%-^	Person is Picasso
%-)	Cross-eyed
#-)	Blotto from drinking all night
|-P	Bleah!

[:-)	Wearing a Walkman
[:-|]	Robot
<:-)	Dunce
:^(	Nose is out of joint
|-|	Asleep
&:-)	Has curly hair
P-)	Pirate
:-)=	Buck-toothed
:-"	Puckering up for a kiss
}:-(	Bull-headed
:-[	Vampire
:-#	Smiley with braces
:*)	Drunk

A second class of emoticons depicts (largely) inanimate objects:

o=	Burning candle (person is flaming)
-=	Extinguished candle (flame is out)
{	Alfred Hitchcock
@>—>—	A rose; given as a peace offering
2B|^2B	"To Be Or Not To Be"
...—...	SOS!

Then there are the large emoticons such as the cow:

```
(__)

(oo)

 \/——\

   ||       | \

   ||—W||    *
```

Or Bart Simpson:

```
 |\/\/\/|

   |         |

   |         |

   |  (o) (o)

   C       _)

   |  ,___|

   |    /

  /_____\

 /        \
```

The fun thing about emoticons is that, for whatever bizarre reason, new ones are being designed and used every day. The preceding examples are designs culled from on-line messages and the dozens of "definitive" emoticon guides making the rounds of the BBSs. All you need is a keyboard and a screen!

Parting Shots

In this chapter, you've absorbed a few tips about how to conduct yourself on line, and you've learned some new ways to express yourself and boost throughput at the same time. :-)

In general, do your best to be a good on-line citizen. Be kind to your sysop, watch your language, be polite to your on-line cohorts, flame infrequently, and use emoticons sparingly. Follow those simple rules and you'll go months, if not years, without angering or offending anybody.

In the next chapter, you'll move on to more powerful stuff—you'll learn how to connect by modem to another individual (rather than a BBS or on-line service), how to set up your own BBS, and the basics of writing telecom scripts.

9

Advanced Telecommunications

Telecommunicating person to person, running a BBS, scripting, and other ways to put your modem to work

You should now know most of what you need to know to telecommunicate. The next two chapters are bonuses. For example, you *need* to know how to make your modem work, how to log onto services, and how to download and upload files. But you could live a long and happy life without learning what's involved in running a BBS of your own.

In this chapter, you'll get an introduction to some things that can help you take even better advantage of your modem— telecommunicating person to person, scripting, and several other advanced topics as well as a bit about how to run your own BBS.

Telecommunicating Person to Person

Telecommunications usually involves linking people to a faceless bureaucracy of some sort. On-line services are *friendly* faceless bureaucracies, but some of you will want to learn how to connect directly to someone else's Mac, avoiding the middlemen. Or women.

The most obvious benefit of avoiding intermediaries is when you want to exchange a file or two with a friend who uses a different BBS or subscribes to a different on-line service.

Since you both have modems, you can simply transmit the files directly, no matter what software you're using. You have three options: you can use regular telecom software, host modes, or specialized software.

Using Telecom Software

The hardest part of transferring files directly is making sure your friend has all the details down and has set up his or her Mac properly.

Start by launching your usual telecom program. If you're using a program that uses the Macintosh Communications Toolbox (see Appendix C), open up a connection using the serial tool, so you can communicate directly with your modem.

Set communications parameters to 8 data bits, 1 stop bit, no parity, and select the highest communication rate possible with your modem. Also, turn on Local Echo in your software.

Here comes the hard part. Until now, you've been dealing with computer hardware that does what you tell it to do, when you tell it to do it; now, you're about to deal with a live human being. (They're usually the weakest link in a network.)

Call your friend, and have him or her fire up his or her telecom software. Make sure your friend is using the same communication settings as you are—8/1/N. Also, find out what the highest speed of your friend's modem is. If your friend is using a 2400 bps modem and you're using a 9600, you have to change your speed setting to match your friend's.

If your friend has done everything you've asked, give one final command: "Have your machine call my machine in five minutes."

During those five minutes, you're going to put your modem into auto-answer mode. That means your modem assumes that any incoming phone call is a modem trying to connect to your Mac, and so answers and establishes the connection. Either choose auto-answer from the appropriate menu in your telecom software, or manually send the following command to the modem:

```
ATS0=1
```

The modem responds with its usual OK, and the modem's AA light (if it has one) should come on. You've just changed one of your modem's S-registers—locations in the modem's memory that store various low-level settings (see Appendix B for a summary of these settings). S0 holds the number of times the phone rings before the modem answers. Usually it's set to 0, which means it doesn't answer the phone. Here, you tell it to answer on the first ring.

> Some modems make things even easier by putting a Voice/Data push button in the front panel. That way, you can call up your friend, say howdy, and if he or she is ready to do a transfer you just push the button. Instantly, the call is switched from two humans talking via telephone to two Macs communicating via modem.

Now it's all in your friend's hands. As soon as his or her modem calls, your modem should answer right away. Then, after you hear the same carrier and data noises as when you connect to a BBS, the speaker is silent, and you're connected.

In this case, the big difference is that there's no BBS program running to smooth things over with welcome screens and menus. You have simply a connection between two Macs. Whatever you type appears in the your friend's window, and vice-versa.

Next, make sure the connection is up and humming. Type a message—any message—on your screen. If everything's working, a response from your friend should appear on your screen. If it doesn't, make sure your communications settings are what they should be and that you're connected and on line (your modem's CD and OH lights are on). If you can't see what *you're* typing, then you probably didn't turn on Local Echo. Turn it on! What you type gets sent out the modem, but doesn't necessarily get sent back for you to read; Local Echo sends what you type to your telecom program's terminal window as well as to the modem.

Now that you've established a solid connection, you need only give your telecommunications program an upload command, and, about ten seconds later, your friend has to give a download command.

So long as you're both using the same file-transfer protocol, that should be all there is to it; the only problems that crop up will be the fault of your friend at the other end. Make sure your friend waits about ten seconds or so after you type **HERE IT COMES!**; your friend has to give you time to give an upload command to your telecom program, plus a head start to establish the transmission.

> By the way, if you have a DOS laptop or a pocket organizer with serial ports, you can use much the same procedure to transfer data from your Mac to it, and from it to your Mac. If you have modem cables for both your Mac and the other device, you need only stick a $5 device called a null modem adapter (it takes the place of a pair of modems) between the two cable ends and launch your telecom programs, and a link is automatically created. Match communications settings, and you're ready to transfer files.
>
> If the cabling setup doesn't work, you may have to look at the pinouts for the two serial interfaces and wire up your own null modem adapter (that's beyond the purview of this book, but you can find some pinout diagrams in Appendix F).
>
> For what it's worth, *beyond the purviews* are a little like personal fouls in the NBA. They give the authors/players a cheap out from a tough situation, but they're hardly polite and you can't get away with too many of them.

That's all there is to it. Once the file transfer is completed, be sure to turn off the auto-answering mode on your modem, with a menu selection or by typing **ATS0=0** before you go to bed. If you forget to do this, the next person who calls you will hear the shriek of your modem.

Using Host Modes

If you do a file transfer manually, you have to be at your computer checking every step from start to finish. The most convenient way to handle a file transfer is to run a mini-BBS or host mode on your Mac, leave it switched on, and go do something else while the program does everything for you.

Many software producers have incorporated limited BBS features into their telecom software. All you have to do is supply passwords for basic functions, as shown in Figure 9–1, engage the host mode, and the Mac becomes a mini-BBS.

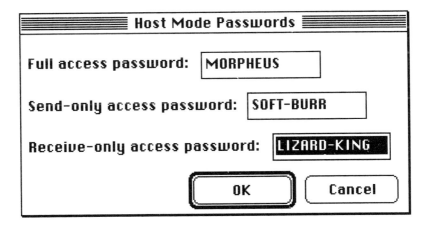

Figure 9–1: White Knight's host mode configuration

Its capabilities are certainly limited; as you can guess from Figure 9–1, most host modes have lax security, and host modes don't display a system of menus and file lists for callers. You have to brief your friend on what he or she has to do once your Mac answers the phone ("Type in **LIZARD-KING** for a password, then enter **SENDZ Red:Final Report** to start the transfer"), but the selling point still remains: while your friend is making his or her way through your host mode, you can be parked in front of the tube with some popcorn and a cold drink.

Some telecom programs don't incorporate host mode features as integral features but as scripts you can run when necessary. Software Ventures MicroPhone II includes MiniBBS (shown in Figure 9–2), a script-based host mode, that supports multiple users with various access levels and has a slicker user interface than many host modes for those logging in.

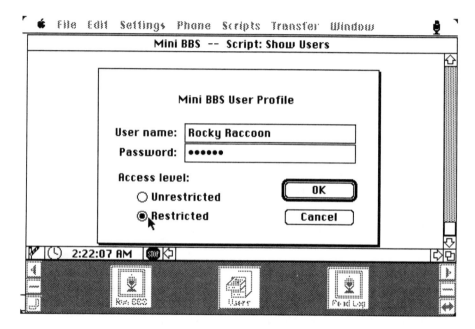

Figure 9–2: MicroPhone II's megarobust Mini BBS script.

Using Specialized Software

Baseline's DoubleTalk and FreeSoft's Okyto (which comes free with White Knight) have specialized features for direct Mac to Mac communication. They try to completely shield you from the telecom process, to make file transfers almost as simple as using Font/DA Mover. Click a couple of buttons to make a connection and you see a scrolling list of files available from the remote Mac.

DoubleTalk is spiffy on its own, and Okyto is a great addition to White Knight, but frankly, I don't understand their appeal for direct Mac to Mac communication. They're not as convenient as the hands-on techniques, because to be effective the same program has to be running at both ends of the connection. If your need for direct file transfers is infrequent, it's hard to justify the extra expense (at least if you buy a copy of DoubleTalk). If you do direct file transfers regularly, you'll appreciate the extra versatility of White Knight's built-in host mode, or a scripted host mode such as MicroPhone's MiniBBS.

Running Your Own BBS

A member of the British Parliament once described his job thusly: "This is a lousy, undoable job which ruins family life, which you can never live up to, but which is done mainly out of dumb, depressing duty." If he had thrown in a line about not getting paid and having to throw his own good money out the window besides, he would have described the job of running a BBS.

The thought of running your own BBS holds that same sort of allure that opening your own bookstore or movie theater does. You want to build an entity that caters to your tastes, offering unique services to the community at large. Your best reward is the continued and enthusiastic patronage of a great number of people.

Life as a sysop means spending your days in either mind-numbing tedium, dealing with boring maintenance tasks, or four-alarm panic, as major things begin to go wrong all at once. Furthermore, you need to buy more hardware and software. The following sections should give you added respect for the sysop of your favorite BBS, even if this brief outline doesn't convince you to start your own BBS.

Buying Lots More Hardware

For most folks, setting up a BBS involves buying some new hardware and getting a second phone line installed for the BBS. You can *tell* everyone your BBS is going to be running only from midnight to six A.M., but folks won't believe you. Unless you enjoy hearing the shrill whine of a modem when you answer your phone, get that second phone line.

After installing the phone line, the next most important purchase is a sturdy modem that can run 24 hours a day, seven days a week. Warning: Cheaper modems can turn to molten slag after the first week.

You also want a new hard drive. You can never have enough storage space for a BBS, and the drive will be running 24 hours a day. Do you want all *your* important data on a drive that could collapse at any second?

A BBS program can run in the background of your main Macintosh. But do you want your $8000 Quadra to run about as fast as a $1000 Mac Classic? Of course not. Considering that you can get a used Mac for $500 or so, a serious attempt at a Mac BBS requires a dedicated Mac.

Finally, as your BBS grows you have to consider adding extra serial ports to your Mac to support more than one user at a time. If there's anything that frustrates a BBS user, it's a busy signal. And with extra serial ports comes extra modems and extra phone lines.

Heresy: Consider running your BBS on an IBM PC (or clone). It makes most folks itch, but a PC is cheap (you can get a whole system for less than $300), there's far more BBS software available for it than for the Mac, and getting it to work with lots of serial ports and lots of modems all at once is a trivial affair. At least think about it.

Another advantage of the PC—at least for user groups and other nonprofits—is that so many companies make PC clones. If the Mac running your BBS blows up, you can only beg Apple for a free replacement. When a PC detonates, you can beg dozens of companies for a handout.

Buying Some Software

Luckily, there's only one thing to buy in this category: BBS software. Unluckily, on the Mac, there isn't a lot to choose from. PC users can choose from dozens of major BBS packages, suiting every level of sophistication. The Mac pool of BBS software is just as deep—some great software exists—but it's not as varied as that available to PC folks.

For all practical purposes, your choices are as follows:

- **Hermes and WWIV** Two shareware BBS programs, available from local user groups and downloadable from on-line services. Either program is fine for learning about how a BBS works, but I wouldn't recommend them for regular operation of a BBS. To the folks who log on, a BBS is only as good as the software it runs on, and neither program has proven to be either as solid or as feature-laden as the alternatives.

- **Second Sight** The BBS counterpart to White Knight, written and published by the same company (FreeSoft). It's the best BBS program for Macintoshes. It's easy to install and configure, and it's well-supported by its publisher. Moreover, since it is the *de facto* standard for BBS software among Macs, a lot of third-party software is available for extending Second Sight's capabilities.

- **TeleFinder** I agonized over this one, I assure you. It's not as good or as feature-laden as Second Sight, but Spider Island Software's TeleFinder has a couple of strong points. It's easy to set up, and it's unique in offering the option of a graphical user interface, if the user logs in with special TeleFinder software.

> Second Sight is the only serious program to consider when running a BBS on a Macintosh. You can start off with a trivially simple BBS, and years later have an internationally based system mangling thousands of messages a day.

The Final Word on BBSs

Putting together a mediocre little BBS is ridiculously simple. Putting together a great BBS is simply ridiculous.

No BBS program works out of the box. The BBS software acts more like a skeleton, more of a *means by which* you can create a BBS than a complete BBS ready to go. You have to do a lot of thinking and reflection as you design your menu structure, decide how your message bases should flow, determine what database services you want to enable, decide if you want to offer regular bulletins and news, and decide whether to implement a Premium Services package, and so on.

After all that work, after you've designed all the visual and behind-the-scenes elements of your BBS, after you've decided on a cool name for it, your evenings will be spent impatiently wondering why folks aren't calling. It's a catch-22 situation: You'll feel like a failure if they don't call, but if they *do*, your work will be increased a thousandfold.

Scripting

Scripting is certainly one of the most powerful and useful features of any telecom program. To have your telecom program handle things for you automatically, you write a list of instructions for your Mac to follow.

To log onto a BBS, for instance, you can write a script that dials the phone; dials again if it's busy; presses the Return key when the modem says *CONNECT*; and types the correct response when the BBS says *Name?* and *Password?* You could do it manually, but it gets tedious after a while.

Every scripting language is different (although some base their languages on a popular language such as C or HyperTalk), but you use a core group of scripting commands to automate repetitive commands (commands in your telecom program can vary):

- **DIAL** Dials a phone number or on-line service.

- **PROMPT** Waits for the following string of text to come in through the modem.

- **TYPE** Sends the following string out the modem as if you'd typed it.

Those three words are the most useful ones. Here's an annotated script that logs me into CompuServe. My password, as you might expect, has been changed to protect the guilty.

```
DIAL  444-0566              Dials the number
PROMPT  "CONNECT"           Waits for the modem to announce you're connected
TYPE  "^C"                  Sends a Control-C to let CompuServe know you're here
PROMPT  "User ID:"          They want my ID number
TYPE  "76004,2076^M"        Type it in, followed by a carriage return (Control-M)
PROMPT  "Password:"         They want my password
TYPE  "NOT@DVORAK^M"        Type it in, followed by a carriage return (Control-M)
```

You don't even have to write scripts yourself if you don't want to. Most telecom programs also offer an autopilot mode, where the program watches what you type as you log onto a BBS (or do whatever you want automated), and then the program writes the script *for* you.

Most communications programs also allow you to attach these scripts to on-screen buttons or menu items; logging into CompuServe can be reduced to clicking on an icon, making the telecom process Mac-like.

Of course, almost all scripting languages feature more than three commands! First, every command that you can send by pulling down a menu can generally be executed from a script. You can change communications parameters, upload and download files, turn a capture file on, and so on.

> One of the finest uses for scripting is to execute a late-night run on a BBS. While you're sleeping, have your script autodial a busy BBS in the middle of the night, move to the message areas of interest, and capture every message to a text file, for calm perusal along with your morning coffee.

You can use simple scripts to make up for some of the holes in an on-line service. CompuServe, at this writing, doesn't support batch downloads unless you're using Navigator or Information Manager. With simple scripting, you can have your software download file after file, sending the right commands at the right time, saving you from having to babysit your expensive hardware.

Some scripting languages are so robust that you can implement nearly any element of the standard Macintosh user interface in your scripts: buttons, windows, dialogs, scrolling lists, and so on. For example, in Figure 9–3, with the exception of the menu bar, everything you see—including the buttons and dialog boxes—is the result of a MicroPhone II script.

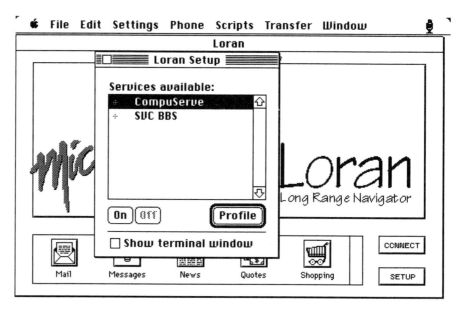

Figure 9–3: MicroPhone II's scripting in action

Although Loran was created by Software Ventures employees, who were paid for doing it, creating buttons and dialog boxes with MicroPhone II is easy. You can assemble custom dialogs with some help from the tools that come with your telecom software (MicroPhone comes with Dialoger Pro, a professional-level dialog builder). This makes it easy for a script writer to customize MicroPhone II and make it more intuitive for the inexperienced user.

Other Advanced Topics

The rest of the chapter is a potpourri of stuff that didn't fit anywhere else. For example, most telecom programs don't implement every feature you want. Fortunately, you have the power to correct any glaring oversights: write your own telecom software, from writing scripts of instructions for MicroPhone II or White Knight to follow to your own stand-alone applications.

Another neat use of your modem: If you have an E-mail package (such as QuickMail or Microsoft Mail), you can install special *gateways* that make it easy to send mail messages from your E-mail program to commercial on-line services quickly and easily.

In another vein, you can use your modem to play games head-to-head with other telecom nuts, or use special software to control a Mac at another location by remote control.

Finally, you can use a modem to access data stored on your desktop computer remotely from anywhere in the world.

Writing Your Own Software

Moving up a magnitude or two in terms of complexity is writing your own, stand-alone communications software, a double-clickable application that exists separate from any commercial program.

In this section, I'll teach you all about C and Pascal programming, and you'll learn the ins and outs of the Macintosh Toolbox. Then, I'll tackle the arcane problems of implementing file-transfer protocols and terminal emulation.

Just kidding.

In fact, no single book can teach you everything you need to know to write your own telecom program, but I'll acquaint you with the whys and hows.

First, why. There are a couple of big drawbacks to writing big scripts: You're operating under someone else's software, implementing what *you* think a telecom program should be within the framework of someone else's vision. If you decide that you want no menus, you're stuck. You want your program to play a QuickTime movie while you download a file? Sorry, that feature isn't supported. Worse still, if you want others to be able to use your program, they have to buy whatever program you built the scripts in before they can take advantage of them.

Now for the how: lots of education and hard work. Normally, it takes a nonprogrammer about two or three months to begin to learn how to program in C or Pascal, the most popular languages. After that, it takes another couple of months to learn how to program with the Macintosh Toolbox, the built-in set of routines that are used for drawing menus, windows, and everything else you associate with Macintosh software. Then you're ready for the *hard* part, learning how to write communications software. Even implementing the simplest file-transfer protocol is a test of programming skill.

If you want to write your own telecom program, one alternative to all this hard work is Visual Programming. A visual programming system (such as Serius's Serius Programmer) reduces programming to bare elements. Rather than writing code from scratch, you merely drag together Lego-like blocks of prewritten code and fill in a few blanks. It's a great solution in that you can have a simple, stand-alone (CTB-based) telecom application running in a day. Your application will be much larger in size than a comparable program written in C or Pascal, and it won't run nearly as fast, but if you want more control than scripting can give, a visual programming system such as Serius is unbeatable.

Modem Games

A depressing offshoot of the computer revolution that people now treat their computers as mere tools. Years ago, people had real, personal contact with their machines. You booted up and were welcomed with a generic system prompt. You'd write applications, hammer together utilities with the computer's built-in programming language, and print documents by sending them to a specific address in memory. Nowadays, you use your computer as a tool for word processing or number crunching.

So, too, with modems. More and more applications use modems in wonderful ways that have nothing to do with logging into BBSs and getting messages.

The true power of a modem is the way it connects people to other people. As usual, the game manufacturers were the first to jump on this concept and write programs that can allow several players with modems to play together in one competition. For example, Falcon (Figure 9–4) can be played interactively.

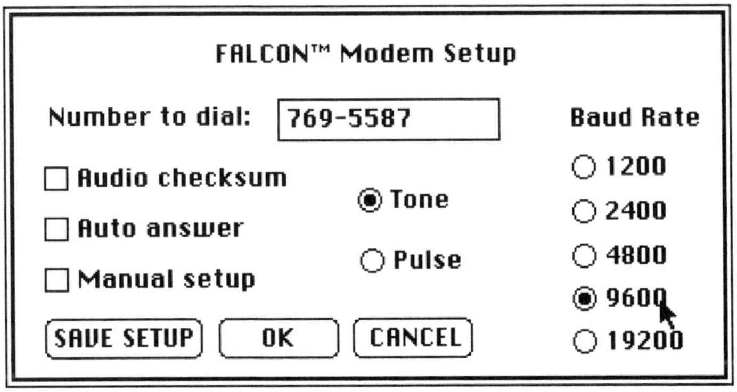

```
┌─────────────────────────────────────────────────┐
│  ┌───────────────────────────────────────────┐  │
│  │          FALCON™ Modem Setup              │  │
│  │                                           │  │
│  │  Number to dial: │ 769-5587 │   Baud Rate │  │
│  │                                           │  │
│  │  ☐ Audio checksum              ○ 1200     │  │
│  │                     ● Tone     ○ 2400     │  │
│  │  ☐ Auto answer                            │  │
│  │                     ○ Pulse    ○ 4800     │  │
│  │  ☐ Manual setup                ● 9600     │  │
│  │  ( SAVE SETUP ) ( OK ) (CANCEL) ○ 19200   │  │
│  └───────────────────────────────────────────┘  │
└─────────────────────────────────────────────────┘
```

Figure 9–4: Falcon allows multiple pilots to join in via modem

Once Falcon dials the phone and finds another copy of Falcon at the other end of the line, your dogfight arena features two planes: one piloted by you, one by your friend. Many games, from flight simulators and war games to poker and solitaire, support multiplayer modem action.

Bridging Networks

"No Mac is an island." The Macintosh makes the linking of computers, printers, and other hardware throughout an entire office a standard rather than an expensive, limited option. In this context, a modem is just another connection tool.

AppleTalk Remote Access, which comes with all portable Macs sold in the U.S. (it's also available separately for $199 from your local Apple dealer), is the niftiest and easiest implementation of remote access. Once you install it on any pair of Macs with modems, you can have one Mac call the other Mac, then use or copy its files by pointing and clicking. You can even get a file from a Mac in Athens, Greece, sent to the printer on your desktop in Athens, Georgia.

It's one of Apple's most elegant inventions, and it's simple to install and even easier to use. I set it up and tested it without cracking the manual; it was up and running in less than fifteen minutes.

Please don't take this as permission to skip the manual. I was making a point. I did, of course, read it from cover to cover (56 pages, lots of pictures) the next day.

For what it's worth, I always read manuals from cover to cover, even the ones that are unintelligible (which, unfortunately, is too many of them.)

I truly believe the old saying, RTFM (read the manual). Just pick up a copy of my magnum opus, *Dr. Macintosh, Second Edition*. You'll see it in there at least three or four times!

If that's not enough for you, Shiva's NetModem and NetSerial do the same job as AppleTalk Remote Access, and more! They perform two functions: They can make a nonnetworkable serial device (such as a label printer or a modem) available to everyone on your AppleTalk network, or a pair of them can link two remote AppleTalk networks. Once you're up and running, it's as if you had 2,000 miles of cable running between you and the remote location.

E-mail Gateways

CE Software's QuickMail, Microsoft Mail, and other packages give your office the equivalent of a slick, graphically oriented on-line service, using AppleTalk instead of modems to communicate. You can increase the usefulness of these systems a thousandfold with the use of *gateways*, electronic links that connect your network E-mail system to a larger on-line entity.

Gateways can link your office E-mail systems to other mail sites across the world, to CompuServe, the Internet, MCI Mail, AppleLink, common bulletin board systems, and even to fax machines! One relatively simple front end—such as QuickMail or Microsoft Mail— can, in theory, pull in your mail from every on-line entity on the planet. You can send an AppleLink to your industry contact within the same framework as your office mail system, without having to fire up a separate program for AppleLink access. All incoming mail and faxes are presented to you within the single, unified shell of your mail server!

If you have electronic mail on your office network, ask your network administrator about installing a gateway for on-line services you use to send and receive messages. Once you've tried it, you'll wonder how you ever did without it.

Controlling Macs Remotely

Seize complete control of another Macintosh anywhere in the world without leaving your chair!

Microcom's Carbon Copy Mac (Figure 9–5) and Farallon's Timbuktu Remote allow you to put on your desktop a window containing the desktop of *another Mac*.

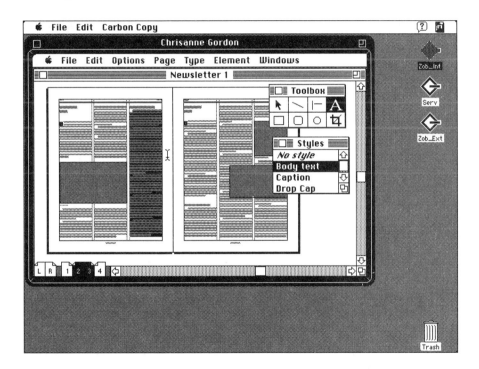

Figure 9–5: Carbon Copy Mac allows your Mac to control another Mac running PageMaker

The software can be a lot of fun. It's also good for solving someone else's problems from afar. Instead of trying to explain to a friend or coworker what to do, you can bring up the friend's (or coworker's) screen on your Mac and solve the problem *for* him or her. Furthermore, you can check on the progress of a job running on your office Mac from your own bed. All the number-crunching is going on in the remote Mac; *your* Mac is just updating its own screen to reflect what's going on at the office.

Parting Shots

Though you probably don't need to telecommunicate with another individual, run your own BBS, write scripts, play modem games, set up an E-mail gateway, or access your Mac from a remote location today, someday you might. That's when the fact that you once read this stuff will come in handy.

You'll probably find a place to use some of this info.

You'll thank us for this someday.

In the next (and final) chapter, you'll learn that if you take a few precautions, the well-publicized virus threat is nothing to worry about, plus a brief interlude about choosing a good password and keeping it safe and secure.

10

It's Nothing to Worry About, Really

Follow these few simple rules and you'll never be bothered by viruses or stolen passwords.

Hazards are involved in telecommunications, but don't allow them to interfere with the pleasure of using your Mac. Hazards are involved in everything in life—walking along a city street, eating dinner, hang-gliding over an alligator pit—but every danger has an effective countermeasure. If you know the countermeasures, you'll be almost 100 percent safe.

The game you just downloaded can come with a hidden bonus, a *virus* that can infect and cripple your Mac. Someone can snatch your secret CompuServe password and run up alarmingly high bills.

Unfortunately, these bugaboos have received more than their fair share of publicity over the years. Certain ill-informed persons in the major newsweeklies have been writing articles that serve to alarm computer users about the dangers of viruses and security breaches, rather than reassuring them about the solutions to these problems. Indeed, the risks are slim, especially if you know the countermeasures.

The title of this chapter was chosen for a good reason. If at any point in this chapter you start to panic, just look at the top of the page and repeat "It's nothing to worry about, really" until you feel better.

About Viruses

It's only prudent to begin with a discussion of the well-publicized software virus. A software virus works something like a biological virus does. Think of a human being with the flu. (It's a rough analogy, although dealing with a software virus is about as unpleasant.) One way or another, a virus manages to sneak its way into a host organism, infecting it. Once inside, the virus makes the host cells crank out jillions more viruses, each one identical to the original bug. These viruses then burst out of the host cell, where they infect more and more healthy cells, and the cycle repeats itself.

> On other kinds of computers, there's the additional threat of worms and Trojan horses.
>
> Worms are like viruses, only instead of replicating themselves after being installed in memory, they munch a path through your hard drive, destroying data as they move along.
>
> Trojan horses are programs that purport to be friendly little games or utilities or whatever, whose benign facades conceal a sinister purpose. While you play that arcade game, the program is secretly trashing all the files on your hard drive.
>
> Fortunately worms and Trojan horses haven't made any significant appearances in the Mac world. Thank heaven, because unlike most viruses, their function is to actively destroy data.

Meanwhile, the host organism (like the downtrodden flu sufferer) gets more and more sluggish; instead of applying its efforts to useful endeavors, most of its energies are used to combat the virus.

Software viruses are constructed by deviant offshoots of the programmer community. The legitimate members of that community have several technical terms for these people, of which only one is printable: loser.

The loser composes the virus code and then "hides" it inside an existing, benign piece of software destined to be widely distributed. Almost any program will do, but games are popular virus carriers; they tend to get passed around from user to user quite a bit. Finally, the loser uploads the newly infected program to a public BBS.

Now here you come, an innocent, trusting, peace-loving telecommunicator. You download the game, not knowing that it's been infected, and run it on your Mac.

Here's where the action begins. When the infected program is run, the virus code implanted inside it wakes up and installs itself inside your computer's memory, independent of the host program. That virus program remains inside your computer for the rest of your session, until you switch off your Mac and its memory is thereby erased. While in memory, the virus has one goal: to find *more* clean, uninfected programs, and infect them by making copies of itself and inserting the code inside the application.

One of the things that makes viruses so sinister is that once installed, they run as independent entities. You can quit the host program (the infected game or whatever), and even delete it from your hard drive, but that virus program runs continuously and infects other programs until you turn the machine off.

And just as every Mac program operates differently, every virus operates in its own distinct manner. Most viruses infect only applications, but some attack only your System file (as the System file's code is executed every time you start your Mac, it's an easy target) or your Finder. Some can also attach themselves to documents, and more still infect the invisible files (such as the Desktop files) that your Mac uses for its own housekeeping.

Viral Symptoms

Up to this point you have no idea that your computer has been infected. However, the virus can indeed have an effect on your Mac's speed. Computer viruses generally wind up slowing your machine down, because more and more of your Mac's time gets devoted to generating new copies of the virus. Worse, dozens of copies of the same virus can be wreaking havoc in your system all at once!

And you don't just take a performance hit. Viruses are usually tiny (generally taking up less than 5K on your hard drive), but as more copies are made and more programs become infected, those 5Ks keep on adding up until you discover that your 40Mb hard drive, which as far as you know contains just a 5Mb System Folder and 4Mb of applications and documents, has no free space left.

Finally, the viruses often have an effect that their loser designers didn't intend: They can cause good software to create system error after system error. When a virus copies itself into memory, it isn't polite about where it installs itself. If it sticks itself into a chunk of memory that your word processor needs, your word processor can bomb.

This is just a generic operational scenario. With some viruses, you don't even have to run an infected application for the virus to infect your system! The mere act of inserting an infected floppy infects your system.

The rest of this section contains nothing but encouraging information.

Encouraging Information

Your Mac can't become infected by a virus that was designed for a different type of computer. So folks who use PCs have to cope with over a *thousand* different kinds of viruses, but the Mac community has only about a dozen to deal with.

Actually, let's gloat on this a bit (we're Mac owners—we're good at gloating). The Mac is harder to program than a PC, which in this case is an advantage; the losers generally don't want to expend all the effort involved in writing a Mac virus.

A Viral Rogue's Gallery

Though new viruses appear every now and then (maybe several per year), four account for most Macintosh infections: Scores, nVIR, INIT29, and WDEF.

Scores is one of the first Macintosh viruses. According to legend, it was written by a disgruntled programmer, after being canned by his or her employer, a computer-game publisher. Scores was supposed to prevent the company's games (which were never released, as it turns out) from running properly. The most obvious indication that your Mac has been infected by this parasite is when you find that your Scrapbook file and Note Pad file have acquired generic document icons, as shown in Figure 10–1.

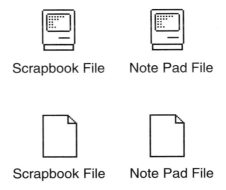

Figure 10–1: Scrapbook and Note Pad icons in their normal state (top) and after Scores infection (bottom)

One of the nasty aspects of nVIR is that it comes in two varieties: nVIR A and nVIR B. And if a disk has been infected by both, the two viruses can spawn new viruses containing parts of both varieties! It entertains as it infects: If you have MacinTalk (a software-based speech synthesizer that worked with System 6 and earlier versions) installed, nVIR occasionally causes your Mac to exclaim "don't panic!" when infected programs are run. If you don't have MacinTalk, your Mac just beeps.

Whereas the first two viruses are so widespread because they've been around for a long time, INIT29 is extremely virulent, spreading quickly. An infected Mac generally presents you with a message saying that your disk needs minor repairs, and asking if you want to repair it.

The WDEF virus is historic; it's regarded as the first virus specifically designed to avoid detection. WDEF infects the invisible Desktop file found on all disks and hard drives. The Desktop file is used by the System and so is opened the instant the disk is inserted (or mounted, in the case of a hard drive). WDEF is clever; as soon as you stick in a disk, the virus is installed and copied onto any other Desktop files it can find. On the bright side, as it only infects Desktop files, it's practically impossible to contract a WDEF infection from a file you download from a BBS.

There are a bunch more, of course, but again these four are the most popular. So to speak.

How to Eradicate a Virus

I've saved the best news for last: With a minimum of effort, you can configure your Mac so that any existing infections are completely eradicated and, moreover, your Mac is protected against further infection! At least it's safe from known Mac viruses. The known viruses contain snippets of distinctive code that sit conspicuously on your hard drive. Just as your word processor can search for a specific word in a document, a special virus-seeking program can search for, and remove, known viruses from your hard drive.

Several such search-and-destroy programs exist, but none can top Disinfectant, a freeware program written by John Norstad of Northwestern University.

Disinfectant (available from must bulletin boards, on-line services, and user groups) is an example of everything that's good and decent in the Macintosh community. When viruses first began to appear, many different programs were written and sold or given away to combat them. When Disinfectant came along, the entire Macintosh community decided to band together and support this one free, commercial-quality program. No one makes a dime from Disinfectant; the program exists purely for the good of the community. Commercial virus-killing programs are available—more on them later on—but they cost money and won't protect you a lot better than Disinfectant.

Disinfectant was designed for simplicity. You run the program and click on the Disinfect button, shown in Figure 10–2. While you go make yourself a sandwich, the program goes off to battle.

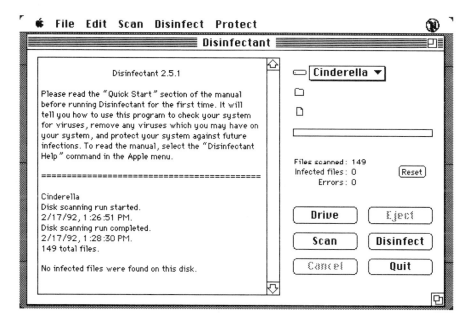

Figure 10–2: Disinfectant's operational window

Disinfectant then examines every file on every mounted volume for viruses. If your hard drive is clean, you see the screen shown in Figure 10–3.

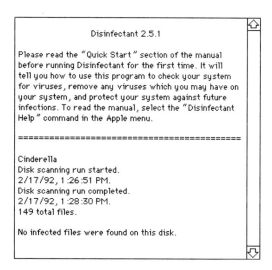

Figure 10–3: A clean bill of health

If Disinfectant comes across a virus, however, you get a message like the one in Figure 10–4:

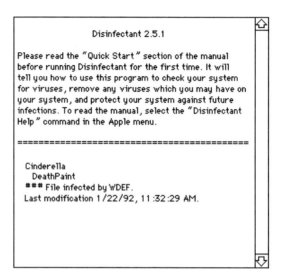

Disinfectant 2.5.1

Please read the "Quick Start" section of the manual before running Disinfectant for the first time. It will tell you how to use this program to check your system for viruses, remove any viruses which you may have on your system, and protect your system against future infections. To read the manual, select the "Disinfectant Help" command in the Apple menu.

===

Cinderella
  DeathPaint
File infected by WDEF.
Last modification 1/22/92, 11:32:29 AM.

Figure 10–4: Disinfectant found an infection

Disinfectant then removes the virus from the infected file (in this case, DeathPaint). Disinfectant is always as good as its word; if it tells you it's found no viruses on your drives or that it's found and removed them, you can be sure that your drive is clean—just about (see the next section).

For best results, get into the habit of regularly scanning for viruses. If you run your virus-eradicator once a week or so, you can stop an infection before it affects your whole hard drive.

The Catch

There's a catch. A program like Disinfectant is trained to search for specific patterns of data on your hard disk—patterns known to represent malignant viruses. Unfortunately, the losers who write viruses keep writing newer viruses, with which your current version of Disinfectant may not be familiar. Remember, Disinfectant has to know about a particular strain of virus for it to be recognized. So if I were to write a new virus on May 28, 1993, your copy of Disinfectant, released on February 8, 1993, wouldn't give it a second glance.

Still, that's no reason to worry. As soon as you hear about a new virus—on line, in a magazine, in a user group newsletter, or wherever—get a new, updated version of Disinfectant. Information about new viruses travels to Disinfectant author John Norstad much faster than the viruses themselves can spread.

If you want to make sure your drive doesn't become infected in the first place, you can either take a defensive posture and try to avoid any exposure to any viruses, or an offensive posture and resign yourself to the fact that viruses *will* find your system eventually, but try to render them impotent before they infect.

Defense: Avoiding Hotbeds of Viral Activity

Viruses can be everywhere, theoretically, but certain environments and activities enhance your chances of contracting a virus. Most viruses are found on bulletin boards, in public computing areas, and on networks.

Bulletin Boards   If you're a loser and you want your new virus to be exposed to as many innocent users as possible, attaching the virus to a popular shareware program and uploading it to a BBS or commercial on-line service is a good plan. Home users shouldn't worry about the software you download, though; almost all services (public BBSs and commercial on-line services) "quarantine" all newly uploaded software in a special file area. The system operators screen these programs for viruses before releasing them into the general file areas. On some BBSs, you can download these new files, but they're always clearly labeled as *untested*. If the untested label worries you even a little, wait a few days for the sysop to test the program in question.

Public Computing Areas   Most viruses are passed from disk to disk rather than on line, so it follows that any spot where people insert diskettes into a computer is going to be a hotbed of viral activity. In places like desktop publishing service bureaus (where dozens of people bring diskettes with documents to be printed) and college computing laboratories (where students insert and eject disks all day long), use caution. Push open the write-protect tab on your diskette (as shown in Figure 10–5) before sticking it in the drive; this makes it impossible for any data (viruses included) to be written onto it.

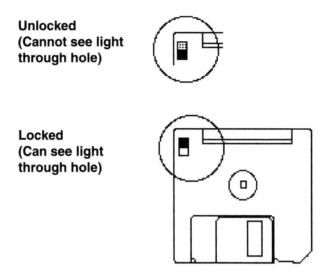

**Unlocked
(Cannot see light
through hole)**

**Locked
(Can see light
through hole)**

Figure 10–5: Lock your disks before inserting them into a Mac that's in a public place

If this isn't feasible (you have data of your own you want to put on the disk, say), then bring in a copy of Disinfectant and scan that hard drive before inserting your floppy.

Networks   Unfortunately, the network that shares files can also share viruses. If your Macintosh network shares only printers, then there's nothing to worry about. If your network uses file servers (volumes on a remote computer that you can mount on your desktop as if they were built into your own Macintosh), or you use System 7's built-in file sharing feature, you can run into some virus trouble. Imagine Bob and Sally on a network, both using the office file server. If Sally inserts an infected disk in her machine, the virus will eventually infect both her internal hard drive and the file server, since the file server is just another volume, and viruses will try to infect every volume it can find. Bob has the file server's volume mounted on his desktop, too, so the viral contamination can infect his hard drive through the remote volume.

This scenario is a nightmare for the people who run large networks. There can be a hundred Macs on the net, and if even *one* Mac becomes infected, the entire network eventually slows down to a crawl.

Unfortunately, if you're on a network, it's almost certain that your network administrator will demand that you keep your office Mac connected, so in this case the only solution is to go on the offense.

Offense: Preventing Infection Before It Happens

If you're worried about viruses running amok in your Mac's memory, you need special software in memory, too, searching for viral activity.

Disinfectant comes with a special Protection INIT that does exactly that. When installed, this INIT looks for the presence of known viruses in your computer's memory. If you attempt to launch an infected application, the INIT immediately quits the application and presents you with an alert, as shown in Figure 10–6.

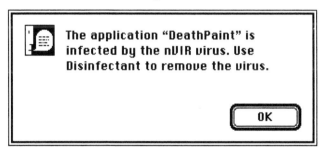

The application "DeathPaint" is infected by the nVIR virus. Use Disinfectant to remove the virus.

OK

Figure 10–6: Disinfectant's Protection INIT alerts you as soon as you try to launch an infected application

It's *not* "OK," of course, but click the OK button anyway. Now run the Disinfectant application to remove the virus from DeathPaint. Disinfectant's Protection INIT also prevents the virus from spreading to other disks. Your files are safe.

If you're still worried, you need SAM (Symantec Anti-Virus for Macintosh). With the SAM Control Panel installed, SAM scans *every* disk you stick inside your Mac for viruses before your Mac knows that the disk is there. If the disk is clean, SAM hands it to your Mac. If it isn't, the disk is immediately ejected; viruses have no chance of infecting your Mac because infected disks never get mounted! Devious!

Of course, the Disinfectant Protection INIT and the SAM Control Panel have the same Achilles' heel as other virus-scanning programs: They have to know specifically what viruses to scan for. Though SAM has an expert mode that can detect suspicious activity from a virus it knows nothing about, the number of false alarms you receive in this mode almost negates its worth.

Similar to SAM's expert mode is Gatekeeper. Like Disinfectant, it's free—a Control Panel written by Chris Johnson for the good of the community. Rather than looking for known viruses, Gatekeeper looks for any activity that seems suspicious, as in SAM's expert mode. Most viruses work in similar ways: by modifying existing code, installing new resources inside files, and so forth. Whenever the Gatekeeper Control Panel sees a program engaged in suspicious activities, it "vetoes" the attempt, blocks the action, and snitches on the naughty program, as shown in Figure 10–7.

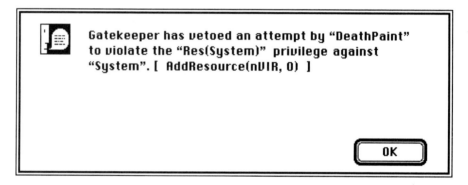

Figure 10–7: Gatekeeper's veto alert

In this example, Gatekeeper suspects that DeathPaint is an infected program because it attempted to add a new resource to the System file, a popular activity for viruses. In addition to the alert, Gatekeeper maintains a log of all suspicious activity it's ever encountered.

But some nonviral applications perform legitimate actions that are on Gatekeeper's "hit list." Font/DA Mover, for instance, also installs resources into the System file. They're nonviral resources known as fonts and desk accessories—but Gatekeeper still blocks the action. To prevent false alarms, Gatekeeper allows you to create a list of excepted applications, as shown in Figure 10–8.

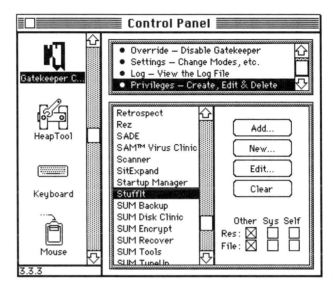

Figure 10–8: The Gatekeeper Control Panel lets you create an exceptions list

Here, for instance, you give permission to the decompression program StuffIt to fiddle with external files and resources without Gatekeeper's interference.

Gatekeeper is invaluable when teamed with a virus-hunter INIT like Disinfectant's. The one danger of Gatekeeper (or SAM in its expert mode) is that too many false alarms may cause you to trash the program after a few days.

If the freeware is so good, why buy a commercial virus-eradicator like SAM (Symantec Anti-Virus for Macintosh) or its main competition, Virex (from Microcom)? One of the advantages of the commercial programs is that you can update the program yourself without having to wait for a new version to be released. Or, for a small fee, you can have updates sent to you automatically whenever a new virus appears on the scene.

SAM and Virex both allow you to type in a search string (the pattern of data that identifies the newly discovered virus) to update your software so it can recognize new viruses. These search strings are easy to come by—Symantec posts them on line, usually within days after a new virus is discovered, and it also has a telephone hot-line you can call to learn the latest search strings.

Another advantage of the commercial offerings is that they are a complete solution—both SAM and Virex include an application that lets you scan for and eradicate viruses *plus* a Control Panel to keep your Mac safe from infection without any intervention on your part.

Electronic Break-ins

Some people are apprehensive about having a modem connected to their computers. Doesn't that mean a hacker, armed only with your home phone number, can call in from across the country to plunder the files on your hard drive?

Actually, you shouldn't use the term *hacker* in this context. A hacker is a true software artist, one who writes software solely because he or she enjoys the programming art. Someone who writes viruses and breaks into computer systems should be properly referred to as *moron* or *loser*.

Many of the popular newsweeklies improperly identify computer criminals as hackers. When this happens, I'm always sorely tempted to send them an angry letter and a dead fish.

Such an attack is extremely unlikely to happen. No one can break into your system unless you leave the modem on, leave the computer on, leave a BBS program running, and set up an account for the miscreant, complete with full access to your entire hard drive, beforehand.

If you're using AppleTalk Remote Access (ARA), an electronic break-in is slightly more likely, if a loser knows your modem's phone number and manages to guess your password. If this bothers you in the least, be sure to use ARA's callback feature, which verifies your identity by automatically dialing a predetermined phone number—where you and your modem are—before allowing access.

In any event, the chances are slim that anyone *wants* to break into your Mac.

Password Security

A password is a computer's sole means of determining whether you are exactly who you say you are.

If you're logging onto a simple, free public BBS, it's a trivial problem. But when you start using commercial services such as CompuServe or America Online, the stakes go up. When an evening of spirited on-line activity can result in a three-figure bill, the importance of a secure password is evident.

Even on free BBSs, though, the idea of someone else logging in under your name should make your flesh crawl. A stranger reading mail intended for your eyes only? Someone sending public mail under your name? Exploiting the extra privileges you've earned as a valued BBS user?

Good, now you're all riled up. Let's start with the basics.

How to Protect Your Password

Here are some guidelines for keeping your passwords safe and secure.

Don't write down your password *anywhere*. Memorize it! No kidding, people actually scribble down their password on a piece of paper and leave it right in their desks! I've even seen some terminals with passwords written on them!

Don't share your password with *anyone*—not your friends, not your spouse, not your mother. A secret password becomes immediately and irrevocably tainted the instant you share it with someone else. The other person might write it down somewhere where total strangers can see it. Resist the temptation to share, no matter how much you trust or love the other person.

Use a different password on every system. On most of the larger services, passwords are encrypted so that the system managers have no idea what they are, but most of the public BBS programs lack that feature. If a sysop is unscrupulous, he or she may take the password you use on his or her system and use it to try to get into some of the other systems you use!

Change your passwords regularly—once every month or two. This helps to minimize the damage that can occur if a moron or loser manages to learn your password; then, if someone else is using your account without your knowledge, it's for three or four weeks at most.

Change your password the *instant* you think it may have been compromised. If you suspect that someone was looking over your shoulder as you logged onto CompuServe, immediately change your password. Remember, evildoers need only a few hours to run up hundreds of dollars in on-line charges.

Finding a Bulletproof Password

Now that you know how to protect a password, let's talk about how to select one. The big weakness of passwords is that to be effective, they have to be memorized. Therefore, a lot of people choose passwords they know already, such as their own names, the names of their spouses and children, birthdays, anniversaries, and the like.

Avoid these passwords like the plague; people who have *any* idea of who you are can guess your password with a minimum of trial and error. Similarly, if everyone knows you're an avid Beatles fan, a password like LENNON will be a miscreant's fourth or fifth try.

The best of all passwords is a random string of letters and digits, such as 8skdl–12, but this can be difficult to memorize. You want to find a happy medium between easy-to-memorize (your name) and easy-to-forget (random passwords). A lot of the trivial information stuck in your brain makes good fodder for passwords. The license number of your grandmother's car, the name of a memorable grade-school teacher, the capital of North Dakota—they're all bits of information that you won't forget but no one else would ever connect with you. This simple solution works for most of your password needs.

I have about forty different accounts on various systems, each with a unique password that is changed monthly. Even if you use only eight or nine passwords, you may need a system to keep all your passwords straight. A famous dodge is the use of a key book—a novel or reference that acts as a source of new passwords. For some time, Andy used *The Book of Lists* in this way; if he forgot a password, he'd remember that it had something to do with blues singers, and after rereading the relevant article and making a few guesses, BLIND-LEMON would let him right in.

One of the best systems is to memorize one ridiculously long, random password (such as 82IDJD92839DKI209), and use that password to encrypt a file containing all of your system passwords. Many commercial programs such as StuffIt (or shareware programs, such as MacDES) can take a standard file generated by your word processor and turn it into psychedelic spaghetti. If someone attempts to read the file without entering a special password, the document appears to contain nothing but gibberish characters. It's a perfectly safe way to record passwords; when I lose one, I can now use that huge password to unscramble my master list and read off the forgotten password.

These are just suggestions, of course. The best password scheme, like the best diet plan, is the one you like enough to stick with for the duration.

Password Scams

Finally, I'd like to fill you in on one of the oldest scams in the book. You've logged onto your on-line service. You've been working solidly for a half an hour when your terminal burps and displays a message like this:

```
Connection to host lost.   Please log in again.
Password:_
```

Beware! It's possible that this message isn't being generated by the on-line service, but by some vile miscreant trying to swipe your password! The miscreant has written a program that displays that message on your screen, stashes your password to a special file, then returns you to the on-line service. Later, he or she logs back on and picks up a file containing the hundreds of account names and passwords the fake logon program managed to collect.

If you're ever asked for your password a second time for any reason, your best bet is to hang up your modem and log in all over again. If it was a genuine error, then you've lost nothing; if it was a scam, you've protected your password!

Parting Shots

If you heed a few precautions and use common sense, you'll never experience viral infection, nor will your computer ever be broken into.

At the least, download a copy of Disinfectant or Gatekeeper, or both. They're free, so you have nothing to lose but a few minutes of downloading time. It's well worth it for the peace of mind they provide. If you want more peace of mind, buy SAM or Virex.

I've used SAM since the day it was introduced, and I'm happy to report that my system has never become infected. SAM has indeed alerted me to the presence of an infected disk or file on several occasions, but I've never had a raging infection.

Finally, be sure to protect your passwords. Failing to do so could have dire consequences for your reputation and your wallet.

See You On Line

Let me know how you're doing. Please, feel free to send me a note via electronic mail the next time you log on. You'll find me at 76004,2076 on CompuServe, LEVITUS on America Online, MCI Mail, and AppleLink, and R.LEVITUS on GEnie.

Glossary

Appendix A

archive A special file format that applications and files are generally transformed into before they're uploaded to an on-line service. A special archiving program can take multiple files—an application and its documentation files—and combine them into one file so all the program's components can be downloaded together. This combined file is then compressed to make it smaller. The archived file, after downloading, must be restored with a compatible dearchiver. The most popular archive formats are Aladdin Systems StuffIt (signified by a .SIT at the end of the file name) and Bill Goodman's shareware program Compact Pro (formerly known as Compactor; signified by .CPT at the end of the file name). Some archived files are self-extracting (signified by .SEA at the end of the file name), which means they extract automatically when you double-click on them, so no dearchiving software is necessary. Most archiving programs can create self-extracting archives.

ASCII American Standard Code for Information Interchange. The international standard for assigning numbers to characters; for example, capital A is 65 and a space is 32.

asynchronous communication Means of sending data from one device to another. *Asynchronous* means that characters are not sent at a constant rate; pauses of any length can occur between characters.

AT Command Set Standard set of commands (developed by Hayes and often referred to as the Hayes Command Set) for controlling the operation of a modem. Called the AT set because with few exceptions all commands begin with the letters AT (attention!).

autoanswer Refers to either a feature or a mode of operation of a modem. A modem with autoanswer can automatically answer the phone when a call comes in. Usually, you turn this feature on with the command **ATS0=1** or off with the command **ATS0=0**.

autoredial A feature in both modems and communications software that allows a busy number to be redialed automatically until a connection is made.

batch A special mode of downloading or uploading where a list of several files can be sent one after the other without any intervention on the part of the user.

baud/baud rate The speed of transmitted data; the rate at which discrete signals leave the modem, not taking into account stop and parity bits. Baud is short for *bits audible*. Commonly, but incorrectly, used to denote modem speed. For the correct term, see *bps*.

BBS Bulletin board service or system. BBS can refer to any service you can access by modem, but usually means a small, local public system as opposed to a large commercial service.

Bell 212A An old standard for communications at 1200 bps. Almost all modems have Bell 212A compatibility.

binary System by which numbers can be represented as 1s and 0s. Also, in Mac telecommunications, refers to a transmitted file that is not a text file and not in Macintosh format; for example, an application for MS-DOS computers.

bit A single binary digit, either an on or an off signal. All data travels through your modem as bits of information.

bits per second See *bps*.

block A piece of data being transmitted from one place to another. When you download a file, the file is split into blocks of identical size and transmitted one at a time. The size of the blocks (how much data they contain) varies depending on which file-transfer protocol you use.

board Short for BBS.

bps Bits per second. Correct term to denote how fast two modems are communicating. See also *baud* and *cps*.

bulletin board See *BBS*.

byte Eight bits of information, representing a single number or character.

carriage return The Return key on your keyboard, which usually brings the cursor to a new line. ASCII code 13. Sometimes shortened to CR.

carrier The noise your modem makes across the phone line as it's communicating with another modem. A message such as *NO CARRIER* or *CARRIER LOST* from your modem or a telecom program that means the modem can no longer sense the presence of another modem on the line.

CCITT The international organization (part of the United Nations) that develops and defines the standards used by modems and other phone equipment. CCITT stands for International Telephone and Telegraph Consultative Committee (translated from the French). Any modem standard that begins with V. (as in V.42) is a CCITT standard.

character A transmitted entity (a letter, number, or symbol) that represents real data, as opposed to numbers being transmitted as part of an error-checking scheme or info transmitted as part of the communications protocol. See also *cps*.

chat mode Using a special area on a BBS or other on-line service to communicate interactively with another user. In chat mode, communication is usually one-on-one. See also *conferencing*.

checksum A number that describes data that's just been sent. The receiving computer calculates a checksum for the info it has received and compares it with the checksum provided by the sending computer. If they're not identical, an error occurred in transmission.

commercial Refers to software or to on-line services that you pay for. Compare to *BBS, freeware, shareware*.

communications parameters A group of settings that determines how data is transmitted and received. Parameters usually include bps rate, data bits, stop bits, and parity settings.

Communications Toolbox The Mac's special set of built-in routines for establishing connections, emulating terminals, and transferring files. The toolbox is built into all versions of System software later than 7.0, and it is available as a system extension for earlier versions. See also Appendix C, The Macintosh Communications Toolbox.

communications tools Drop-in modules for the Communications Toolbox that add extra features to all programs built upon the toolbox. Three classes of tools exist: connection, terminal, and file transfer. See also Appendix C, The Macintosh Communications Toolbox.

compiler A feature of a telecom program's scripting language that translates scripts into faster, more efficient machine code.

conferencing Using a special area on a BBS or other on-line service where several users at a time can discuss a subject live. In conference mode, what you type can instantly be seen by all other users in the conference area. See also *chat mode*.

connection An open line of communication between two computers.

control key A special key that sends a character when you use it with another key on the keyboard. Ctrl–C means "hold down the Control key and press C. On older Macs that don't have a Control key, another key stands in, typically Option.

cps Characters per second. Refers to the rate at which *actual data* (characters you've typed, the numbers that make up a file being downloaded or uploaded) are transmitted. Looking at cps or *throughput* of a transmission is more valuable than the simple bps rate, as CPS tells you how much speed was gained with a data-compression protocol (like V.42bis) or how much was lost either to an inefficient protocol or a noisy phone line. Multiply CPS by ten to get an approximate bps rate. If the throughput of a V.42bis download was 1380 cps, it means that the data compression gave you the speed of a 13,800 bps modem.

CRC Cyclical redundancy checking. An error-checking technique used in many file-transfer and modem hardware protocols, most notably the XMODEM CRC file-transfer protocol.

Ctrl key See *Control key.*

CTS Clear to send. A hardware signal between computer and modem that signals that one of the two is ready to receive data from the other.

cursor The place on the screen, usually represented by a solid or flashing block or underline character, where the next thing you type will appear.

data bits The number of bits that make up each character of data. As part of the communications parameters, it's generally set to 7 or 8 (8 is more popular). Sometimes referred to as *word length.*

DCE Data communications equipment. Technical term for a modem, most accurately the modem that establishes a communications link.

dedicated phone line A phone line that's used for telecommunications exclusively, as opposed to one that's used for voice and data.

default A setting that a modem, telecom program, or BBS chooses for you until you change it yourself.

direct-connect A connection between two computers that's made without the use of modems or telephone lines, usually by cabling one machine's serial port to the other's.

disk capture In a communications program, refers to saving all data into a text file as it comes in.

doors Special areas of a BBS where you leave the BBS and temporarily use a different program. Typically, doors are games, databases, and specialized mail readers.

download To have data transmitted from the on-line service to your Macintosh. Can refer to all data (messages, listings, and so on), but usually refers to files. Can also be used as a noun ("Get this file, it's a good download").

DTE Data terminal equipment. A technical term that usually refers to your computer.

DTR Data terminal ready. A hardware signal generated by a computer or a modem that says it's ready to communicate.

dumb terminal Keyboard and monitor with no processor of their own. Used for accessing mainframe and minicomputers. Macintosh telecommunications software can often emulate dumb terminals, making it possible to log onto a mainframe or mini from your Macintosh instead of a dumb terminal.

echo A message base shared with several BBSs across the country. Also short for *Local Echo*.

E-mail Electronic mail. Can refer to any message you send to someone else via a modem, but usually means a private message that can be read only by the sender and the receiver.

error checking   Any scheme by which transmitted data is verified at either the sending or receiving end.

escape   A special keyboard character that's often used to terminate an activity or back up. On older Macs that lack an Escape key, you can usually use the tilde key (~).

external modem   A modem that exists as a separate component and connects to your Mac via a serial port. Compare with *internal modem*.

file-transfer protocol   A scheme for breaking up a file into efficient blocks that can be transmitted from one computer to another and reassembled at the other end. See also *FTP*.

flow control   A scheme that stops and starts the flow of data as necessary. For instance, it can prevent data from being transmitted when the receiving modem isn't ready for it.

forum   An area on an on-line service dedicated to a special interest group.

freeware   Software that may be freely copied for personal use.

FTP   A file transfer protocol used largely on UNIX systems. The term FTP is also used on the Internet to designate special sites offering software for downloading (as in *ftp.apple.com*).

full-duplex   A communications mode where data can flow in both directions simultaneously.

gateway   A link between one on-line service and another. For example, an America Online or CompuServe user can send mail to someone on the Internet (and vice versa) by means of a gateway.

half-duplex   A communications mode in which data can flow in both directions, but only one direction at a time. Half-duplex usually involves turning on Local Echo so you can see what you're typing.

handshaking   Scheme by which two devices synchronize their operations so communication can take place.

hardware-handshaking cable   A special modem cable wired for hardware handshaking.

Hayes Command Set   See *AT Command Set*.

Hayes-compatible   Denotes a modem that uses the Hayes or AT command set (but doesn't necessarily come from Hayes Microcomputer Products). Almost all modems are Hayes-compatible.

host mode   A special feature in some communications programs that turns your computer into a miniature BBS and allows other people to exchange messages and files.

host system   The computer you dial into and connect to.

HST   High-speed technology. Proprietary communications protocol of USRobotics.

initialization string   A string of AT commands a telecom program gives to your modem every time you launch the application. You use an initialization string to set certain modem features (echo, maximum transmission speed, turning off the speaker) that you'd normally use only with this specific program.

installer   A special program that's used to install certain applications and perform upgrades to System software.

internal modem   A modem that installs inside your Mac, mounted on an expansion card.

Internet   An international network connecting almost every computer system on the planet to every other system, including most commercial services.

K   Short for kilobyte; 1024 bytes of data.

Kermit   A file-transfer protocol used chiefly on mainframe computers.

keyboard buffer   A feature of telecom software where what you type goes into a one-line editing window and is sent to the modem only when you press the Return key. Until you press Return, you can edit the line using the mouse and other Mac features such as cut, copy, and paste.

LAPM   Link access procedure for modems. An error-checking protocol that is part of V.42.

leased line   A special kind of phone line that maintains a direct link between one computer and another.

library   An area on an on-line service where files are available for downloading.

line editor   A primitive word processor that lets you work on only one line of text at a time. Once you go to the next line, it's difficult to make changes to a previous line; you have to type the whole line again. Most BBSs and on-line services provide a line editor for composing messages.

line noise   The background static you hear on phone lines. Major line noise can make communications difficult if not impossible, causing random bursts of nonsense characters to pour into your terminal window.

Local Echo   Feature in telecom software and modems that automatically sends whatever you type to the terminal window as well as to the service you're connected to. Turn Local Echo on if you're communicating at half-duplex or you are directly connected to another computer via a serial cable.

logging off   The procedure for terminating your on-line session and disconnecting the phone call.

logging on   After your modem has connected to an on-line service, the procedure by which the service grants you access to the service. Usually involves typing in your name and password.

MacBinary   A scheme by which the two forks of a Macintosh file are combined into one when it's uploaded to a non-Macintosh computer, and separated again when downloaded by another Mac.

macro   A simple (usually one-line) series of commands that your telecom software can attach to a single button or keystroke. See also *Script*.

mainframe   A large computer usually found in colleges and corporations. Also the computer running most large commercial on-line services.

MNP   Microcom networking protocol. Microcom's standard for error checking. Levels 1 to 4 are in the public domain and built into many modems as part of V.42. Levels 5 and above include data compression and are available only in Microcom modems.

modem   The device that takes the data from your computer, transmogrifies it into noise, and sends it across the phone line. Likewise, it takes whatever noise is sent to it, transmogrifies it to data, and sends it to your Mac. Short for modulator/demodulator.

modem driver   In some telecom programs, a special file that prepares the program for a specific modem.

multiuser   Type of on-line service that can accommodate many users on the service simultaneously.

null modem   A special cable or adapter that allows two computers to be directly connected to each other with serial cables instead of modems.

NVRAM   Nonvolatile RAM. A special kind of memory in most modems that maintains your modem settings when you turn the modem off. You can store settings to NVRAM by using the command **AT&W**.

offhook   The modem status equivalent to having the phone's receiver off the hook (but not necessarily being connected to an on-line service).

offline   Not connected to another system.

onhook   The modem status equivalent to the phone's receiver being on the hook.

on line   Having an active link to another system.

on-line service   Denotes any other computer you connect to with your modem. Sometimes used to refer specifically to commercial services as opposed to free, public BBSs.

originate mode   Modem status in which the modem is the originator of the phone call.

packet   A chunk of data comprising a part of a transmitted file with some error-checking and file-transfer protocol data. Similar to a *block* but more specific.

parity   A rudimentary method of error checking. After sending some data, the sending computer sends a parity bit, which indicates whether an even or odd number of binary 1s were transmitted. Supplanted by more modern schemes, parity these days just means even or odd, a setting in your communications parameters.

password   A special word that, theoretically, only you know. An online service uses a password to confirm your identity when you log on.

post   To leave a message for public consumption. Sometimes used as a noun: "I read your post yesterday."

protocol   A standard set up for certain procedures, as in handshaking protocols, file-transfer protocols, error-checking protocols, and so on.

QuickB, B+   Proprietary file-transfer protocols used by CompuServe.

round-robin dialing   Special dialing mode in some telecom software. A list of on-line services is dialed one at a time, until connections have been made with each of them.

RS-232   International standard for serial communications.

RS-422   Type of serial ports on the Macintosh, basically RS-232 with a few enhancements.

script   A list of instructions you can write and have a telecom program follow. Many telecom programs include scripting capabilities. A script can do simple tasks (automatically log onto a service for you) as well as complex tasks (serve as a graphical front end to an on-line service or turn your Mac into a BBS of its own). A script is more versatile than a *macro*.

serial communications   Method of transmitting data from one device to another, where all bits of data are sent one at a time, single file.

serial port   One of several of your Mac's connectors that support serial communications. On most Macs this is either the modem or the printer port, both of which use the RS-422 standard. You can also add more serial ports by buying an expansion card.

Shareware   Try-before-you-buy software. If you use a shareware program for longer than the stated evaluation period, you're honor-bound to register your copy by sending the developer a check.

start/stop bit   The communications parameter, usually set to either 1 (by far the most popular), 1.5, or 2, that defines how one machine signals that the flow of data is about to begin or end.

sysop   Short for system operator. The person who runs a BBS and has complete power over it and those who use it.

terminal   Any device used to read and write on-line information. As opposed to a modem, which takes information and moves it someplace else.

terminal emulation   A feature of telecom software that allows your computer to perform like a dumb terminal. The most popular terminal emulation is VT100/VT102.

terminal window   In a telecom program, the window in which info you type gets sent to the modem, and in which the info that's received is displayed. Only what's typed into the terminal window is transmitted.

throughput A speed rating that reflects how fast data was sent or received, not taking into account overhead such as communications data, information sent as part of a file-transfer protocol, and so on. Usually given in *cps* (characters per second).

TTY Short for teletype. The simplest form of terminal emulation.

upload To transmit a file from your Mac to an on-line service.

V.22 The CCITT standard for 1200 bps communications.

V.22bis The CCITT standard for 2400 bps communications. Compatible with Bell 212A.

V.32 The CCITT standard for 4800 and 9600 bps communications.

V.32bis An improvement to V.32 that adds 7200, 12,000, and 14,400 bps speeds.

V.42 The CCITT standard for error-checking modems that includes LAPM and MNP error control.

V.42bis An extension of V.42 that adds on-the-fly data compression and uncompression.

VT100/VT102 The most widely used form of terminal emulation.

window Part of a Mac screen, or a block of data transmitted with a file-transfer protocol.

word length See *data bits*.

word-wrapping On some on-line text editors, the ability to automatically put a word on a new line if it doesn't fit on the line you're currently typing in.

XMODEM File transfer protocol. Also known as XMODEM checksum. One of the most widely supported (but not most widely used). Alternative versions are called XMODEM CRC and XMODEM 1K.

XON/XOFF   A scheme of software flow control (as opposed to hardware flow control) where two ASCII characters signal when the flow of data should be paused and resumed.

YMODEM   File transfer protocol. An improvement over basic XMODEM, faster because it sends eight times as much data before pausing to check if the data was sent properly. A special version, YMODEM-G, is better for use with error-checking modems.

ZMODEM   File transfer protocol. Currently runs the fastest and offers the most features.

The AT
Command Set

Appendix B

This appendix summarizes all the commands your modem understands. Its purpose is to give you a good reference. When you need to figure out why you can't get error checking to work on your modem, for instance, you can skim through this list and find the command you need.

All of the most useful and popular commands—dialing, answering phone calls, setting parameters—are the same for all modems. Less common commands can be different for different modem brands, however. You may find one or two commands here that don't work with your modem. Remember to use your modem's manual as your primary reference, and treat this appendix as a *companion* to your modem's manual—not a replacement. Your manual will contain a detailed list of all the AT commands that work specifically with your modem.

This appendix has two lists of commands: the basic command set and the extended command set.

Basic Command Set

The basic command set controls day-to-day modem use. Nearly all modems, from the cheapest to the most complex, support most of these commands.

> When you see a lowercase italic *n*, it is a placeholder for a numeral. For example, S*n* means you type an S followed by a numeral. Also, the character 0 is always the number zero, and not capital O, except in the ATO commands.

+++   **Escape**   When you're on line, type three plus signs in rapid succession, then type nothing for a second or two, to switch the modem from on-line mode to command mode. On most modems, your link to the remote system remains active and you can switch back to on-line mode by entering **ATC** or **ATO** at any time. A few modems hang up before entering command mode, though, so beware. Usually you can enter a command to modify this behavior; check your modem manual.

A/   **Repeat last command**   The last command given to the modem is executed again. Useful for manually redialing a phone number.

A>   **Repeat last command continuously**   The last command given to the modem is executed over and over again until you hit any key. Dialing commands are repeated a maximum of ten times (as mandated by a Canadian telecommunications law).

(any key)   **Cancel**   Pressing any key stops whatever the
                  modem's busy doing at the moment. If it's dial-
                  ing the phone, it stops and goes back to com-
                  mand mode. If it's repeating a command, it stops
                  repeating.

AT   **Attention**   Lets the modem know that what
                  follows is a command to be carried out and not
                  data to be transmitted. With the exception of the
                  four commands already listed, all modem com-
                  mands must begin with **AT**. You can concatenate
                  many AT commands in one line. For instance, the
                  command **ATM0E1&K0DT 555-1827** turns off
                  the modem speaker, enables Local Echo mode,
                  disables all error-checking modes, and dials the
                  phone. The command is executed only when you
                  press Return at the end of the line.

> All of the following commands begin with AT. You can concatenate
> commands by using **AT** only at the beginning of a line.

A   **Answer**   Forces the modem to go off hook and
                  try to answer whatever's going on in the phone
                  line at the time. You use the A command when
                  you're talking on the phone with someone who
                  wants to send a file to you. You both turn on your
                  telecom programs, your friend enters **ATD**, you
                  enter **ATA**, and that phone call switches from
                  two people talking to two computers communi-
                  cating. You can also use this command to have
                  your modem answer a phone while it's ringing.
                  Don't confuse this command with **ATS0=1**,
                  which tells your modem to answer the phone
                  automatically whenever it rings.

B*n*   **High-speed modulation**   The number *n* determines what handshaking method the modem uses when establishing a connection with another modem. The number varies from one manufacturer to another. For instance, on a USRobotics Courier HST, **ATB0** (the default) allows the modem to make connections using the V.32 protocol. **ATB1** forces the modem to establish connections using its proprietary HST protocol *only*; if the modem you're trying to connect to is *not* an HST, no connection is made.

C*n*   **Transmitter enabled/disabled**   The transmitter is that part of the modem that transmits a carrier signal across the phone line, which allows it to transmit data. If you enter **ATC0**, this transmitter is disabled and the modem can only receive data. The default is **ATC1**, which allows the modem to both transmit and receive. There are some brands of modem that don't support this command— check your manual.

D   **Dial**   The most popular command. This command forces the modem to go off hook and dial a phone number you specify. To dial 555–8817, you enter **ATD5558817** or **ATD 555-8817**. Most modems ignore hyphens, parentheses, and spaces. Usually, when you don't specify a dialing method, pulse dialing is used.

The next eleven commands allow you to modify the dialing string. Just as you need enter only one **AT** in a command line, you need enter only one **D** on your command line, followed by as many single-character dialing commands as you need. See the DW entry for an example.

The D commands are listed in the approximate order of their usefulness.

DT	**Touch-tone dialing** Dials the number using touch-tones, as most push-button phones do. It's a faster way to dial the phone.
D,	**Pause** A comma causes the modem to pause for two seconds in the middle of dialing the phone. Use a pause if your office phone system requires you to dial a 9 for an outside line. If two seconds is too long or too short for you, you can modify the delay with the S8 command. Also, additional commas add two seconds each.
D;	**Return to command mode after dialing** Normally, after your modem dials a number it waits to see if another modem answers your call, and it establishes an on-line connection if one does. Putting a semicolon at the end of the dialing command, however—as in **ATDT 555-2882;**—forces the modem to go back to command mode immediately after dialing. This command is handy if a pal asks you to dial his or her computer. If his or her spouse answers the phone before your pal's modem does, your modem won't shriek in the spouse's ear. If a modem does answer, you can connect by typing **ATD**.
DP	**Pulse dial** Dials the number using pulses instead of tones, as a rotary phone would.

D"   **Dial the letters that follow** On some modems, a straight quote symbol dials the letters that follow as numbers. For example, **ATDT "HOG–WILD** is the same as **ATDT 464–9453**.

D!   **Flash** The equivalent of holding down the switch-hook of the phone briefly. On some phone systems, you do this to transfer a phone call.

DW   **Wait for a second dial tone** When your modem comes to a W in the dialing string, it pauses and listens for a second dial tone before proceeding. If you use a calling card to dial a toll-free access number, wait two seconds, enter a code, and then wait to get a second dial tone before dialing the number, you can use a string like this: **ATDT 1 800 555–2918, 12345 W 555–1928**.

D@   **Wait for silence** Halts the dialing command until a predefined period of uninterrupted silence occurs. Useful if your office phone system re-quires you to listen to the entire introductory sequence before you can dial the extension you want. **ATDT 555-2938 @ 7726** dials the number, waits until the electronic voice stops, then dials the extension.

DR   **Reverse mode** Some old modems are originate-only, and you can connect to them only by add-ing an R at the end of the dialing command.

DL   **Redial** Redial the last dialed number. Use **A** / to repeat the last command, whatever it was; use **ATDL** to redial the last number even if you've been giving the modem other commands since your last try. This command is not supported by all modem manufacturers.

DS*n*   **Dial stored number**   Many modems allow you
to store a short list of phone numbers in memory,
each associated with a digit (usually 0–3). **ATDS0**
dials whatever number has been stored at posi-
tion 0 in the list. To store numbers, use the AT&Z
command (in the Extended Command Set section
of this chapter).

E*n*   **Echo command characters**   In command mode,
ATE1 (the default) echoes each character you
type back to you as you enter commands. If you
type **ATE0**, no characters are echoed in command
mode.

F*n*   **Echo transmitted data**   By default, this setting is
ATF1 (Local Echo OFF), which means that what
you type gets sent over the phone line and that's
it. If you enter **ATF0** (Local Echo ON), the modem also echoes what you type back to you. Use
ATF0 when you're on line and you can't see what
you're typing (or have your telecom program
generate Local Echo for you, which is easier).

H*n*   **Hook control**   **ATH0** (or **ATH**) hangs up the
phone (putting it on hook). **ATH1** picks up the
phone, taking it off hook (but does not establish a
connection).

I*n*   **Information**   Gives a status report on some
component of the modem hardware; each *n* tells
you something different about the modem.
Usually, **ATI0** displays a product code that
identifies what make and model modem you
own, and **ATI1** and **ATI2** calculate checksums on
the ROM and/or RAM of the modem. Otherwise,
I*n* varies from one manufacturer to the other.
USRobotics, for example, has codes that tell you
all the modem's current settings, how long the
last phone call lasted, what kind of connection
was made, how it was disconnected, and so forth.

Ln

Speaker volume   Sets the volume of the modem's built-in speaker, from a low of 0 to a highest setting of 3.

Mn

Speaker control   Determines when your modem's speaker is on. **ATM1**, the default, leaves the speaker on while dialing and turns it off once you're on line. You can silence the speaker with **ATM0**. **ATM2** keeps the speaker on all the time, even while on line, and **ATM3** leaves the speaker off while dialing, turns it on while the connection's being made, and then turns it off when you go on line.

Nn

Negotiate connection   On some modems, **ATN**n defines how your modem connects to another modem—specifically, how speed should be negotiated between the two, the order in which various connection protocols are tried, and so on.

On

Return on line   If you're connected to another modem and you use the escape code (**+++**) to go off line for a moment (to give your modem a few commands), **ATO** puts you back on line. **ATO1**, used rarely, and only at 2400 bps, forces your modem and the one it's connected with to renegotiate their connection.

Qn

Result codes   Your modem sends you the messages *CONNECT 2400*, *BUSY*, and *NO CARRIER* to let you know how a certain operation went. Under the default setting, **ATQ0**, these codes are displayed as necessary. **ATQ1** suppresses them completely, and **ATQ2** suppresses them only when the modem has answered a phone call.

S*n*=*x*   **Set S-register value**   Your modem's S-registers are variables in its memory that determine certain technical aspects of how your modem operates. The number of S-registers in a modem can range from a handful to several *dozen*. I've listed the ones you'll want to know about.

The next nine commands control a specific S-register parameter, where *x* is the setting you can change.

S0=*x*   **Specify phone rings before answering**   Specifies the number of times the phone rings before your modem answers an incoming call. **ATS0=0** (the default) means "Don't answer the phone at all!" **ATSO=6** lets the phone ring six times before answering. This gives you (or your fax machine) an opportunity to answer first. This is probably the most important S-register for casual users.

S2=*x*   **Change escape character**   Contains the ASCII code for the modem's escape character. Normally it's 43 (the plus sign), but if you have to use exactly that same sequence to do something on line, you can change the escape sequence to something else (such as *** or @@@) by entering that character's ASCII code (*x*) in S-register 2.

S6=*x*   **Seconds to wait before dialing**   Sets how many seconds the modem waits, after it's gone off hook, before dialing a number. Normally, it's two seconds, but if your phone system takes a long time to give you a dial tone, you can increase this number as needed.

S7=*x* **Seconds to wait for carrier** Sets how many seconds the modem waits, after dialing the number, for the other modem's carrier signal. Increase it if your modem keeps hanging up before the remote modem has a chance to emit its shriek.

S8=*x* **Seconds to wait per comma** Determines how many seconds the modem waits when it runs into a comma in a dialing string. The default is two seconds.

S9=*x* **Tenths of a second to wait for carrier** Determines how many tenths of a second your modem waits for the other modem's carrier signal.

S10=*x* **Tenths of a second to wait to reestablish carrier** Determines how many tenths of a second your modem waits before hanging up when the carrier is lost. If your lines are noisy, your housemates pick up extensions while you're on line, or you have call waiting, your modem may not be able to detect the remote modem's carrier signal on the phone line and may hang up. By increasing this number, your modem waits longer for the carrier to be reestablished before it hangs up.

> If your problem is call waiting, a better solution is merely to insert a ***70** before the number you want to dial; on most phone systems, this turns call waiting off for the duration of the call. Call your phone company if *70 doesn't work.

S11=*x*   **Specify touch-tone notes** Determines, in tenths of a second, the duration and spacing of touch-tones generated by your modem. Increase the number if your modem is dialing too quickly for your phone system to keep up.

S12=*x*   **Wait before command mode** Determines how long (in fiftieths of a second) your modem waits, after you type **+++**, before going into command mode.

S*n*?   **Return S-register value** Returns the current value in S-register *n*. To find out how long your modem waits when it encounters a comma, enter **ATS8?**. If you haven't changed this setting from the default, the answer is 2.

V*n*   **Verbal/numeric result codes** When the modem tells you what kind of connection was made, you can specify English (*No Carrier*) or a cold, inhuman number (*3*)? Usually the default is ATV1, English, but you can switch to numeric mode with ATV0.

X*n*   **Result code set** Determines how full a range of result codes you want the modem to return to you. At **ATX0**, the modem typically gives you only one of five messages (*OK, CONNECT, RING, NO CARRIER*, and *ERROR*). At its highest setting, it gives you the speed, error checking, compression level, and so on. The number of different levels available and the info each level provides varies depending on your modem.

Z   **Reset modem** Hangs up the modem if it's off hook and restores all the modem's settings to what they were the last time you used **AT&W** to save modem settings. On some modems, you can flip a switch and use **ATZ** to restore the modem to its original factory settings.

Extended (Ampersand) Command Set

The extended command set addresses more subtle, more device-specific modem features than the basic command set. If you want to use any of these commands, check your modem manual to make sure your modem supports the command.

All extended commands are also preceded by AT.

&B*n*   **Mac-modem communication speed**   Defines how fast the Mac and the modem send data to each other. Under the default, **AT&B0**, the modem always changes the speed at which it communicates with your Mac to match the speed of its current on-line connection (if it's getting data from a BBS at 2400 bps, it sends data to the Mac at 2400 bps). With **AT&B1**, no matter how fast or slow the modem's talking to the BBS, it maintains the same speed exchanging data with your Mac. Set modems with built-in data compression to **AT&B1**.

&C*n*   **Carrier detect modem to Mac**   With computers other than Macs, the modem can maintain a carrier with the computer just as it maintains a carrier with the BBS with **AT&C1** (the default). Being a Mac user, you should use **AT&C0**, which tells the modem to always assume the carrier is present.

&D*n*   **Data terminal ready (DTR) signal Mac to modem**   Determines how DTR is to be used between Mac and modem. If you aren't using a hardware handshaking cable, and you have a cable that supports DTR, use **AT&D2**, which enables use of the DTR signal. It can be used to force the modem to hang up. If you don't have a hardware-handshaking cable, issue an **AT&D0** command to override reliance on DTR (otherwise, the modem won't accept any commands from your Mac).

&F   **Restore default settings**   Restores all the modem's original factory settings. Useful when you've been issuing commands willy-nilly and now nothing works. To make those factory settings permanent, enter an **AT&W**.

&H*n*   **Hardware flow control of transmitted data**   If you have a hardware-handshaking cable, use **AT&H1** to have the modem use the clear to send (CTS) signal to control the flow of data from the Mac to the modem. If you don't have a hardware-handshaking cable, use either XON/XOFF software flow control (**AT&H2**) or (if you like to live dangerously) no flow control at all (**AT&H0**).

&I*n*   **Software flow control of received data**   Similar to &H*n*, but without the hardware option. **AT&I0** (the default) disables software flow control, and **AT&I1** uses XON/XOFF flow control.

&K*n*   **Data Compression**   If your modem has V.42bis or MNP data compression, this command lets you define how (or if) it's used. **AT&K0** disables data compression, and **AT&K2** makes data compression always available (as long as the modem you're connected to has data compression). **AT&K1** enables data compression when you've set **AT&B0** (constant modem/Mac communications rate, which is required for data compression to work properly), and disables it when you haven't set **AT&B0**.

&L*n*   **Leased line**   If you're using a leased line, use **AT&L1**. If not, use the normal phone line setting, **AT&L0** (the default).

&M*n*   **Error checking enable/disable**   Turns the built-in error-checking features of your modem on or off. With the default, **AT&M4**, the modem tries to make a connection that uses hardware error checking, but settles for less. **AT&M0** turns off all ARQ error checking (you use it if ARQ negotiation is interfering with your connection). **AT&M5** forces the modem to accept only an ARQ connection and hang up if that's not possible.

&N*n*   **Variable modem/modem communication speed**   Normally, two modems chat with each other to decide the fastest speed both can use to communicate. If you're running a BBS and want to ensure that only 2400 bps callers get through, however, you can use **AT&N*n*** to set the speed of communication; all others are disconnected. Check your modem manual for the *n* settings for your modem.

&R*n*   **Received data hardware flow control**   If you
             have a hardware handshaking cable, use **AT&R2**.
             Otherwise, use the default, **AT&R1**, which
             overrides hardware flow control.

&S*n*   **Data set ready**   For the most part you can accept
             the default (**AT&S0**) which ignores DSR signal-
             ing. To use a system with DSR signaling, use
             AT&S1.

&T*n*   **Test mode**   Initiates technical self-tests to verify
             that your modem is operating OK. Use this
             command when you're trying to get technical
             support for your modem over the phone and the
             rep from the modem company tells you what
             tests to run.

&W   **Write**   Save any changes you've made to the
             modem's settings to a special area of its memory
             so you won't lose the changes when you turn the
             modem off.

&Z*n=x*   **Store phone number**   Stores phone number *x* at
             position *n* in the modem's built-in phone book. If
             I entered **AT&Z1=16178640712**, then whenever I
             gave the command **ATDS1**, the modem would
             dial the BCS•Mac BBS for me.

&Z*n*?   **Show stored phone number**   Shows what phone
             number has been stored in position *n*.

The Macintosh
Communications Toolbox
Appendix C

You don't need to use the Macintosh Communications Toolbox (CTB) to go on line, but it's an important part of System 7 and Apple's new modular System software strategy. If you use Macintosh communications software, chances are you'll have to deal with the CTB someday.

The Macintosh telecom software market has three kinds of applications:

- **CTB-ignorant** These applications have no Comm Toolbox features whatsoever, which is a shame.

- **CTB-savvy** The programmers have decided to augment a more or less standard telecom program with CTB features of their choosing. This is probably the most powerful level of CTB support, as it gives you the best of both worlds. ZTerm 0.9 is still a hands-on program, but it allows you to use any serial port registered with the toolbox. Software Ventures

MicroPhone II 4.0 can work directly with the hardware and use built-in functions, but it can also use just about any CTB tool. Hayes Smartcom II gives you the option of turning CTB support on or off; with the features switched off, all the Connection menu items and the like are wiped away to reveal a standard Mac telecom program interface.

- **CTB-dependent** These programs embrace the Comm Toolbox, depending on it for all communications functions. Done right, a CTB-dependent application is great—PacerTerm is probably the cleanest-looking telecom program for the Mac, considering all its power. Done wrong, however, a CTB-dependent program is awful.

Background

Over the years, Apple Computer has made hundreds of millions of dollars on the Mac, and for a simple reason: simplicity. All programs work in much the same way, with consistent commands. When you buy a new printer, all you have to do is drop a driver for it into the System Folder, and all Mac programs can print to it. Ditto for fonts and Control Panels, but not telecom software.

All communications software does the same things (dial the phone, emulate a terminal, download a file), but each program does things in a different way. And what if you want your Mac to emulate a different terminal? Or connect to another computer over AppleTalk instead of a modem? Or use a new, faster file-transfer protocol? The simple solutions to all three problems is to buy a new telecom program.

At least it was that way in the past. Recently, Apple has created an extension to the Macintosh System, dubbed the Macintosh Communications Toolbox, to make communications easier for both users and programmers.

When the CTB succeeds, it succeeds admirably. Indeed, communications software that integrates the CTB's features is the simplest and most functional telecom software available for any computer. But it doesn't always succeed. In this appendix, you'll learn about the Communications Toolbox—what it is, what its components are, how to install it, its advantages, and how it works.

What Is the CTB?

The Macintosh Communications Toolbox is a standard package of built-in routines that all Mac programmers can call upon in their programs. Dozens of such packages exist, either burned into your Mac's ROM chips or tucked away inside your System file. All Mac programs use windows and menus (and all Mac windows and menus look alike) because all Mac programs use other toolbox functions— such as the Window Manager and the Menu Manager—to include those features. Instead of writing code from scratch, programmers need only write a few simple lines that call upon functions that Apple burned into Mac. The programmer can write a really hot program with relatively little effort; the user sees standard routines that look and behave the same way.

Where to Find the CTB

The Communications Toolbox, being a relatively new concept, isn't burned into ROM; it's part of your System file. All copies of System 7 come with the CTB already installed, but if you're using any version of System 6, you'll have to install the Comm Toolbox routines to make any CTB features available to your software.

This is one of the great things about the Mac. Whenever there's a need for a new feature, there's no need to buy a new piece of hardware, or even a new version of the System software; just install the new feature. If the new feature is universally cheered and reasonably compact, like 32-bit QuickDraw, it's eventually burned into the ROM of all new Macs.

If you're running System 6.0.x, the Comm Toolbox lets you know it's been installed by displaying its icon in your welcome screen shown in Figure C–1. Every copy of System 7 has the CTB already installed so you won't see a special icon at startup.

Figure C–1: Icons denoting that the CTB has been installed and loaded (left) or not loaded (right)

You can also detect the presence of the Comm Toolbox in your System Folder. If you're using System 7, open your Extensions folder within the System Folder. If you're using System 6.0.x, look for the Communications Folder, shown in Figure C–2.

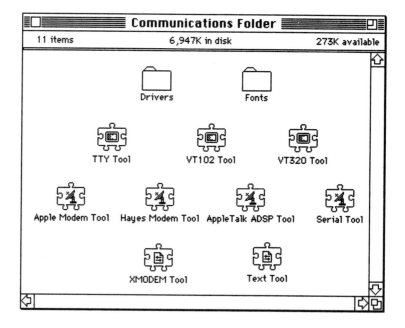

Figure C–2: The System 6.0.x Communications Folder

What's wrong with this picture? Apple says the Comm Toolbox makes telecommunications simple, and has modular tools that all work together seamlessly. But look at those icons: They're jigsaw puzzle pieces and *none* of them can fit together properly!

Better to have impossible icons and a great piece of software than the other way around.

The Communications Folder (System 6) or Extensions Folder (System 7) holds the collection of modular tools that perform most telecommunications functions.

What the CTB Contains

The Comm Toolbox performs only three types of functions, so it has only three kinds of tools: connection tools, terminal tools, and file-transfer tools, as shown in Figure C–3.

Figure C–3: Icons for connection tools, terminal tools, file-transfer tools (left to right)

- **Connection tools** You use connection tools to establish a connection between two computers. Most of you establish a connection using two modems and a large phone company, but that's one of a myriad of ways to link two computers. You can use an AppleTalk network, to chat with someone in the building a few floors up; a direct serial connection, so you can link with a DOS laptop and exchange data; or a satellite-based communications system, to get data from a field office in Istanbul.

- **Terminal tools** You use terminal tools to provide terminal emulation (see Chapter 3). If you need a new terminal emulation not included with your CTB-savvy telecom program, merely obtain that terminal tool and drop it into the Communications Folder (System 6) or Extensions Folder (System 7).

- **File-transfer tools** You use the file-transfer tools to send a file from one computer to another. The more file-transfer tools you have, the better. If your CTB-savvy telecom software doesn't support a new and more efficient file transfer protocol, merely obtain a file-transfer tool for that protocol and drop it into the Communications Folder (System 6) or Extensions Folder (System 7).

Advantages of the CTB

The three types of CTB tools leave the wetware (you) out of much of those three processes. The connection tools, for instance, operate completely in the background. When you tell your telecom program to connect to a remote computer, you needn't know all the technical details involved. You need not know that it's activating your modem, dialing a phone number, waiting for a response, then establishing a connection at a particular speed and with particular parameters. You need not know that an AppleTalk connection is made by sending packets out through the network port, looking for a specific target, and so on. To set the process in motion, all you do is issue a command that results in a connection to another computer.

The second benefit the CTB offers is selective expandability. A telecom program written for the Comm Toolbox will never become obsolete. When a new file-transfer protocol comes along, you need only put the tool for that protocol in your the Communications Folder (System 6) or Extensions Folder (System 7), and your communications software will support it.

Or, if you buy a pocket electronic organizer (for example, a Sharp Wizard or Casio BOSS), you need not rely on its substandard organizer-to-Macintosh data-transfer program if the manufacturer enclosed a special connection tool, which you could use with your favorite CTB-savvy communications software.

Though Casio and Sharp don't currently offer connection tools for their products, Apple's handheld personal digital assistants (codenamed Newton and scheduled for release in early 1993) probably will.

A non-CTB communications program is like a Swiss Army knife. I never leave the house without mine, but if I needed a new tool, I'd have to leave the old knife at home and buy a new one that had the tool I needed.

The third benefit—a minor point—is that the Comm Toolbox offers a simple way to use as many serial devices as you want. Normally, once you've plugged something into the printer port and the modem port, you can't use any more serial devices (unless, of course, you're using a TelePort ADB modem; see Chapter 2). The Comm Toolbox, however, offers infinite flexibility. Devices such as expansion cards with multiple serial ports, modems available for use only on a network, and modems that plug into an ADB port need only register themselves with the Comm Toolbox, and all those devices can be available to your Mac at the same time. It's a trivial thing for most of you, but essential for folks who want to run their own BBS from a Mac, for instance.

Finally, the Comm Toolbox works hard to bring something of a standard interface to telecommunications. All the tools have their own standard user interface items, so if you know how to configure the Apple modem tool in MicroPhone II, you'll know how to deal with it in Smartcom II.

Another minor point: The CTB makes telecom software easier to *write*. The simple task of writing a program that dials a modem and opens a terminal window can exercise most programmers, but with the CTB it's reduced to two easy pages of code. This makes it cost-effective for software publishers to incorporate telecommunications features into their software.

Imagine a spreadsheet program that, upon command, could dial into a corporate database, grab the data it needed, and plug it into a spreadsheet. Without the CTB, this feature's limited value would not be worth the substantial development time. With the CTB, such a feature could be implemented in a couple of days.

Arguments Against CTB

The CTB is another layer between you and your hardware. I've railed on this subject before; keep in mind that your modem has lots of built-in features, and to take advantage of them you need a program that lets you talk to the *modem*, not just to the CTB.

Second, the standard Comm Toolbox tools (the ones Apple gives you for free) aren't so great. The first (and current, at this writing) version of the Apple modem tool doesn't give you access to modem functions such as error checking and data compression. None of the file-transfer tools offer an *efficient* file-transfer protocol. The standard terminal tools seem to have a hard time keeping up with the flow of data when used on a slow Mac such as a Plus or a Classic.

To be fair, the idea behind the Comm Toolbox is for programmers to write and distribute their own improved tools. Hayes, for instance, already has its own Hayes modem tool, which is a vast improvement on the Apple tool whether you're using a Hayes modem or not. At this writing, though, the Comm Toolbox has been out over a year and third-party tools are still scarce.

Installing the Macintosh Communications Toolbox

If you're a System 7 user, you can skip to the following section. System 6 users who do not see the startup icon shown on the left in Figure C–1 (and thus don't have the CTB installed), have to go through the installation process.

Using the Installer (System 6 only)

The Comm Toolbox arrives on two floppies, and it usually accompanies all communications software that requires it. You can also get the CTB package from many user groups, as well as online services and APDA (Apple Programmers and Developers Association).

The Installer disk contains a working System and Finder, the Installer program, the Installer script for the Comm Toolbox, and a text file that lists any major changes or warnings you ought to be aware of. The disk has all the tools necessary to open your System File, implant the Comm Toolbox code, and close it again.

Warning: Don't cut the power to your Mac while the Installer is running!
It's writing data to your System file, and any disturbance could damage
your System file.

Here's how to use the Installer disk: Shut down your Mac, put the
Installer disk in the floppy drive, and start the Mac. Your Mac boots
from the floppy disk rather than your hard drive, thus making it safe
to perform the installation on the System file on your hard disk.
Double-click on the Installer, click on OK in the welcome screen, and
you should see the greeting in shown in Figure C–4.

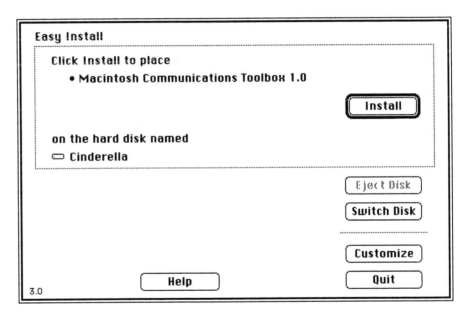

Figure C–4: The Comm Toolbox Installer

Apple makes the Installer simple and foolproof. Click on the
Switch Disk button until the name of the hard drive you want to install
the toolbox on appears where you see *Cinderella* in Figure C–4, then
click on the Install button. After a few minutes, the CTB will be
installed.

By the way, to remove the Comm Toolbox from your hard disk—it takes up a fair amount of memory and disk space, and not everyone wants to use it—hold down the Option key while running the Installer. The process is similar to installation, except that the result is the removal of the Comm Toolbox from the selected drive.

Installing the Basic Connectivity Set.

The second disk contains the individual CTB tools, known as the Basic Connectivity Set. If you're using System 7, chances are excellent that these tools have yet to be installed. Drag the tools onto your System Folder and the System will put all the tools in their proper place. If you're using System 6, open the System Folder and drag the tools into the Communications Folder. When you restart your Mac, the Comm Toolbox is securely installed inside your System.

Using the Communications Toolbox

Probably the biggest paradox of the Macintosh Communications Toolbox is that it was designed and executed by Apple, and yet it's modal, violating one of the prime directives of Macintosh software design. With the CTB, rarely can you decide to do something, then quickly do it; to do almost everything, you must stop and call up a modal dialog box, which prevents you from doing anything else until you're through with it. Conversely, most applications allow most functions to be accessed by a simple, nonmodal menu command.

Still, all CTB applications have a common user interface and the info in this section can help you learn to use almost anything based on the toolbox.

Connection Tools

The connection tools do nothing more than establish a link between two computers. Generally, a Comm Toolbox application has two menu items dealing with connection tools: Open Connection and Close Connection. The Open Connection option opens the connection to the remote computer if you're not on line. Thus, if you've selected the modem tool, it dials a number, waits for a computer to answer, then goes online. The Close Connection option severs the connection if you are on line—it hangs up the modem. The Comm Toolbox insulates you from the details of how these tasks are accomplished.

If you are interested in having some control over the connection, you can use the Configure Connection option. Selecting this option brings up a dialog like the one shown in Figure C–5:

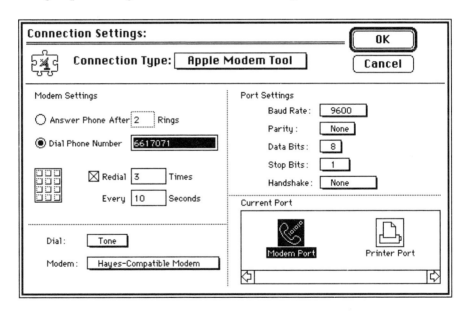

Figure C–5: The configuration dialog for the Apple modem tool

Figure C–5 shows the configuration dialog for the Apple modem tool, but all configuration dialogs for the CTB tools work the same. The top section contains a simple pop-up list of all the tools of that type (connection, in this case) that are currently available. The rest of the dialog box contains items for configuring the particulars of each different tool.

You get several standard Apple connection tools on the installation disks: the Apple modem tool, the serial tool, and the AppleTalk ADSP tool.

The Apple Modem Tool Apple offers standard, modem-based tele-communications with the Apple modem tool. Most of the items in the dialog box shown in Figure C–5 are self-explanatory, but two of them bear closer inspection. In the lower right corner of Figure C–5, you can choose between the printer or the modem port. In fact, it's a scrolling selection; if I had a TelePort or four extra serial ports on an expansion card, icons would appear for each additional port, thus allowing me access to any available serial device.

Second, the Apple modem tool can handle the peculiarities of several different brands of modems. A pop-up list, shown in Figure C–6, gives your Mac information to avoid some of the shortcomings of each model. It's a minor point, since almost every modem you can buy is Hayes-compatible.

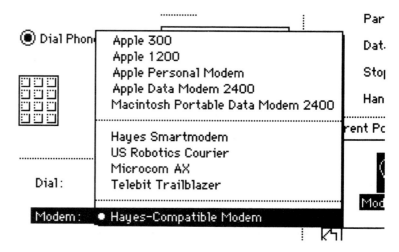

Figure C–6: Alternate modem configurations in the Apple modem tool

This is as good a time as any to slander the mothership. See those first four Apple modems on the list? Don't buy any of them. When folks leave messages on BBSs along the lines of "Hey, my modem's acting screwy and I don't know why," the first question everyone usually asks is "Is it an Apple modem?" and the response is usually "Yes."

Apple designs many things very well, but modems aren't one of them. Apple modems are almost always overpriced, underpowered, and problematic. Remember the AppleFax modem? The one that rarely worked properly and was eventually withdrawn from the market?

Once you've specified configuration parameters as shown in Figure C–5, you connect to a remote service merely by issuing the Establish Connection command.

The Hayes Modem Tool   A superior alternative to the Apple modem tool is the Hayes modem tool, written and distributed by a major manufacturer of telecommunications hardware and software.

Remember the discussion in Chapter 4? You want to make sure your Mac talks to your modem faster than the modem talks to the remote BBS.

The Apple modem tool is useless with V.42bis or any other mode of data compression. You can set the speed to 38,400 as we recommended in Chapter 4, but when you connect, the Apple modem tool slows down the terminal speed to *match* the 9,600 bps communications speed. To communicate at a faster speed, use the Hayes modem tool (Figure C–7), which is smarter.

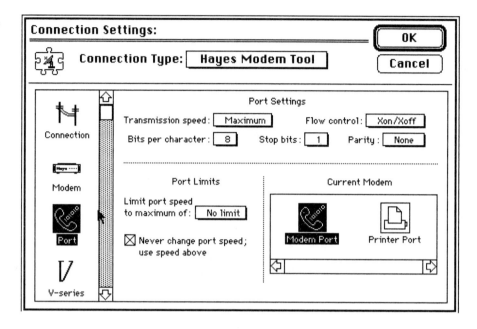

Figure C–7: The Hayes' modem tool

Figure C–7 shows one of the five dialogs for configuring the Hayes modem tool. In this dialog, you can instruct the tool to always connect to the modem at the highest speed possible, and to always keep the Mac to modem speed constant, no matter how fast or slow the modem is sending data through the phone line.

You can also fine-tune the dialer, specify numerous setup strings, turn the modem speaker on and off, and so on. You can't use all the Hayes tool's features with modems manufactured by makers other than Hayes, but even so, the Hayes modem tool is a necessity if your software uses the Comm Toolbox.

The tool is free, but Hayes maintains tight control on how it's distributed. Most free software can be sold by user groups or downloaded from public bulletin boards, but the only way to get the Hayes modem tool is to buy a Hayes product or to download the tool from Hayes' corporate BBS. The Hayes BBS is a free call at 800-US-HAYES.

Serial Tool   The simplest of all the connection tools is the serial tool. It opens a direct serial connection to whatever serial device is hooked up to the selected port. The dialog box in Figure C–8 shows the settings for the serial tool.

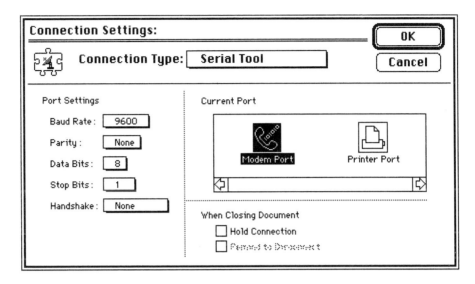

Figure C–8: Connection settings for the serial tool

Use the serial tool to link with a laptop computer you've plugged into a serial port, or to create a "direct" connection to your modem, as you have with almost all non-CTB software. With the Apple and Hayes modem tools, the modem can't see what you type until it has made a connection to a remote system; with the serial tool, you give your modem configuration commands and get responses as you press Return.

Unfortunately, when you use the serial tool, you lose a lot of user-interface items. You have to dial the phone by manually entering a dialing command, and you can't use electronic phone books.

AppleTalk ADSP Tool In the context of this book, you probably won't use the AppleTalk ADSP Tool often; it establishes a direct connection between any two Macintoshes on an AppleTalk network. You can use this tool to swap files from office to office, but the file sharing feature of System 7 already does that. You can also use this tool to chat with someone a few floors away, but that is handled more elegantly using QuickMail's conference feature.

File-Transfer Tools

If you're going to be downloading files using a Comm Toolbox application, you *have* to buy some third-party file-transfer tools. Until you do, here's a rundown of the mediocre set of tools you get for free: the XMODEM tool and the text tool.

Use the file transfer tools like the connection tools: Normally, you just type Command-S or Command-R or choose Send or Receive from a menu, and the program sends or receives using whatever protocol's been set, with whatever settings. You are prompted for a file or file name if necessary. To change the transfer protocol or its settings, pull up the dialog box.

The XMODEM Tool The configuration dialog for the XMODEM tool, shown in Figure C–9, shows mostly the features you learned about in the discussion of XMODEM in Chapter 5, so I'll hit some of the high (or low) points.

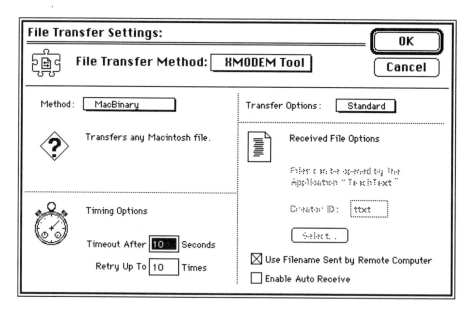

Figure C–9: The XMODEM tool

As shown in Figure C–10, you can turn off MacBinary when you're transmitting non-Macintosh binary files.

Figure C–10: Various methods of file transfer under the XMODEM tool

In the Transfer Options pop-up shown in Figure C–11, you can see the CRC and 1K Blocks options, with 1K being the most efficient protocol available here. CleanLink is more or less standard XMODEM, with no error checking. Use it where the hardware is doing the error checking for you already (as is the case with a V.42 or MNP-equipped modem). Unfortunately, CleanLink is only supported in Comm Toolbox applications, so it has limited use.

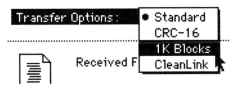

Figure C–11: XMODEM transfer options

Text Tool   The text tool, whose settings are shown in Figure C–12, is used for transferring text with no error checking. This tool is merely an aggregation of the menu commands a non-CTB application would give you for dealing with incoming and outgoing text; the left half is for pacing how fast a text file is sent to the remote computer (some systems fail if you send text too fast), and the right half decides what formatting is imposed on the file as it's received.

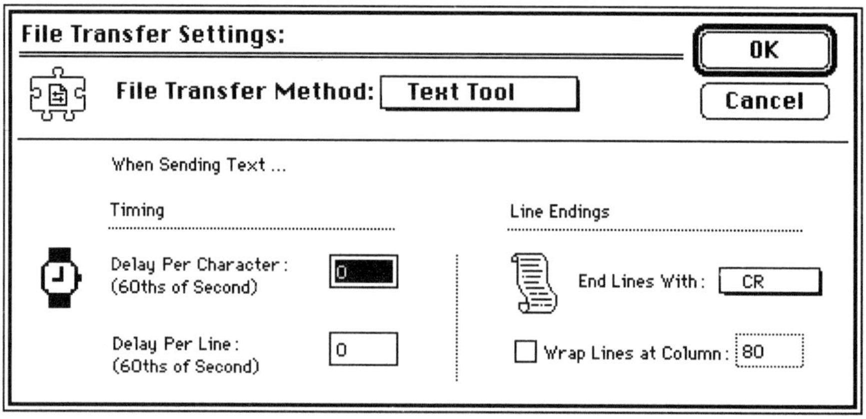

Figure C–12: Text tool

Terminal Tools

Most folks need only the most basic terminal emulation: Send what I type through the modem, and take whatever comes back and put it on the screen. The CTB offers the VT102 tool and the TTY tool.

The VT102 Tool   You can choose the VT102 tool as your modem tool. The VT102 tool handles basic terminal text admirably, and it also allows on-screen graphics modes such as boldface text and the drawing of lines and boxes and other special graphics characters. The terminal settings for the VT102 tool are shown in Figure C–13.

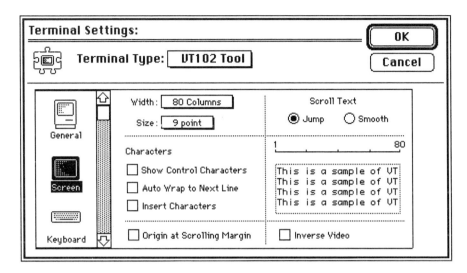

Figure C–13: Terminal settings for the VT102 tool

Only two highlights are worthy of mention. First, the VT102 tool can use inverse video (in your terminal window, you see white letters on a black background rather than the usual black-on-white). If your Mac doesn't have Color QuickDraw (a Classic, SE, Plus), however, this feature may not function properly.

Second, look at the Scroll Text radio buttons. Do you want text to bump up one line at a time (quicker) or to scroll smoothly up, as if it was being inched up on a roll of paper (prettier and more like what a dumb terminal would do)? Whatever you choose, it doesn't affect operations.

The TTY Tool   For the simplest level of emulation, use the TTY tool. It's basically a typewriter: It takes whatever comes in and puts it on the current line. When a carriage return comes across, it goes to the next line.

Use it in the rare cases when a system has trouble dealing with your VT102 tool. The terminal settings for the TTY tool are shown in Figure C–14.

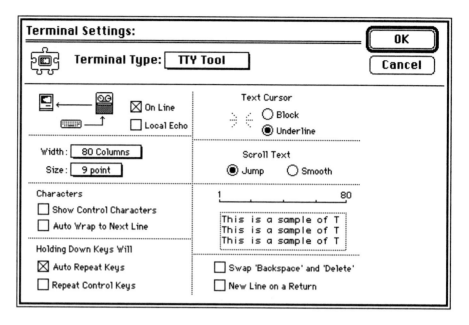

Figure C–14: Terminal settings for the TTY tool

Parting Shots

You don't have to deal with the CTB if you don't want to; programmers will always be able to choose how much Comm Toolbox support they're going to incorporate into their software.

At this writing, your best bet is to look for CTB-savvy software and hope for better third-party tools.

Manufacturers' Addresses

Appendix D

Accu/Weather (On-line service)
60 Leveroni Court
Novato, CA 94949
(415) 883–3000

Aladdin Systems (StuffIt)
165 Westridge Drive
Watsonville, CA 95076
(408) 761–6200

America Online (On-line service)
8619 Westwood Center Drive
Vienna, VA 22182
(800) 827–6364
(703) 883–1509

Applied Engineering (QuadraLink)
PO Box 5100
Carrollton, TX 75011
(800) 554–6227
(214) 484–1365 (fax)

Baseline Publishing (DoubleTalk)
1770 Moriah Woods Boulevard, Suite 14
Memphis, TN 38117
(901) 662–9676

CompuServe (On-line service)
5000 Arlington Centre Boulevard
Columbus, OH 43220
(614) 457–0802

Creative Solutions (Hurdler)
4701 Randolph Road, Suite 12
Rockville, MD 20852
(301) 984–0262

Dialog (On-line service)
3460 Hillview Avenue
Palo Alto, CA 94304
(415) 858–3785
(415) 858–7069 (fax)

Dow Jones & Company (On-line service)
PO Box 300
Princeton, NJ 08543
(609) 520–4641
(609) 520–4662

Everex Systems (Modems)
48431 Milmont Dr.
Fremont, CA 94538.
(800) 628–3837 or (510) 498–1111

Farallon (Timbuktu Remote)
2000 Powell Street, Suite 600
Emeryville, CA 94608
(510) 596–9000
(510) 596–9020 (fax)

FreeSoft (White Knight, Okyto)
105 McKinley Road
Beaver Falls, PA 15010
(412) 846–2700
(412) 847–4436 (fax)

GEnie (On-line service)
401 North Washington Street
Rockville, MD 20850
(301) 340–4000

Global Village (Modems)
1204 O'Brien Drive
Menlo Park, CA 94025
(415) 329–0700
(415) 329–0767 (fax)

Hayes Microcomputer Products (Modems)
PO Box 105203
Atlanta, GA 30348
(404) 441–1617
(404) 441–1238 (fax)

Lexis/Nexus (On-line service)
PO Box 933
Dayton, Ohio 45401
(800) 227–4908

Logicode Technology, Inc. (Modems)
1817 DeHavilland Dr.
Newbury Park, CA 91320
(805) 499–4443

MCI Mail (On-line service)
1111 19th Street NW, Suite 500
Washington, DC 20036
(800) 444–6245

Microcom (Modems, Carbon Copy Mac, Virex)
PO Box 51489
Durham, NC 27717
(919) 490–1277
(919) 490–6672 (fax)

Pacer Software (PacerTerm)
7911 Herschel Avenue
La Jolla, CA 92037
(619) 454–0565

Practical Peripherals (Modems)
31245 La Baya Drive
Westlake Village, CA 91362
(818) 706–0333

Prodigy (On-line service)
445 Hamilton Avenue
White Plains, NY 10601
(800) 776–3449

Prometheus (Modems)
7225 SW Bonita
Tigard, OR 97223
(503) 624–0571

Radio Shack (Teleprotector; phone jacks and phone cords)
2000 stores nationwide
consult your Yellow Pages

Serius (Serius Programmer)
1981 E. 4800 South
Salt Lake City, UT 84117
(801) 272–7788
(801) 277–2440 (fax)

Shiva (NetModem, NetSerial)
1 Cambridge Center
Cambridge, MA 02142
(617) 252–6300
(617) 252–6852 (fax)

Software Ventures (Microphone II)
2907 Claremont Avenue
Berkeley, California 94705
(800) 336–6477
(510) 848–0885 (fax)

Spider Island Software (TeleFinder)
4790 Irvine Boulevard, Suite 105–347
Irvine, CA 92720
(714) 669–9260

Supra (Modems)
7101 Supra Drive SW
Albany, OR 97321
(503) 967–9075
(503) 967–2401 (fax)

Symantec (SAM—Symantec Ant-Virus for Macintosh)
10201 Torre Avenue
Cupertino, CA 95014–2132
(408) 253–9600
(800) 441–7234

Synergy Software (VersaTerm Pro)
2457 Perkiomen Avenue
Reading, PA 19606
(215) 779–0522
(215) 370–0548 (fax)

Telebit (Modems)
1315 Chesapeake Terrace
Sunnyvale, CA 94089
(408) 734–4333

USRobotics (Modems)
8100 North McCormick Boulevard
Skokie, IL 60076
(708) 982–5001
(708) 982–5235 (fax)

Zoom Telephonics (Modems)
207 South Street
Boston, MA 02111
(617) 423–1072

A Smattering of BBSs

Appendix E

Sometimes, the most difficult step when you begin to telecommunicate is the problem of finding the number of a local BBS. Once you have one number, you can ask other folks on that BBS for others.

Although I assembled the modest list in this appendix from many sources—BBS listings downloaded from BBSs, requests on commercial services for people to give me BBS numbers, and word-of mouth—it's hardly comprehensive; no list is.

The most reliable method of finding a Mac-oriented BBS in your area is to call your local user group. Call Apple at (800) 538-9696, extension 500, and ask for the name and number of the closest Macintosh user group.

Finally, remember a basic rule of etiquette: For these and any other BBS numbers you obtain, *always* voice-dial the number first at a reasonable hour of the day, in case the number belongs to a real person and not a computer. After all, this list was put together months before you're reading it, and BBSs do have a tend to fold up now and then.

(201) 387–9232	The Rock Pile BBS
(212) 645–9484	NYMUG BBS
(212) 597–9083	Metro Area MUG BBS
(214) 739–0645	MACRO Mouse
(214) 644–4781	The Mac Shack
(214) 644–4781	Mac Shack
(214) 394–9324	MacExchange
(215) 895–2579	DragonKeep IV (Drexel U.)
(215) 895–2579	DragonKeep IV
(303) 444–5175	MacLeisure
(310) 549–9640	Mac–HACers
(401) 739–6403	MacStation
(404) 447–0845	Atlanta Macintosh Users Group
(410) 922–7743	INS BBS
(419) 893–0121	Zephyr
(419) 691–0279	Amy's Place
(419) 536–8967	MacToledo
(510) 849–2684	BMUG
(514) 935–4257	MAC–LINK
(518) 381–4430	MECCA
(519) 672–7661	Wonderland

(601) 992–9459	MacHaven BBS
(602) 495–1713	Arizona Mac User's Group BBS
(606) 572–5375	MacCincinnatus
(607) 257–5822	Memory Alpha
(608) 221–3841	Mad Mac BBS
(617) 864–2293	BCS•Mac 9600
(617) 864–0712	BCS•Mac 2400
(617) 849–0347	The Graphics Factory
(617) 354-8873	Channel 1
(617) 739–9573	The World
(619) 576–1820	San Diego MUG BBS
(702) 359–4999	Nevada Mac/AMUG
(717) 285–2535	The Mouse House
(719) 637–1458	Scorpion
(802) 388–9899	Green Mountain Mac BBS
(818) 965–6241	The Drawing Board
(908) 388–1676	New Jersey Mac Users Group BBS
(912) 764–7701	MicroLine
(914) 562–8528	Mid–Hudson Mac
(916) 455–3726	MacNexus

Serial Wiring Diagrams

Appendix F

You'll rarely need to know what signals go through what wires in a Macintosh serial cable. Say you get a new laptop computer, and you can't find a proper cable to connect it to your Mac. With these pinout diagrams, you'll be one step closer to making your own cabling solution.

The Macintosh Serial Connector

Figure F–1 shows a diagram of a Mac serial connector, seen from the cable's end.

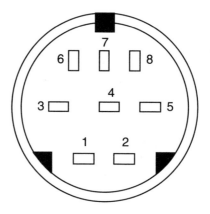

Figure F–1: Mac serial connector

The signal assignments are as follows:

Pin	Function
1	Output handshake
2	Input handshake
3	Transmit data (-)
4	Signal ground
5	Receive data (-)
6	Transmit data (+)
7	General purpose input (not all models)
8	Receive data (+)

The RS-232 Connector

Most serial devices have a 25-pin connector. The end of such a cable is depicted in Figure F–2.

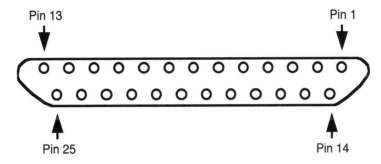

Figure F–2: RS-232 25-pin connector

The important pins are these:

Pin	Function
1	Protective ground
2	Transmitted data
3	Received data
4	Request to send (RTS)
5	Clear to send (CTS)
6	Data set ready (DSR)
7	Signal ground
8	Carrier detect (CD)
20	Data terminal ready (DTR)

Index